Narratives of Place, Culture and Identity

D1388727

IMISCOE (International Migration, Integration and Social Cohesion)

IMISCOE is a European Commission-funded Network of Excellence of more than 350 scientists from various research institutes that specialise in migration and integration issues in Europe. These researchers, who come from all branches of the economic and social sciences, the humanities and law, implement an integrated, multidisciplinary and internationally comparative research program that focuses on Europe's migration and integration challenges.

Within the program, existing research is integrated and new research lines are developed that involve issues crucial to European-level policy-making and provide a theory-based design to implement new research.

The publication program of IMISCOE is based on five distinct publication profiles, designed to make its research and results available to scientists, policymakers and the public at large. High-quality manuscripts written by IMISCOE members, or in cooperation with IMISCOE members, are published in these five series. An Editorial Committee coordinates the review process of the manuscripts. The five series are:
1. Joint Studies
2. Research
3. Dissertations
4. Reports
5. Textbooks

More information on the network can be found at: www.imiscoe.org

IMISCOE **Dissertations** include dissertations of IMISCOE members. There are more than 100 Ph.D. candidates in the various affiliated institutions working on doctoral research within the IMISCOE framework.

Narratives of Place, Culture and Identity

Second-Generation Greek-Americans Return 'Home'

Anastasia Christou

IMISCOE Dissertations

AMSTERDAM UNIVERSITY PRESS

Cover design: Studio Jan de Boer BNO, Amsterdam
Layout: Fito Prepublishing, Almere

ISBN-13   978 90 5356 878 1
ISBN-10   90 5356 878 6
NUR   741 / 763

To all the migrants and refugees whose tears soothe the grounds
I walk on and whose smiles give colour and light to my journeys...
I still have the hope that resistance will no doubt, one day,
set us all free to new awakenings and faded dreams...

Table of contents

Acknowledgements

The genesis of the research project that this book is based on can be traced back in time and space to several multilocal and multicultural experiences that encapsulate imprints of memories, thoughts, conversations and questions in a life of diaspora, in both its academic and everyday facets. This book involves many stages of my own 'migranthood' and an evolving process that explores issues that have been both fascinating and troubling over the years but always of great importance. This manuscript is the product of over a decade's challenging work, and I have been extremely fortunate that many friends and colleagues shared my agonies, stimulated my thinking, inspired my writing and above all provided continuous support and generous assistance. This is a group of people from several countries whose contributions to this book have been fundamental.

But first and foremost to my parents and brother, migrants themselves, return migrants of different generations but similar reasons, I am grateful for all your emotional support and love. Thank you for believing in me, respecting and tolerating my dreams, decisions and life choices and always having to pay the price of missing me. I know I wasn't there where you were most of the time but you were always with me.

From the very beginning of my research, the unconditional help, friendship, love, patience, support and guidance of Dr. D. Mentzeniotis, which constantly increased as my fears and anxieties reached 'dangerously' high peaks, are clearly more than any utopian idealised Platonic perspective could capture but nonetheless coming from an incredible philosopher and person. Thank you for generously sharing your genius with me, abundantly providing honesty, a wealth of research material, time and timeless wisdom. I will never be the same since I met you...!

I am also greatly indebted to the numerous people who have accompanied and guided me throughout my research journey. My supervisor at the University of Sussex, Professor Russell King, who guided my doctoral research so expertly; I owe my warmest gratitude for his valuable feedback, comments and suggestions that have shaped my research and study and made it possible to develop into a complete thesis. His constant presence – at the University and at a distance – his patience, support, stimulating contributions and his trust in me went beyond anything I could have possibly wished for. Through his work he introduced me to the richness of geography and migration studies and instilled in me an appreciation for interdisciplinary perspectives. I will always be inspired by his example of engagement with the subject matter, the breadth of his knowledge and scholarship, the quality of his research and above all his modesty and integrity. I shall forever be indebted to him.

I am grateful to Professor Richard Black and the academic committee for selecting me and offering me a prestigious Marie Curie Research Fellowship in Migration Studies as part of the Migration and Asylum Research Training Initiative of the Sussex Centre for Migration Research. Professor Black's support has been instrumental and highly appreciated. My fellowship at the University of Sussex was an exceptional academic experience. Many colleagues and fellow researchers generously offered their time and friendship. The list is long and I am genuinely grateful to all. Special thanks go to Jenny Money and Clare Rogers who always saved the day, no matter how challenging it was! To Nayla Mourkabel and Antigoni Papanikolaou, thanks for their support, love, understanding, patience, generous hospitality and making the friendship last beyond Brighton. To the Raza family I owe infinite gratitude for their most generous hospitality and genuine friendship. Many distinguished scholars from a range of disciplines sharing the same interests, always beyond the call of duty, carefully read excerpts of my preliminary work and spent time with me clarifying many points of uncertainty and will always be mentors for me. From the University of Sussex: Professors Jane Cowan and Ralph Grillo, providing their expertise of many years in Anthropology and themes related to my thesis; Dr. Al Thomson for guiding me in oral history, life stories and the magic of narratives; Professors Mick Dunford and Alan Lester for discussing Epistemology and Methodology in Geography and listening to my sometimes 'radical' theoretical endeavours of analysis. Many courses I followed in the Migration Studies, Geography and Anthropology programmes, the Research Methods coursework and in general the interdisciplinarity of the University of Sussex were all memorable experiences that reinforce the desire of wanting to remain a 'professional life-time student'! Professors Jane Cowan and Paul White read and commented on this text in its earlier format as a doctoral thesis. I am especially grateful for their guidance and written feedback and for the pleasure of a lively scholarly discussion. I have also enjoyed several enlightening conversations and benefited from the scholarship of Professors Anne Buttimer, Ayse Caglar, Peter Carravetta, Barbara Einhorn, Ivor Goodson, David Harvey, Michael Herzfeld, Doreen Massey, Mirjana Morokvasic-Muller, Norma Moruzzi, Tom Nairn, Demetrios Papade-metriou, Nikos Papastergiadis, Harry Psomiades, Shalini Randeria, Saskia Sassen, Gayatri Chakravorty Spivak, Imogen Taylor, Paul Thompson, Hans Vermeulen and Steven Vertovec.

My friends and colleagues from the State University of New York and St. John's University, despite their numerous transnational com-mitments, have generously offered their support and technical assis-tance. Again, I am so grateful that the list is very long and forgive me if I can't mention everybody on this occasion. From Athens to Finland to New York, Professor Carole Ford has been a mentor and a mom! To Professor Frank LeVeness, thanks for always encouraging me and stop-ping by Athens and Brighton from different continents to make sure that all is well! From various Universities in the United States and Eur-ope, a special thanks to Professors Constantinou, Bonnabeau, Bragle, Buttimer, Ford, Leets, Klimt and Konstantellou for sending articles and books across the ocean when I desperately needed them. Many collea-gues at conferences, seminars and summer schools throughout the years have carefully and patiently listened to my long presentations and provided constructive feedback and valuable commentary; this added to my research and list of international friends! My work has benefited from several enriching experiences of an interdisciplinary academic dialogue and the stimulating and fruitful discussions of my research with many colleagues who generously offered constructive guidance and critical observations. I am grateful for the numerous invi-tations from several universities in the United States, the United King-dom, the Netherlands, Finland, Denmark, Sweden, Germany, Austria, Hungary, Poland, Estonia, France, Italy and Greece to present pieces of my research at conferences and workshops, from early on at the start of my fieldwork to the completion of this manuscript. The wisdom of my colleagues who served as discussants on conference panels in which I presented papers but also commentary from the audiences on these occasions has been a guiding source of revision in framing my reflection, analysis and writing. I thank the various individuals who in-vited me and for their helpful comments and questions. The list is long and for that I owe much to all, truly thank you!

I had the privilege in 2004 of an incredible academic, learning and research opportunity during my stay as Visiting Assistant Professor at the Institute for History, International and Social Studies, University of Aalborg and as a postdoctoral researcher at the Academy for Migration Studies in Denmark (AMID). I would like to express my deepest grati-tude to the Director of AMID, Professor Ulf Hedetoft for this opportu-nity and for being a mentor and a continuous source of intellectual in-spiration. The experience and resources available to me during my stay at the University of Aalborg proved to be invaluable. I am also grateful to Julie Larsen for her enduring administrative support and to my colleagues at AMID and SPIRIT (School for Postgraduate Interdisciplinary Research on Interculturalism and Transnationality) for their warmth, interest in my work, enthusiasm, friendship and constructive feedback at seminars I offered during my stay. I am also thankful to Dr. Garbi Schmidt from the Danish National Institute of Social Research (SFI) and to Dr. Ninna Nyberg Sørensen and Dr. Simon Turner from the Danish Institute for International Studies (DIIS) for their hospitality and for inviting me to give lectures on my research. From the University of Copenhagen, Trine Stauning Willert has generously offered endless support and genuine friendship and from the University of Roskilde, Lily Varidaki-Levine has provided much invaluable assistance.

During the Autumn 2005 term, as Lecturer in Cultural Geography at the University of Sussex, I had the opportunity to design and teach a *Cultures in Time and Space* as well as a *Cultural Geographies* course during which I benefited greatly from the many inspiring discussions I had with my students at lectures and seminars. I am so very much touched by their eagerness to learn, to collaborate and to critically question the world surrounding them. They were such a rich source of inspiration and encouragement. What an enormous gift it is to be a teacher! I am also indebted to my colleagues for their support, assistance and friendship. I owe special thanks to the Head of the Department of Geography, Professor Russell King, to the Director of Cultural Studies, Dr. Filippo Osella, to Professors Brian Short and Tony Fielding, and to Dr. Simon Rycroft and Dr. Michael Collyer. Dr. Eugenia Markova has been an intellectual and 'diasporic' companion but most importantly a very caring friend.

Thanks to friends, family and colleagues from Athens and New York who, in spite of e-mail, called long distance to check up on me – you know who you are! I am indebted to many friends who have stood by me all this time, during all the journeys, ups and downs, the joys and traumas. They are too numerous to cite here, and I have chosen to thank them privately. I think I may need a whole manuscript just for the acknowledgements. I have to resist that and briefly but honestly say that you all mean so much to me, and you have shaped my personal and research journey in such significant ways. You are in my heart.

At the University of Amsterdam Press, I am extremely thankful to Dr. Maria Berger for her tremendous assistance, encouragement and sustained confidence in my commitment to the materialisation of this book. I am truly grateful as well to the three anonymous referees whose commentary and suggestions were indispensable during revision of the manuscript. As always, I remain solely responsible for any errors or shortcomings. To "*me *myself and *I", well, what can I possibly say? As I am getting sad with the completion of something that seemed so passionately to be a life commitment, I shall reassure myself that this is just the beginning...!

Last, but to no extent least of all, to those who participated in the research, 'my participants', I genuinely thank you for accompanying me in this journey and allowing me to enter your own. My deepest thanks and most heartfelt gratitude to the 'return migrants', the Greek-Americans, women and men who offered so much, for sharing their experiences and deep reflections with me, their generosity of time, history, heart, mind and soul; this has been unpredictably unprecedented. It is with overwhelming admiration that I thank the participants for their time and patience in recounting their life stories without which I would not have been able to achieve a portion of my dream and to narrow the existing gap in research relating to Greek-American return migration. I am forever indebted for each and every encounter, the wonderful conversations, the enjoyable moments we spent, their warmth and unselfish *filoxenia*. In dedication to all – in the spirit of Diaspora – the poem by Olga Broumas, 'Artemis':

We are ethnics committed to
a politics
of transliteration, the methodology
of a mind

stunned at the suddenly
possible shifts of meaning – for which
like amnesiacs

in a ward of fire, we must
find words
or burn.

A note on transliteration

There is no consensus among scholars as to how modern Greek should be transliterated into English. The aim has been throughout the book to present terms so that non-Greek speakers will be able to more or less pronounce them, and Greek speakers to be able to recognise them. I therefore tried to maintain source citation consistency (filotimo/philotimo or filoxenia etc. as cited in the literature, when quoting from English sources, I kept Greek transliterations as originally published) along with, on occasion preserving familiar English spellings or borrowed prefixes (hence, Philippinesa from the Philippines). Transliteration of modern Greek terms has followed a modified phonemic system, excerpt names are given in a form that would be more accessible to non-native speakers, that is, an international audience. However, I have not invented modifications inconsistently, but based on the International Phonetic Alphabet, when there was a source. Again, for similar reasons of decreasing complexity, I have not used accent marks. Furthermore, as indicated the majority of narratives were offered in English with the exception of two and for which I have provided any translations necessary of excerpts used from the Greek texts. Finally, although the book follows the UK English standard spelling, all narratives expressive of participants' oral and written words follow the US English standard spelling.

1   Introduction

1.1   Narrating diasporic migrancy – conceptualising ethnic ancestral 'return' migration

I have always been compelled to perceive the quest for knowledge as an endless journey of multiple, new and fascinating meanings. It was always the journey that mattered, not the destination, if there even was one for that matter. When I embarked on the journey of my research project, I realised that the project in itself was a collection of stories of journeys, those of others but yet so alike and so like my own. The stories and journeys are those of second-generation Greek-American return migrants, a distinct group that has not been adequately researched by academics nor understood or assisted by policy makers and service providers. Yet, these individuals have in most cases made a conscious decision to *move* to their parents' country of origin, some of them even fulfilling their parents' dream of return since in many instances the latter are left behind and only the children have returned. In speaking of second-generation migrants, for lack of an appropriate term, I call this relocation process *return migration* although in reality they are not returning because they never left in the first place. They were born, raised and educated in the United States but their search for an *identity* and a *home* has brought them to a different place, Greece. Greece is their ethnic ancestral homeland but does it ever become their *home*?

The image of people moving back and forth across and beyond national borders has become very vivid in our times. Mobility has saturated all facets of contemporary life and society. However, the imaging and representation of *home* has become ever more blurred and confused. Migration is a phenomenon which has brought about unprecedented changes not only in the movement of peoples but also in their identifications, which, although negotiable, are at the same time intimately and ultimately connected to the notion of *place*. This new type of movement extends to new kinds of *social spaces* and *cultural fields* that question previously stable notions and fixed entities. Return migration challenges, translates, defines, narrates and constructs new meanings of the *who I am* in connection to the *where I am*. These processes are both a challenge and an opportunity to attempt to comprehend, at least to an extent, the current metamorphosis of Greek society and the transformations that occur in relation to return migration. Migrant stories can become narrated insights into the depths of the meanings attached to specific experiences, and through their interpretation they can reveal, in addition to feelings and views, alternative understandings of individual and collective identities that transcend static notions of bounded affiliations to nation-states. Contradictory to what may initially seem as scepticism towards fixed loyalties, this fluid sense of belongingness may surprisingly prove to be even more robust and durable than previous frameworks. This alternative view fills the void of chaotic discrepancies between agency and structure by illuminating the role of the individual as *active actor* who shapes and is shaped by the social world. This type of *embodied agency* begins with the returnees' decision to move and continues its trajectory from the return stay to the integrated (re)settlement involving a personal plan of action, both *ideological* and *geographical*.

This book is a product of an in-depth qualitative study of second-generation Greek-American return migration conducted through a three-stage methodology of a relatively small sample numbering forty participants. During the first stage the participants engaged in deep self-reflection, and through semi-structured and unstructured interviewing they shared thoughts, feelings and personal data about their return experience. During the second stage the participants wrote about their experiences without having their stories interrupted or distracted by conversation. This was in the form of personal journals. The third phase was a final meeting with the participants some months later in order to balance my role as researcher, listener and conversationalist by going over my preliminary interpretations of their stories, both oral and written, to verify that none of the information was misrepresented or misinterpreted from their viewpoint. At its final stage this study endeavours to bring the case of current Greek-American return migration to academic attention and substantially contribute to debates on issues of identity. It aims at advancing our theoretical and empirical understanding of return migration and identity construction. This understanding is quite absent in the current literature. Moreover, my technique of collection and analysis of new primary data as described above fosters the intention of being a methodological contribution in the area of ethnic and migration studies. The fundamental notions of *self*, sense of *home* and *belonging* can be best articulated and illuminated through the qualitative insight that participant observation and in-depth interviewing provide; therefore, my plan was to conduct in-depth interviews and collect life stories from a relatively small group of participants. My aim was to address a variety of fundamental questions in depth and to explore the meanings attached to these research questions, which are not easily quantifiable.

Life history and ethnography are two closely complementary qualitative methods that can capture the meanings of the returnees' life experiences. In the particular methods that I employed during my ethnographic study, I attempted to maintain reflexivity throughout my engagement in the research process. In being reflexive in this relationship between me as researcher and the participants as subjects, once the fieldwork was completed as well as during the writing-up stage, I proceeded to give this role as 'author' to my participants who became not only readers but also 'authors' of the work. The meaning of the word 'author' that I employ is of one who 'authorises' the work, that is to say the participants themselves had a second chance of authorship. In addition to submitting their written journals, I asked them to read my analysis of their contributions and to provide me with feedback. In a sense this ethnography therefore has a component of being their 'auto-ethnography'. This way the study benefited from a variety of explorations of the self and self-inscriptions. The reconsideration of the analysis and interpretations of meanings deriving from personal narratives enriched the context of this project; it challenged and resisted any hegemonic tendencies in discourse; it provided an additional layer of authenticity of the 'ethnic voice', and it reinforced self-reflexivity.

There is always a dialectical and dialogic relationship between the 'narrated-self' and the 'narrating-self', and this dynamic reinforces an in-depth exploration that can highlight meanings and become very revealing of both social and cultural forms. Through this process I hope to promote a neutralisation of predispositions of bias and to offer an alternative multi-tasked method that contributes a less-biased, if not completely unbiased, way through which social and cultural biographies are constructed and depicted. This particular perspective is accentuated by what Deborah Reed-Danahay means when she raises questions about the voice and its authenticity: 'Who speaks and on behalf of whom are vital questions to ask of all ethnographic and autobiographical writing. Who represents whose life, and how, are also central topics of concern in our current age of bureaucratisation. ...The ability to transcend everyday conceptions of selfhood and social life is related to the ability to write or do autoethnography. This is a postmodern condition. It involves a rewriting of the self and the social' (1997: 3-4). In my attempt to allow my participants to 'rewrite themselves' I am also offering myself the opportunity to understand their rewriting of the social world. If, as Reed-Danahay claims, 'one of the main characteristics of an autoethnographic perspective is that the autoethnographer is a boundary-crosser, and the role can be characterized as that of a dual identity' (1997: 3), then the dual identities or the *double consciousness* of my participants will transcend the simplifications of shifting identities and their lives and discourses will not only document these changing social forms but will also provoke further dialogue beyond the textual one.

The theoretical framework that underpins and guides this analysis is the triple or triangular notion that return migrants construct ideologies of home, return and self which in turn reinforce and respectively construct geographies of place, culture and identity. To be more explicit, the ideology of home corresponds to the geography of place, the ideology of return to the geography of culture and finally the ideology of self to the geography of identity[1]. This is not, however, a division into three distinct blocks of meanings. The symbolic and real interaction of these cultural constructions is the generation and expression of new modes of geography. The dialogic and dialectical relationship between social beings and social spaces is the channel through which geographies are articulated, as will emerge more fully during the course of this book.

The primary question that arises in relation to second-generation Greek-American return migration, integration and construction of identities is the following:

> Do second-generation returnees construct their return migration project as a search for identity, and if so, is this identity constructed in relation to place as the manifestation of home and cultural belongingness?

Subsequent questions that arise in connection to this are:
1. What exactly motivated second-generation migrants to move to Greece?
2. What coping mechanisms and strategies (if any) have the return migrants implemented in order to adjust to this new environment?
3. Are they continuously constructing and negotiating an identity? Do dual or multiple identities exist in their case? And how are they explained and understood by the migrants themselves and subsequently by others?
4. What are the existing social and economic activities of return migrants and their social networks? Do transnational practices exist in their case?
5. How has Greece impacted them?
6. What are their current experiences and expectations? What would they do the same and what different?

1.2   Entering the field – processing the fieldwork experience

> *'Truth is not to be found inside the head of an individual person,*
> *it is born between people collectively searching for truth,*
> *in the process of their dialogic interaction'*
> Bakhtin

My personal reflections on return migration and identity construction commenced more than a decade ago. When embarking on the journey of studying return migration I realised that interdisciplinary fields of study such as migration and identity draw on a broad and eclectic set of epistemological perspectives. My research study is broadly situated within the theoretical tradition of social and cultural construction[2], along with feminist[3] and phenomenological perspectives[4]. I assume that identity is socially constructed, shaped by a variety of cultural, political, economic and historical influences as well as institutions and practices, and is modified throughout life in the migration and return migration process. The spatial constitution of social life, as it relates to return migration, is articulated and shaped by the returnees themselves, and the epitome of this is the very process of their identity construction. During the narrative analysis of my informants' journals and my thematic analysis of their oral narratives, I held on to Holland and Ramazanoglu's (1995) indication that we cannot read meaning in texts, allowing them to pose their own meanings, without also reading into them. On the other hand, while accepting the need to take individuals' experiences and accounts seriously, Cain reminds us of the need 'to take our own theory seriously' and to 'use the theory to make sense of the experience' (1986: 265).

The return migrants were seen throughout the research as socially embedded, active, intentional agents who influence, as much as they are influenced by, the social context in which they are located. This approach was adopted in the study by encouraging the returnees to engage in a process of self-reflection and to attempt to relate their actions, feelings and thoughts to the wider socio-cultural context of their changing place and positionality. This reality is what guided me towards constructionist readings of cultural and ethnic identifications.

The pragmatic and practical reality that I (without any predetermined intentions) engaged mostly with female returnees redirected me towards a new set of readings in feminist methodologies, feminist geographies and feminism in oral history. My initial plan was to interview an equal number of women and men from a variety of socio-economic and educational backgrounds. The fieldwork experience, however, resulted in an abundance of female returnees willing to fully commit their time and life stories to the study and a rather limited number of male returnees who could sign up to the study. Often, when we did meet in person at a scheduled time and place for an interview, the male participants were very cooperative, friendly, and talkative. Within the snowball sample there was an additional quota of more than ten male returnees with whom I had been in contact for several months, but in the end, I did not manage to have them participate in the study. Several appointments were cancelled, rescheduled, cancelled again; numerous reasons and difficulties were proffered on their behalf as obstacles in meeting despite my own flexibility in terms of time and travelling. Hence the fact that most of the participants[5] were women redirected me towards an interest in feminist methodologies and women's studies. In fact, I found the usefulness of the feminist perspectives employed in human geography not limited to the female returnees but also useful in my encounters with male returnees.

To work to unveil the structures, the meanings and processes of return migration and identity construction entail the continual discovery of the self. This is what the auto-ethnographer strives for. To know that the self and the subject are intertwined in the local and the historical moment of an individual's research is the path towards emancipation from essentialist notions and the forum for a genuine cross-cultural and interdisciplinary exchange[6]. Many things happen during the course of auto-ethnographic reflection and writing. It is a continuous conversation and a multi-channelled creative experience. I attempted to maintain reflexivity throughout the research project: eventually I realised that self-reflexivity was what I was doing from the very start.

In engaging with volatile and yet still shadowy concepts and in attempting to understand both myself and others, my research focus became even more blurred when I realised that several discourses had to be addressed, including those pertaining to the dialectics of *nationalism* and *ethnicity*, *place* and *space*, *belonging* and *remembering*, *being* and *becoming*, the *self* and the *other*, *home* and *away*, *here* and *there*, *us* and *them*, and many others factually and fictionally ingrained in the research. The constructionist[7] epistemology became both my compass and invisible critic that engaged in an inner dialogue with me throughout the research preparation, fieldwork, data analysis and writing-up stages. It was also an additional template that became the medium between the experiential world and writing the returnees' world – their *geographies of return*. Thus all narrative approaches to identity and all self-narratives were validated or invalidated by means of the social context in which they took place. In reading, analysing and interpreting the returnees' oral accounts and written narratives, I was aware that this process is constructive and therefore not neutral; thus I had to continuously locate and confirm my position not only as researcher but also as reader and writer in relation to the text.

This process was not only innovative but also a challenging experience, both for the participants and for myself. Being a second-generation Greek-American return migrant, I shared but also disputed many of the social and cultural issues regarding identity construction and return migration. In their choice of written narratives and in-depth interviews, participants explored the ways in which their personal experiences and interpretations had shaped their ideas of self-identification. Individuals as active agents are constructors of knowledge in their lives, influenced and assisted by the prevailing social and cultural discourses and their own experiences. As a result of this interaction, an evolving set of meanings are continuously created from individuals' understanding of their interactions and experiences in their world. This phenomenon is fluid, and so are identities. It is only through the interaction of the self with socio-cultural processes that we can know the emerging self. This is a constructed self, a constructed identity. The phenomenological perspective ingrained in this type of research seeks to understand how a person lives a life in a particular culture.

What I cannot emphasise enough is the creative potential of doing fieldwork: the interactiveness of various situations and the emergence of information on multiple levels. Boundaries in the field can be pre-established but they also can be altered, and in my case they were. In order to develop the research design, I spent one month in the United States (New York) in spring 1999 and several months in 2000 with second-generation Greek-Americans; about a year later I conducted a five-month intensive fieldwork study with second-generation Greek-American return migrants in Athens, Greece. Based on an initial sample of ten participants, this part of the fieldwork, from May to September 2001, formed the pilot study of my research. The analysis of that data and their writing up were completed during my stay as Marie Curie Research Fellow at the Sussex Centre for Migration Research. Some results of this first phase of fieldwork were published in Christou (2002).

The second part of my fieldwork resumed with my arrival back in Greece in April 2002. A total of thirty new in-depth interviews were completed and participants' journals collected until August 2002. The third and final part of the fieldwork study and empirical analysis of the forty life stories took place from September 2002 to the summer of 2003. The final stage included meetings with participants to discuss transcript interpretation. The names (pseudonyms) and basic biographical characteristics of the sample of 40 participants are set out in summary form in the Appendix.

From the pilot study I concluded that it was essential to the research design that participants met certain criteria. The project was designed to include only those return migrants who were second-generation

Greek-Americans, specifically those born in the United States to Greek immigrant parents. The participants had to have had a minimum return stay of at least six months. The six-month period was decided on after ongoing discussions with people involved directly or indirectly with return migration and the perception of *initial adjustment*. After speaking with officials from Greek-American organisations and social clubs, it was ascertained that six months is the minimum required time for the 'actual return' to start taking place. Finally, it was also critical that all participants in the study expressed their willingness not only to dedicate their time but also to engage in deep self-reflection and to disclose personal and even intimate data about their return experience. Consistent with a phenomenological approach the themes presented in the study illustrate the shared experience of the participants. The presentation of the data in narrative format retains the essence of the data, which is the participants' own voices.

The qualitative interviews were the primary strategy for data collection. These life stories were used in combination with observation, written narratives (personal journals), archival research and document analysis. I also looked at newspaper accounts, special reports in Greek and American newspapers, and published work by Greek-Americans (migrants and returnees), including academic research but also poems, novels, songs and movies. This textual engagement with the Greek diaspora offered insights into other aspects not always directly related to my research but nevertheless constructive. Electronic (e-mail messages, mobile text messages) and phone conversations with participants served as additional sources of information. In recording the primary data I also used extensive field notes. My observation strategies depended on the particular circumstance. I would sometimes maintain a passive presence, not directly interacting with the participants, as in my first couple of visits to Greek-American organisations and clubs when my identity as researcher was not fully known to all members. In other instances, for example after completing a formal interview, I was invited to participants' homes as a guest during family gatherings, birthday, name day and holiday celebrations. During those occasions I engaged in natural conversation and interaction but always felt like a researcher in the field soaking up information. Each of these instances had its specific advantages and disadvantages and ethical dilemmas that I carefully examined throughout the research project and will discuss in the following segments. The selection of the particular methodology also aimed at maintaining interdisciplinary triangulation (Janesick 2000) and crystallisation (Richardson 1994). Memo writing assisted in linking analytic interpretation with the empirical reality in making connections and examining patterns and categories. This method helps to move between 'thick description' and 'thick narration'.

As I have already said, the primary form of data collection is in-depth interviewing and the collection of personal narratives. The use of narrative methods in the collection and analysis of the data enabled significant insights into biographical information that in turn facilitated the illumination of issues of identity and belongingness.

The use of written narratives was selected because this method provides the opportunity for participants to account for personal experiences and how socio-cultural processes have been reflected in their lives in their own words. The written narratives allowed the participants to be the creators of the data without any guidance by the researcher, without open-ended questions or probes. The participants reconstructed their experiences and hence their self-identity through reconstructing past events by including or excluding information. The participants were collaborators, co-creators and co-authors of the research project. No particular format was suggested so as not to inhibit the creative writing process. Hence there was a diversity of formats. Subsequent to the written narratives, a further personal interview was scheduled to discuss the narratives in more depth and explore the life stories. This gave me an additional opportunity to understand the returnees and their interpretations of the migratory and return migration project. The particular research methodology implemented, based on continuous dialogue and collaboration, gave me some sense of reassurance that it was as non-hierarchical and non-oppressive as possible.

Revisited again and again, back and forth in the tides of social science, ethics and morality in research surface constantly, at times generating fierce debates. It seems that all of social science has been preoccupied with ethos in research and writing. Recently, with the emergence of new voices in feminism and postmodernism, more cases have been made for a reflexive commitment and awareness in research (Reinharz 1992; Ellis and Bochner 1996; Denzin 1997; Hertz 1997).

My study is the first to utilise a qualitative methodology to research the social construction of identities of a sample of second-generation Greek-American return migrants. The returnees voluntarily and unconditionally shared their life stories and personal interpretations of their self-identities in order for me to complete this study and to thus fulfil not only my academic but also my personal odyssey. Each unique, all of our (theirs and mine) return migration projects were woven together in the ancestral journey of return to locate the home, to locate the self, and to finally locate the self in the home. As I have said already, this academic research endeavour has been a truly self-reflective and enlightening experience for me in many respects. In deciding to have the participants' voices guide the research, I was constantly aware of how and to what degree I was bringing to the study my own experiences and beliefs. This is something I had to be very cautious of, and I continuously struggled to safeguard the 'authenticity' of the participants' representations in the research.

Another issue for which I had to hold myself in constant check was my relationship to the participants. In qualitative, ethnographic research of the kind I was involved in, there is always a relationship 'to' and 'with' the participants. Issues of trust, self-disclosure, power and expectations from both ends are some of the key ethics that need to be addressed and dealt with.

However, another issue stems from the researcher's degree of involvement with the group under study. In my initial contacts with the participants when we discussed my research and their participation and when I reassured them of maintaining the confidentiality of their identities and the privacy of other communications conducted in the future, some of the participants expressed enthusiasm about my work and interest in my own personal background, which I openly shared with them. This I had anticipated, and the information disclosed was to an extent in order to avoid creating any type of distance or power relation between us but enough to build trust. The participants did not feel that they were being exploited for research purposes: on the contrary, they felt useful to the study. This type of openness may have some risks, but it undoubtedly has many strengths: the participants felt a sense of security in knowing that although a researcher, I was really 'one of them', and they appreciated all the efforts I made to provide an atmosphere of trust and colleagueship, which enabled them to engage in deep self-reflection and to share feelings, behaviours and attitudes that are not always quantifiable and are missed in structured interview research. Thus a degree of self-disclosure was anticipated by the participants, and I was just sufficiently cautious not to seem too distant and not, on the other hand, too eager to provide a lot of personal information. However, throughout the interviewing and discussion process I realised that some of the participants sought to verify their ideas and to have me acknowledge their experiences as social realities. They did this by interjecting in the conversation expressions such as 'You know what I'm talking about, right?' and 'You probably experienced this too, right?'. This also served as a means to establish trust and confidence. Gaining trust and establishing rapport were found to be very easy from the first minutes of each encounter.

Interviews were conducted in the participants' native language, which were both English and Greek since all exhibited more or less bilingual native fluency. Conversations would flow without any predetermined choice of language. The participants were asked to select the language that made them feel more relaxed so they could describe their feelings, thoughts and experiences without translating. None exhibited a particular preference in language so most conversations were mixed.

However, English prevailed with the exception of two interviews conducted in Greek and translated into English by the author. In order to protect the anonymity of the participants all names used in the text are pseudonyms. In order to maintain consistency with the idea of the ancestral return, I used ancient Greek names as pseudonyms. Some of the participants' real names were indeed of ancient Greek origin; those names have not been used in the text.

In the journey of writing this book, in sharing the narratives of others and the migrations of all of us involved, whether imaginary or historic, identification has been the apex of locating the self as subject and story. I locate myself in the context of several migrations: my own and my family's experiences and in the midst of this project as a remapping of cultural crossings and strategies in trying to break through a hazy rendering of how identities take shape in the midst of mobility. Clearly my own perceptions and narrations of the social world as I experience it through my surroundings, but also as I critically comprehend it as a socio-cultural and political unit, derive from my class and socio-economic background as well as everyday life events within a working-class migrant family, extending to my political consciousness and my positioning as a feminist geographer, an anti-racist and an activist having received education and training, having lived and worked in both a 'European and American space' of shifting adaptation and diversification. Hence, my narrativisation of sociality is inevitably weaved into the separate textualities of my analysis of the participants' narratives. In this way we view the self as an emergent and changing 'project' and not as a fixed and eternally stable entity. Self-definition then, becomes an ongoing narrative project that reveals multiple selves in varying spatial and temporal locations. As Goodson affirms, 'to locate our ongoing narrative requires sources which develop our social history and social geography of circumstances and in many instances collaboration with others to provide contextual and intertextual commentary. Alongside *narration*, therefore, we need *location* and *collaboration*' (1998: 31; italics in the original). As I have already briefly mentioned, my motivations and research interests lie within as well as beyond an initial inquiry into the realms of my own national consciousness and belonging. Born and raised in the United States, daughter of Greek immigrants, having lived and received education in both the United States and Greece, haunted by Socrates' words *'The unexamined life is not worth living for'*, I can *identify* with Karakasidou's (1997: xix) claim of her academic odyssey:

> Perhaps it was a progressive sense of cultural homelessness, born of spending more than half of my life in a foreign country and returning each summer to a Greece that seemed ever less

familiar, that prompted my growing appreciation of comparative cross-cultural theory in anthropology. In any event, it was undoubtedly my training as an anthropologist that brought me to engage critically the basis of Greek national identity and to historicize modern nation building in the country of my birth. I make no claims to privileged knowledge of Greek culture, be it based on innate genes, national ancestry, or the intimacy of childhood socialization and native enculturation. On the contrary, it is often difficult for native scholars to become conscious of, let alone to liberate themselves from, the assumptions of their own culture. It is the burden of culture that conditions one to look at the world in one way and not another.

I have followed ethnographic practice based on distancing myself from native cultural assumptions, and instead I immersed myself in critical introspection, in-depth reflection and active participation in the social phenomena I have aimed at analysing. My research originated from the very beginning, and continues to this day, to be a social encounter that extends beyond as well as within the research project. After many years of research and fieldwork I was able to 'listen beyond' what was said and explore the issues with greater critical awareness and insight.

During some of the interview sessions I realised that certain participants found these encounters almost 'therapeutic' insofar as they could freely and deeply reflect on their lives. This was another point of my awareness of my constant self-reflexivity. A life story interview may have a profound effect on the participant recalling sensitive issues of their life course. Previous professional experience and training gained in a social work setting compelled me at times to take on a previous role, that of therapist-listener-researcher. I immediately became aware of the potential problems involved and disciplined myself enough to be solely a researcher during all sessions following the advice of Slim, Thompson, Bennett and Cross:

> For most people, recounting their life story is a positive, if emotional, experience from which they can gain much satisfaction and a renewed sense of perspective, but the listener should always ensure that the narrator is comfortable at the end of the interview and is surrounded by the support they need, whether from family and friends (2000: 116-117),

while also sharing the same ethical dilemmas as Al Thomson:

> Interviewing which approached a therapeutic relationship could be damaging for the interviewee as well as rewarding for the in-

terviewer. It required great care and sensitivity, and a cardinal rule that the well-being of the interviewee always came before the interests of my research. At times I had to stop a line of questioning in an interview, or was asked to stop, because it was too painful. Unlike the therapist, as an oral historian I would not be around to help put together the pieces of memories which were no longer safe. (2000: 302)

The research conducted is innovative and illuminating in that it explores the return migratory project along with personal experiences and individual insights, expressed in the participants' words: either verbal expressions of in-depth interviews and discussions or written accounts and narratives of their experiences. Being able to act as both an 'insider' as well as 'outsider' is an important component of the research process. In order for a researcher to fully understand a phenomenon, a culture or a people, the language, which is the primary channel of cultural production, must be understood. This is central to the anthropological approach to research, but it is true for any type of qualitative-based research. The participants, being fully bilingual, expressed themselves in both English and Greek without any kind of intimidation if they could not think of the appropriate words and without the anxiety of being misunderstood. On many occasions participants indicated how comfortable they felt disclosing personal matters and discussing important issues about their lives with someone 'who really can understand what I am talking about' (being one of them). Coming from the same background, speaking the same language(s), and having the same concerns and experiences were instrumental in gaining the participants' confidence and dedication to the study.

Filtering of data through the dual lenses of the participants and the researcher is inevitable in the case of qualitative research. In reflexive ethnographies, the researcher's role is critical. Reflexive ethnographies range along a continuum from starting research from one's own experience, to ethnographies where the researcher's experience is studied along with that of other participants, to confessional tales where the researcher's experiences of doing the study become the prime focus of investigation (Ellis and Bochner 2000). The idea of critical self-awareness and the oxymorous nature of participant observation, which leads most times to the observation of the participant and hence the participation of the participant (Tedlock 1991), all blend together within the ethnographic scene of encounter which in turn becomes the ethnographic dialogue of the self and other. It has been argued that because we cannot study the social world without being a part of it, all social research is a form of participant observation (Hammersley and Atkinson 1983). As Yang notes, 'My fieldwork was my own life and the lives of others in which I had an active part' (1972: 63). This is also what Yans-McLaughlin means when she says that:

> The fieldwork methods of ethnography, which often rely on the personal testimony of informants, make it a likely focus for the initiation of this extraordinary self-scrutiny.... and the 'hidden' authority with the interview situation and behind the ethnographic text, as well as experimentation with ethnographic texts make them overtly 'polyvocal' (admitting not to one but several 'authoritative' voices). Both of the creators of the text – the ethnographer and the informant – are the newly acknowledged authorities...The interviewer is not understood as ferreting out data to be discovered only in the recesses of the informant's memory. Rather, the interviewer is actually creating a text *with* the informant. The interview is understood variously as a 'social act', a 'dialogue', and a 'circular feedback' process in which the investigator and the informant continually influence one another. (1990: 256-257; italics, parenthesis and quotations in the original)

Hence, the crux lies in the researcher's commitment to a critically humanistic method that will study the social world from a gendered, historically situated and interactive perspective. With this kind of complex commitment in mind we can embrace a critical, cross-cultural dialogue. Only then can we give voice to the 'Other', that which lies within and outside the self and the text[8]. Only then can we follow Plummer's 'longing for a social science to take more seriously its humanistic foundation and to foster styles of thinking that encourage the creative, interpretive story tellings of lives – with all the ethical, political and self-reflexive engagements that this will bring' (2001: 1).

To sum up, reflexivity is the process of reflecting critically on the self as researcher, the 'human as instrument' (Guba and Lincoln 1981). It makes us confront our choice of research problem, those engaged in the study, and ourselves, and with the multiple identities that represent the fluid self in the research setting (Alcoff and Potter 1993). I only hope that our work, the participants' and mine, can vocalise this vision and visualise this multivocality.

1.3   Documenting the ethnographic textualisation of the narration of migrancy and identity

Chapter one has introduced the book and presented the importance of the study to me as the researcher, to academic scholarship and to the

Greek and Greek-American communities. This chapter presents my research aims and objectives and demonstrates how this attempt to make sense of return migration and identity construction relates to a broader context of shifting configurations in geographies of the social world. Furthermore, Chapter 1 provides the epistemological, methodological and ethical perspectives and context in which the research was conducted, analysed and subsequently presented. The methodological and ethical issues highlight my position as researcher and provide the broader landscape on which the analysis is based. Finally, the introductory chapter summarises the overall structure of the book.

Chapter two locates the study within the wider academic debate on national and ethnic theorising of issues of place, culture and identity. Place is understood as both a context for the returnees' actions and a source of their identity, existing on a border between the subjective and the objective reality of return. Their cultural interpretation of the symbolic and real sense of place is connected with the social construction of their representation of identity through their understanding of the home-place. Therefore, by examining the returnees' *ideologies of home, return and self* through the framework of *geographies of place, culture and identity* we can capture some of the critical meanings revealing of migrants' relocations which are not merely geographical but cultural too. This will illuminate some of the grey areas in return migration and migrant practices. The theoretical framework serves as a guiding chart to understand how the ethnic, national and cultural components reinforce and influence both agency and structure.

Chapter three unfolds the socio-cultural journey from the emigration-settlement of the first generation to the return-settlement of the second generation. By understanding the multifaceted dimensions of these journeys not only do we interpret the historical and social forces that shaped the migration project but we also start to locate personal internalisations and developments – both implicit and explicit – in the return project.

Chapters four, five and six provide primary empirical data based on long-term intensive fieldwork in Athens, Greece. Through careful analysis of the oral and written narratives and of the ethnographic material, return migration is understood as a process that activates the construction of identities and the reconstruction of place. Return migration can thus be further debated as a fluid cultural process that shapes and influences many aspects of migrants' lives and how individuals relocate themselves and the social world. These three empirical chapters are ordered according to the triangular analytical frame that structures my epistemology. Hence Chapter four is on *ideologies of home* and *geographies of place*, Chapter five is on *ideologies of return* and *geographies of culture*, and Chapter six is on *ideologies of self* and *geographies of identity*.

Chapter seven concludes the book. I provide an overview of my research achievements, and I assess if the analysis has met the aims and objectives outlined in the introduction. I evaluate the success and shortcomings of this endeavour and discuss the findings in relation to the wider debate on issues of identity and belongingness. Finally, I point to additional areas for further research in the field of ethnic and migration studies.

2 Situating and theorising national and ethnic expressions of place, culture and identity

Readings and analyses of studies of nationalism, ethnicity and identity have offered valuable insight into the multiple and shifting notions of home, place and self in the return migration project. Moreover, the understanding of nationalism, ethnicity and identity as complex processes of cultural articulation and signification has informed my research project with a theoretical backbone that exposed otherwise concealed notions of migrant belongingness. Furthermore, the analytical terms used in the conceptualisation of the results were selected and developed on the basis of this framework. This revealed how migrant belongingness can be explained in relation to the social construction of place. The returnees' narratives and life-stories, significant sources for the articulation of migrant life and return migration, were transformed into narratives exposing constructions of nation, self and place.

The critical theoretical exploration of the notions of home, place and self not only enlightens the research process but also provides conceptual challenges to the empirical material gathered. This element of challenge is an additional analytical tool, and its value cannot be emphasised enough. More specifically in referencing, situating and theorising national and ethnic expressions of *place*, *culture* and *identity*, I examine:

1. The social production, representation and construction of place as a concept signified and expressed within a cultural context. In locating the *topos*, we are locating *culture*. Place cannot be understood outside a cultural context.
2. Diasporic and transnational formations are networks of cultural transformation between the country of origin (for second-generation migrants, the country of birth, the United States) and the country of return (Greece). The 'here-there' dichotomy can be understood as the connecting channel through which the 'cultural stuff' (Barth 1969) is articulated.
3. The 'self' is signified and consequently articulated as the culmination of the aforementioned processes – place and culture – within the cultural landscape of the conceptualised 'home'.

Hence, the arena of discussion in this chapter is the theoretical representation of my three key analytical constructs: how *place, culture* and *identity* signify the particular conceptual framework of the migrant sense of *home, return* and *self.*

2.1   Locating the topos: exploring place

> *'Place is the locale of the truth of Being'*
> Heidegger

> *'Perhaps place is the first of all things'*
> Archytas

A review of the literature (Sowell 1996; Hammar, Brochmann, Tamas and Faist 1997; Jacobson 1998; Brettell and Hollifield 2000; Foner 2000; Papastergiadis 2000; Castles and Miller 2003) defines and discusses the social processes of migration and return migration affecting the geographic and cultural context of both sending and receiving countries. The study of sending and receiving countries as cultural landscapes can direct us to the dynamic context of where ethnic groups express culture and ethnicity. Cultural performance and cultural production in this sense are connected to place. The cultural topos becomes not only the place of return for the returnees but also the social space where the return itself is articulated, contested, justified, and finally is transformed by the returnees into accepted action. Thus, the cultural landscape of return is at once the ethnic landscape of arrival. In locating this topos, I will present the most fundamental theories and themes that frame place as an expression of national, ethnic and cultural representations while serving as a platform to discuss identification.

The articulation of narratives of return is a bridge into the future that unites past cultural imaginary into new narrative identities. Indeed, the narratives and their sense of self are constructed out of the 'placeness' that they encounter. The narratives of self are situated, they are 'placed', in the cultural topos of the ancestral homeland. As Pile suggests, 'narratives of the self are inherently spatial; they are spatially constituted. That is, stories about the self are "produced" out of the spatialities that seemingly only provide that backdrop for those stories or selves' (2002: 112; quotations in the original). I will now proceed to illustrate how place is conceptualised in my study and how this is linked to culture and identity. This seemingly abstract theorisation will become clearer and more relevant when we look at the returnees' narratives.

Before I pursue the issue of place in depth, I would like to first clarify some points concerning the 'space-place' debate. Or to phrase it as Olwig does, 'Must place necessarily be reduced simply to a portion of geographical SPACE occupied by a person or thing?' (2001: 107; capitals in the original). Unlike most physical geographers who continue to accept a view of space 'defined as three dimensional Euclidian in which action occurs by contact' (Sack 1980: 56), many human geographers now interpret space as being socially constructed. Apart from whether the critique of postmodernism and the cultural turn is resolved (or justified) or not, what is clear is that discussions in geography have moved (back) toward an emphasis on space. As Mitchell notes, 'so added to the postmodern and cultural "turns" of the 1980s, was a spatial turn. All of a sudden, the language of space and place was everywhere. And geographers, used to being in the margins of academic discourse, sat up and took notice' (2000: 60; quotations in the original). The 'reassertion of space in social theory' (Foucault 1986; Soja 1989) became the scope and agenda for a new cultural geography. That is how we now *read* space, place and landscape and further construct meaning out of that *reading*, because it 'is possible, indeed normal, to decipher or decode space' (Lefebvre 1991: 160).

Foucault referred to the ways space is thought of as 'the dead, the fixed, the undialectical, the immobile' (1980: 149). In rethinking and redefining space, the space we dwell in and inhabit as well as the imaginary and symbolic space that we constitute as real, we then come to understand space as a stage for the performance of identity as space itself is performed (Rose 1996). Space is the backdrop against which life unfolds. Space is the container for social action and for the unfolding of events and processes (Lefebvre 1991). The early approaches were developed by theorists of socio-spatial relations, with key representative Henri Lefebvre's triadic model of *perceived, conceived,* and *lived* space.[1] Giddens relates the separation of space from place with modernity (1990: 18), and Massey holds that 'the spatial' is constructed out of the multiplicity of social relations across all spatial scales, clearly integral to the production of the social world (1994: 4); additionally, she has recently reaffirmed that we live in 'spatial times' (Massey 2005).

In Tuan's early work, the meaning of place and space is conceptualised in the following terms, 'place is security, space is freedom: we are attached to the one and long for the other' (1977: 3). But place is multidimensional and carries many layers. It constructs many identities that are also contested in that they cross geographical, historical and cultural boundaries refracted through prisms of ethnicity, gender, race and class. A critical component of humanistic research in geography is to comprehend how people feel about place, rather than how place is in its natural physical setting. Geographers do make sense of place in a variety of ways: by its physical location, natural resources, environmental conditions, and human interactions with nature and landscape symbolism. A humanist-critical-cultural geography suggests that place should be understood as 'imaginative ground'.

These processes of deconstructing place, taking into consideration the many layers of human experience and emotions, direct us to an awareness of place-identity. People locate and reshape themselves in correlation to place as much as place contains a nation's social history. Place has a definition, a history, a meaning: a container both of facts and of symbolism. Defined often as a region, it exists in its own being but it is also constructed, represented and narrated. It is not simply a geographical notion of a fixed and bounded piece of territory mapped by a set of coordinates. Such fixedness has been challenged so that now human geographers maintain that places are fluid and contested spaces.

It is important, however, as McDowell points out, 'not to be too carried away by the fluidity of this new conceptualisation and representation of relational place, as customs and institutional structures clearly persist through time and "set" places in time and space as it were' (1999: 5; quotations in the original). Socio-spatial associations may persist in time, conditioned by social relations. From a geographic perspective, space–'real', 'represented', and 'imagined'–is a foundational concept in the understanding of world constituents, either collective (community, nation, ethnic group) or self-based (gender, identity, ethnicity, culture).

The relationships between 'worlds' and 'selves' and their equivalents (spaces, places, peoples and identities) have preoccupied human geographers and their theorisations (Jones III 2001). This discussion has crossed disciplinary boundaries and become even more interesting as it drew in other social sciences. As an increasing number of social theorists and geographers have claimed, the 'spatiality' of society (the way in which it uses space) is a matter fundamental to the 'very nature of society and its constitutive processes' (Dodgshon 1998: 2). The declaration that 'there are no aspatial social processes' (Soja 1996: 46) brings us to the notion of marginal spaces, those of 'betwixt-and-between' (Turner 1974: 232) or 'third spaces' (Bhabha 1990: 211), portrayed as an 'interstitial passage between fixed identifications which opens the possibility of a cultural hybridity' (Bhabha 1994a: 4)[2]. On the other hand, even those geographers who were initially sceptical about the space-place contribution, for example David Harvey 'who previously dismissed place as a concept for the ideologically blinded and deceived' (Entrikin 2001: 434), discuss the transformation of 'absolute spaces' to 'relative spaces' (Entrikin 1991: 48) and to 'spaces of hope' (Harvey 2000). Cultural cores alternatively provide the basis for a communal, shared sense of 'sacred space'. In all modern societies, sacred places reflect a living community of consensus and conflict (Entrikin 1991: 67).

Landscape is also a contested topos of place, community and self (Olwig 2001: 95) and this is understood when we look closely at community (collective sense of self) and self (identity) in the domain of place. As Casey notes, 'an effort to assess the relationship between self and place should point not just to reciprocal influence but, more radically, to constitutive co-ingredience: each is essential to the being of the other. In effect, there is *no place without self; and no self without place*' (2001: 406; italics in the original). It will be interesting to see if social science *puts everyone in their place* or whether *everyone has their place in the world* and furthermore if identity is a question of *place*.

One response is that 'as agents in the world' we are always 'in place' as much as we are always 'in culture' (Entrikin 1991: 1). In locating the topos, we can initiate a discussion of topophilia[3], 'the affective bond between people and place' (Tuan 1974: 4). Human construction is what makes places. It is this interaction that poses challenges in interpreting the objective and subjective worlds of reality. As Unwin declares:

> Space by itself is meaningless...place has become a focus for understanding the interaction of the human world of experience and the physical world of existence. The task of critical geography is to enable people to reflect upon this interaction, and in so doing to create a new and better world (1992: 211).

Relph (1976) devotes an entire chapter 'On the identity of place' in his book *place and placelessness*. In noting how fundamental the notion of identity is in everyday life, he looks at both individual and community images of place, presents a typology of identities of places, and elaborates on the development and maintenance of identities of places. His basic premise coincides with the focus of the next section, in arguing:

> Identity is founded both in the individual person or object and in the culture to which they belong. It is not static and unchangeable, but varies as circumstances and attitudes change; and it is not uniform and undifferentiated, but has several components and forms.

He goes on to emphasise a vital point of reference, namely that:

> It is not just the identity *of* a place that is important, but also the identity that a person or group has *with* that place, in particular whether they are experiencing it as an insider or as an outsider (1976: 45; italics in the original).

The images of identities of places are reconciled with the identity of the subject itself, in this case the migrant, the returnee. The images of places are constructed and reconstructed during the processes of social interaction and symbolic representation of culture in the context of a bipolar relationship between the 'host' country (in my case Greece) and the 'home' country (in my case the United States) and the struggle to define their meaning and representation. Of course, in this study of second-generation returnees, notions of 'home' and 'host' countries become confused and interchangeable – which is part of the fascination of this study.

Images of places are defined through the use of common languages, symbols and experiences (Berger and Luckmann 1966: 32-36; 130-132). Identities of places become meaningful, like images of places, on the interaction of what Gurvitch refers to as the three opposing poles of the *I*, the *Other*, and the *We* (1971: xiv), which is exemplified at the stage of 'secondary socialisation', that of group attitudes, interests and experiences (Berger and Luckmann 1966: 163-173). This is precisely what Relph poses as the distinctive element in the individual perception of place:

> Within one person the mixing of experience, emotion, memory, imagination, present situation, and intention can be so variable that he can see a particular place in several quite distinct ways. In fact for one person a place can have many different identities. How, or whether, such differences are reconciled is not clear, but it is possible that the relatively enduring and socially agreed upon features of a place are used as some form of reference point (1976: 56).

This particular reference point is the crucial nexus of 'self' and 'place' that becomes the vital mode of experience in the articulation of identification. This is a particularised sense of collective sharing of the notion of 'home' that is a component of individual and collective (migrant) identifications. We then come to comprehend that the spatial order of migrant existence derives from the social production of migrant space, the construction of human geographies that reflect and configure migrant subjectivities in the world. Finally, this realisation leads us to the 'cultural stuff' represented in both the (trans)national and the diasporic experience.

2.2   Cultural representations: the (trans)national and the diasporic

'*We now have to make sense of a world without stable vantage points; a world in which the observers and the observed are in ceaseless, fluid, and interactive motion, a world where human ways of life increasingly influence, dominate, parody, translate, and subvert one another*'

Derek Gregory

If 'culture is to anthropology what place is to geography' (Richardson 1989: 144), then both are necessary for an interdisciplinary dialogue. Place, the experiential; culture, the symbolic. Place, the world; culture, the worldview. Place, the historically contingent process; culture, the creative, the constitutive.

Undoubtedly, migration represents a fundamental engagement with place (King 1995). Migrants' construction of a 'habitus' (Bourdieu 1977) becomes the cultural representation of their world, what Bottomley (1992) in her study of Greek-Australians terms 'the poetics of ethnicity'. This is what I attempt to address under the triple schema of *ideologies of home, return and self* in relation to *geographies of place, culture and identity*.

International migration at the turn of the century has produced new migration networks and transnational realities that extend beyond borders. Transnational social spaces serve as an important frame of reference in determining new everyday practices, new biographical projects, and newly constructed identities. As Pries emphasises, new transnational social spaces are emerging within multiple geographical spaces; life plans and projects are becoming structured within transnational social relationships and institutions (Pries 1999: 27).

These frameworks pose a new challenge for social scientists to rethink the relationship between national, geographic and social space, redirecting geography towards the *anthropo*-geography of the spatial. These spaces involve cultural, economic and political processes in the form of resources, as types of capital[4] (human, financial, social and cultural), and they denote dynamic interchange, not static notions of ties. Transnational social spaces are defined as 'combinations of social and symbolic ties, positions in networks and organizations and networks of organizations that can be found in at least two geographically and internationally distinct places' (Faist 1999: 40). Moreover, Faist defines space as referring not only to physical features but also to 'larger opportunity structures, the social life and the subjective images, values and meanings that the specific and limited place represents to migrants' (1999: 40). Social activity takes *place* in *space*, and, it has been argued, at the epistemological level space 'is implicated in symbolic and conceptual formations' (Shields 1997: 191). In the next section I will address a core conceptual, symbolic and pragmatic formation, namely identity, while drawing attention to the epistemological and theoretical dialectic of 'society-space' in migration and return migration.

Before any 'commitment' to identity and its socio-spatial formation, I would like to address some aspects of the theoretical debates on culture and society. These debates extend to viewpoints on i) culture and agency and ii) culture versus structure. I will review the concepts pertinent to 'culture as praxis' (Bauman 1999) in order to narrow my focus to the 'spaces of culture' (Featherstone and Lash 1999) constructed by return migrants. This is important in recognising that 'a theory of cultural production cannot be properly developed unless we possess an adequate account of the nature of human agents' (Giddens and Turner 1993: 214).

In the history of social sciences, culture[5] has repeatedly been addressed, explored and explained as a concept having connection to groups, settings and processes. A conference held in 1998 by the Harvard Academy for International and Area Studies and the resulting publication entitled *Culture Matters: How Values Shape Human Progress* (Harrison and Huntington 2000) set the record straight: culture still matters! In full agreement with Vermeulen's declaration that 'the variety of notions and definitions of *culture* is virtually endless' (2001: 3; italics in the original), I cannot disregard Bottomley's remark that 'culture is one of the most commonly used concepts in studies of migration, yet it is curiously unexplored' (1992: 3). Compelled by both these views, I will situate *culture* in the context of my theoretical framework, thus incorporating it as *cultural representation* of ethnic, (trans)national and diasporic dimensions of individual and collective migrant trajectories.

The complexity of the culture-concept, as well as the multiplicity and diversity of agents and structures, requires a redirection from traditional disciplinary boundaries toward an inter-, multi- and cross-disciplinary focus. Anthropologists have developed in-depth frameworks of understanding and analysing culture[6] whilst geographers (not limited to cultural geographers and cultural theorists) have evolved from periods of environmental determinism and cultural relativism to a new cultural geography with a critical scope and breadth of inquiry. If there is any consensus in the new work done in cultural geography (and this in a multiplicity of voices: feminist, post-structuralist, etc.), it is simply that, no matter what the approach or perspective, 'culture' is spatial (Mitchell 2000). Not only geography but also other allied disciplines stress this new cultural theory of space, understanding culture to be constituted through *space* and *as* a space. Spatial metaphors have become indispensable in comprehending culture, and culture is understood to be a realm, medium, level, or zone (Mitchell 2000).

In the midst of much confusion of what seems to constitute culture, we may need to turn away from *explanations* and definitions and move towards *explorations of meaning*. Thus, culture 'is the very medium through which change is experienced, contested and constituted' (Cosgrove and Jackson 1987: 95), hence Jackson's *'maps of meaning* through which the world is made intelligible' (1989: 2). But culture is also fluid and open, a 'text' always subjectable to multiple readings and interpretations (Duncan 1990). Clearly, culture is language, 'text', 'discourse'; it is political[7], social, material. It is central to the construction of such entities as 'identity', 'gender' and 'race'. But an important point to emphasise is that culture and ethnicity should not be conflated (Bottomley 1992).

Ethnicity is another slippery term, difficult to pin down to a single definition or conceptual frame. As an explanatory variable, it can become a resource as much as a liability. There have been numerous trenchant critics as well as inspired adherents. Rather than going through a lengthy review of the term's historical development and usage[8], I will attempt to deconstruct the *ethnic* as well as the *(trans)national* in framing a discourse of return migration that extends beyond the diasporic and the cultural to *praxis*.

Moving away from the assimilationist and pluralist arguments that dominated American immigration literature in the 70s and 80s, the discourse of *transnationalism*[9] and *transmigration* defined migrants as both cultural and political actors in order to emphasise that 'many migrants today build social fields that cross geographic, cultural and political borders' (Basch, Glick Schiller and Szanton Blanc 1994: 7). Under these new circumstances, it is vital to reconsider the concept of identity while maintaining a stance critical of extremes: between those that render identity fixed and frozen and those that consider identity as highly fluid and fragmented. Identity should be viewed as a process that is situational and multiple, emerging from historical and contextual circumstances and articulated through constructions of daily lives that narrate this praxis. Although return migration may resemble stasis (the relocation renders it as action completed), the returnees' *personal plan of action* which encapsulates the (trans)national, the diasporic and the cultural is *praxis*, a creative process of identification.

When culture is viewed as 'maps of meaning' (Jackson 1989), we can proceed to 'cartographies of diaspora' (Brah 1996) through the migrants' encounter with the new reality of the ancestral return. Return migration is not dislocation but a new location, a new space where culture is contested. Diaspora, often visualised as exile or expatriation, the struggle between two places and the conundrum of being at home in neither, can also be considered as a demarcation from the hegemony of the nation-state[10].

Diaspora[11] can also become the means to 'narrate the nation' insofar as it conceals the 'trauma' by reconciling past and present through reconstructing stories and boundaries of the national. As 'imagined communities[12]' (Anderson 1991), nations are represented as spaces within which members of the nation maintain a strong bond with each other and as a collectivity for, as Balibar argues, 'the people is the community which recognizes itself...in the institution of the state...' (1996: 138). The argument advanced by Hall that 'it is only *within* culture and representation that identification with this "imagined community" can be constructed at all' (2000: 229; italics in the original) postulates the dialogic relationship between culture, nation and identity.

Although the notion of diaspora is articulated on three levels – homeland, displacement and settlement – the theoretical weakness of the category of diaspora has been criticised as another way of alluding to essentialised notions of ethnicity (Anthias 1998; Sayyid 2000) and considered as an *anti*–nation (Sayyid 2000: 41). The same holds of course for all the concepts explored in this section, including ethnicity. I would like to keep in focus the fact that research on ethnic processes has pointed to new and exciting fields of inquiry and still has much to offer. At the same time, we need to pay close attention to the advice of Eriksen, 'we ought to be critical enough to abandon the concept of ethnicity the moment it becomes a straitjacket rather than a tool for generating new understanding' (2002: 178).

In trying to understand these processes in order to present an alternative framework to structure my empirical data, I have endeavoured to maintain a critical view in relation to traditional social science perspectives. In the next section I explore the concept of *identity* within the context of the social and cultural fields outlined above to underscore its *place* in return migration. As will become obvious, the shortcomings that arise from one singular perspective emerge from disciplinary limitations and associated conceptual problems.

Identity discourse is a stage to bring together varied frameworks for thinking through subjectivity and an occasion to draw new approaches out of previously confined theorisations: the interdisciplinarity that emerges through the (dis)connections between place and identity, the negotiations between the local and the global, the translation of the imaginary and the produced articulations of culture. As Bauman urges, 'culture, which is synonymous with the specifically human existence, is a daring dash for freedom *from* necessity and freedom *to* create' (1999: 136; italics in the original).

Return migrants, as agents and actors, are able through their actions to interact in processes of cultural transformation. That is because 'culture is not a fixed script which actors are bound to follow....Habitual structures affect the lives of individuals but, in turn, the way agents inhabit these structures in their everyday life, affects the contours and trajectory of these structures' (Papastergiadis 2000: 109). The constant mobile and transformative exchange between the 'objectivities' of a society and the 'subjectivities' of the individual (migrant) will be demonstrated in the following section on identity discourse.

2.3 Signifying the self: identity discourse

> *'All identity formation is engaged in this habitually bracing activity in which the issue is not so much staying the same, but maintaining sameness through activity'*
> Michael Taussig

Retrospective theorising of 'essentialist' discourses on identity formation, a term now resonating almost in a derogatory sense because of the belief it holds in inherent values of identity, fixed and attained without the intervention of agency and placed outside of any socio-historical context, is a perspective that I have also dismissed in my study of identity. Instead, I explored contemporary studies on identity in the humanities as well as in the social, behavioural and cognitive sciences.

What I found was hardly surprising: identity is a complex and multidimensional construct. As the subject of continuous debate and fascination to this day, researchers from diverse disciplines have studied identity from a variety of empirical and theoretical backgrounds (Alba 1990; Phinney 1990; Waters 1990; Smith 1991; Romanucci-Ross and DeVos 1995; Jenkins 1996; Hall and du Gay 1996; Castells 1997; Craib 1998; Holland, Lachicotte, Skinner and Cain 1998; Campbell and Rew 1999). As an elastic concept, identity is often shaped by the researcher's lens of emphasis (Erikson 1968; Epstein 1978; Tajfel 1982; Zavalloni and Louis-Guerin 1984; Trimble 1995; Breakwell and Lyons 1996; Burke 1997; Weinreich 1997; Stryker 2000) while, more germane to my own research, much attention has also been given to the relationship between migration and identity (Gilroy 1993; Benmayor and Skotnes 1994; Chambers 1994; Brah 1996; Clifford 1997; Papastergiadis 1998; Rapport and Dawson 1998; Fortier 2000; Ritivoi 2002).

Identity (from the Latin *idem-identitas* meaning 'the same') was first introduced by Aristotle, employed by medieval theologians, the philosophers Locke and Hume, and in this century by the sciences (mathematics), the humanities and the social sciences. One could write volumes about identity as a concept of social science inquiry. It is not my purpose here to provide a comprehensive overview of the literature but rather to situate and motivate my conception of identity in devising a theoretical framework to excavate the constitution of identity from the narratives of second-generation return migrants.

For the purposes of my analysis I draw inspiration from the idea that 'identity is formed at the unstable point where the "unspeakable" stories of subjectivity meet the narratives of history, of a culture' (Hall 1987: 44). I refrain from using a prefix (ethnic, cultural, social, self, personal) to the term identity because I am interested in detaching any such presuppositions from the empirical exploration of the process of identity construction. In exploring the role of various socio-cultural influences during the investigation without assigning analytic attention to them, I allow the participant voices to communicate and establish the qualities involved in the process of their identity construction. The result of this can be viewed as another form of conscious, reflective and self-evaluative understanding of identity. This will be revealed through the participants' narratives. More specifically, many researchers agree that personal narratives offer unique opportunities to represent the self in the construction of meaning (Gone, Miller and Rappaport 1999) and have described the centrality of the 'life story' for the construction of individual identity (McAdams 1990; Linde 1993; Peacock and Holland 1993) in addition to others who have linked narrative and identity (Shaw 1994; Somers 1994; Schiffrin 1996).

What primarily concerns me in my study is how place is perceived by return migrants, how this particular landscape is constructed, reconstructed and possibly even contested and changed to fit their particular life narratives. The insight to these questions will assist the exploration of migrant identifications. These identifications are found in between the spaces of the *home-host* constructs, and this inbetweenness is found in the *place* of the ancestral homeland. In diasporic conditions, people adopt shifting, multiple or hyphenated positions or identifications (Hall 2000). As Paasi denotes, 'identity is not merely an individual or social category, but also – crucially – a spatial category, since the ideas of territory, self and "us" all require symbolic, socio-cultural and/or physical dividing lines with the Other' (2001: 10).

So place is also an allocated perspective when searching for that inbetweenness and the role it has in social life, the critical dimensions of locational meaning rather than the specific sense of location; that is how place should be comprehended if we are to trace the identity of location and not merely the physical space of location. Space is socially constructed, and place is socially articulated. As Tuan states, 'Place is not only a fact to be explained in the broader frame of space, but it is also a reality to be clarified and understood from the perspectives of the people who have given it meaning' (1974: 213). Place, argues Entrikin (1991), is always understood from a particular point of view, and it is both a context for our actions and a source of our identity, existing always on the border between a subjective and an objective reality. The significance of place in modernity is exactly this kind of 'situatedness' and the interconnected of issues of identity and action. Conceptualising place by a rather critical narrative of such notions, Entrikin emphasises that:

> Place serves as an important component of our sense of identity as subjects. The subject's concern for this sense of identity may be no different in kind from that of the geographer, in that the geographer's aim of accurately representing places can also be tied to concerns for social action and cultural identity (1991: 13).

Apparent in the narratives, as evident in subsequent chapters, is this notion of the returnees' existential as well as cultural interpretation of the material, physical sense of place in terms of the social construction of their conscious representation of identity through the *home-place*. This home-place becomes the embodiment of their comprehension of identity; as they seek to mediate their status as 'insiders' in the country of return, they are simultaneously particularising an identity discourse. Place and identity are then viewed, experienced and articulated from points in between, and the access to this inbetweenness is the significance of their ability to actively implement the *personal plan of action* upon return.

In the same vein, Doreen Massey explains that:

> The identities of place are always unfixed, contested and multiple. And the particularity of any place is, in these terms, constructed not by placing boundaries around it and defining its identity through counterposition to the other which lies beyond, but precisely (in part) through the specificity of the mix of links and interconnections *to* that 'beyond'. Places are viewed this way are open and porous ...Just as personal identities are argued to be multiple, shifting, possibly unbounded, so also, it is argued here, are the identities of place...place is interpreted as being important in the search for identity in this supposedly troubled era of time-space compression (1994: 5-10; italics in the original).

And finally, Massey brings us to a realisation central in the study:

> There is, then, an issue of whose identity we are referring to when we talk of a place called home and of the supports it may provide of stability, oneness and security. There are very different ways in which reference to place can be used in the constitu-

tion of the identity of an individual, but there is also another side to this question of the relation between place and identity. For while the notion of personal identity has been problematized and rendered increasingly complex by recent debates, the notion of *place* has remained relatively unexamined (1994: 167; italics in the original).

The dynamic process of identity construction, or identification, occurs in mundane, everyday life, in collective, communal spaces and forms a component of the interactiveness of thought, action and experience. Identification is simultaneously an individual and a collective act, the reason being that 'people construct community symbolically, making it a resource and repository of meaning, and a referent of their identity' (Cohen 1985: 118) because the nation is the metaphorical space in which people locate their personal histories and thereby their identities (Eriksen 2002: 109).

The dichotomy between social and individual identities is not a helpful notion; as Edensor asserts, 'rather than being understood as distinctive entities they should be conceived as utterly entangled, for individual identity depends on thinking with social tools and acting in social ways, whether reflexively or unreflexively' (2002: 24). This helps us to understand identity as a process, not an essence, continually remade through an 'internal-external dialectic' involving a simultaneous synthesis of internal self-definition and one's ascription by others (Jenkins 1996: 20).

Identity is not only conceivable through an ongoing process of inclusion and exclusion, but it also serves as a tool, as a 'mediating concept between the external and the internal, the individual and society...a convenient tool through which to understand many aspects – personal, philosophical, political – of our lives' (Sarup quoted in Edensor 2002: 24). Admittedly then, identities are 'resources of history, language and culture in the process of becoming rather than being: not "who we are" or "where we came from", so much as what we might become' (Hall 1996: 4; quotations in the original). Crucially then, identity is always in process and is always being reconstituted in a process of becoming by virtue of location in social, material, temporal and spatial contexts (Edensor 2002: 29).

2.4 The arena of discussion: place, culture and identity as signifiers of the migrant sense of home, return and self

'Territorial place-based identity, particularly when conflated with race, ethnic, gender, religious and class differentiation, is one of the most pervasive bases for both progressive political mobilization and reactionary exclusionary politics'
David Harvey

I have discussed the way in which 'place matters' (Adams, Hoelscher and Till 2001) in a 'geography that matters' (Massey and Allen 1984) and that addresses questions of identity because 'spatialities represent both the spaces between multiple identities and the contradictions within identities' (Keith and Pile 1993: 225). Migration creates ambiguities about personal identities (Thompson 1994), but this confusion and ambiguity can also become an opportunity for cultural creativity (Bhabha 1994b).

I have shown that the issue of identity is both complex and multi-faceted. Resulting reconfigurations are fundamental issues in an era of general uncertainty (Christou 2002), demonstrating that although migration continues to be a basic feature of social life, our insight into processes of (re)constructing identity is still rather blurred. In response to this complexity, it is not enough to pose identity as constructed in a vacuum; it is not enough to recognise identities as *multi-faceted, negotiated, translated, (trans)formed, (re)invented,* or even as *fractured* or *fragmented.* The fluidity of identities remains a total vagueness if it is not explored through migration-related experiences and then critically explained and analysed. Migration and identity cannot be explained as a single event in space at a single moment in time. Through the return migration process, individuals constitute themselves as *social subjects* and *active actors* who (re)assert, (re)define and refine who they are where they are. Whether identities are crystallised or crafted remains to be examined in the 'historicisation' of the processes for, as Grossberg affirms, 'identity is entirely an *historical* construction' (1996: 100; italics in the original).

In discussing temporal constructions it is relevant here to look at how the national and the cultural interweave and produce a spatial matrix that encapsulates the notion of 'home'. Edensor (2002) explores the 'emotional' notion of 'home' as often synonymous with nation. He avers that the 'centrality of home to constructions of identity partly testifies to the desire to achieve fixity amidst ceaseless flow, and metaphorically is used to proffer a unified, identifiable culture within a specified space' (2002: 57). *Home* as a useful analytic construct is a 'means of encapsulating, linking and transcending traditional classifications'

(Rapport and Dawson 1998: 4). Traditional classifications linked to fixed spaces fail to convey the fluidity of movement within and between conceptions of *home* because 'home', in Bammer's words, 'is neither here nor there, rather, itself a hybrid, it is *both* here *and* there – an amalgam, a pastiche, a performance' (1992: ix; italics in the original).

In this way, there is an indication that people are always and yet never 'at home' as 'home' is perhaps 'where the heart is'. In narratives of place and identity, in stories of self in return migration, home represents both 'the place from which we set out and to which we return, at least in spirit' (Hobsbawm 1991: 65). Home, then is no longer just a dwelling; it has become more mobile as a habitat, and this conceptual shift is a recognition that not only can one be at home in movement, but movement can be one's very home (Chambers 1994; Rapport and Dawson 1998).

In short, in a world of movement, home has become 'an arena where differing interests struggle to define their own spaces within which to localize and cultivate their identity' (Rapport and Dawson 1998: 17). I might add to this the arena of discussion in my study where stories of movement become the domain of self-knowledge; individual narration constructs relationships between home and movement and hence migrancy and identity. This is not far from the working definition of 'home' suggested by Rapport and Dawson, 'where one best knows oneself – where "best" means "most", even if not always "happiest"' (1998: 9; quotations in the original). Hence, rather than regarding the 'homing desire' (Brah 1996) as a source of nostalgic fulfilment, we can look at 'homecomings' (Markowitz and Stefansson 2004) as acts of discovery of selves and mediation of identities. As such, return migration as process and course of action of a life plan is a performance in time and space that involves both countries of origin and destination (from conception to implementation) but that also intersects with particular social, cultural, historical and political surroundings.

In the next chapter we will come across some of those particular social, cultural, historical and political surroundings in the presentation of the Greek-American experience of emigration, settlement and return.

3 The Greek-American experience: emigration, settlement, return and identity

'New York...that unnatural city where everyone is an exile, none more so than the American'
Charlotte Perkins Gilman

3.1 The Greek-American Diaspora: a brief historical review

In trying to locate a non-essentialist social history of the Greek Diaspora and in particular the Greek-Americans, one committed to a critical overview of the group's migration history and settlement in the United States, I was confronted by a dilemma. On the one hand I found books written by non-Greeks almost a century old[1] (i.e., Fairchild 1911; Burgess 1913) or more recent ones that did not include the Greek case (i.e., Sowell 1981; Takaki 1993). On the other side, I found books authored by native Greeks as *outsiders*[2] who offered little insight into the themes I was interested in addressing (i.e., Hassiotis 1993) or by Greek-Americans who were mostly *insiders* and focused on the group's success stories and achievements (i.e., Monos 1986; Moskos 1999). Although Theodore Saloutos' (1956; 1964) devotion in writing the ethnic history of the Greek-Americans is indeed monumental and recognised (including the sole contribution to first-generation Greek-American return migration), his views, largely accepted until the 1980s, have recently been contested[3]. Nevertheless the wealth of material on the Greeks in the United States collected by Saloutos[4] is a dedication to the collective historical memory of the Greeks of the Diaspora, now held in the Immigration History Research Center of the University of Minnesota (Clogg 1999).

An adventurous interdisciplinary spirit and my frustrated thirst for a history that quenches yet questions fuelled my reading and motivated my discussions with scholars from a variety of fields in the US, the UK and Greece in combination with recurring visits to the archives of research centres and the library shelves. This also led me toward additional formal and informal conversations over immigration history with first-generation Greek-American migrants and returnees. Eventually, I realised that if 'the peopling of America[5] is one of the great dramas in all of human history', as Sowell suggests (1981: 3), I was indeed mostly presented with a 'Greek tragedy': escalating from pain, turmoil, sorrow and struggle and reaching a climax of success[6] mixed with joy, confusion and confrontation. The melodic symphony of the Greek migrant's emotional journey is present everywhere from newspaper accounts to poems, songs, novels and plays (i.e., Kalogeras 1985; 1987).

The historical overview attempted here serves as a general stage that will set the 'historical' scene and a starting-point from where the returnees' oral and written narratives will unfold the writing of their *histories* and the construction of their *geographies*.

Incontrovertible remains the fact that the economic, political and social tides of the times shaped the migration destiny[7] to the United States of a number of Greeks who resumed their journey of literal survival. Emma Lazarus' imagery of 'huddled masses', 'tired', 'poor' and 'wretched' can testify to that, as does the mythology of 'golden door' opportunity. The United States stands in these terms as a benefactor who not only raised the standard of living of many thousands of poverty-stricken Greeks but also offered the adventure that led to prosperity and the advantages of having opportunities to accomplish goals and materialise dreams that others back in the homeland would never have. International and transnational entrepreneurial and scientific success is an illustration of this. Strong desire for economic advancement, social acceptance and academic achievement are all Greek-American characteristics that have been emphasised and explored (Saloutos 1964; Moskos 1999). This synoptic portrait of the first generation's relocation and settlement in the United States may appear to echo the standard US-propagated rhetoric about immigrants' hard work and socio-economic progress, specifically, that everyone who works hard can get ahead when we know that structural obstacles to advancement may condemn some poor people (a large number of whom are immigrants) to continued poverty no matter how hard they work and hence such descriptive accounts may appear as matters of opinion rather than fact and as such, to be somewhat essentialising. However, extensive evidence strongly suggests that, in the case of Greek immigrants, many of whom entered the ethnic-niche small business sector specialising in food and catering, this picture of 'struggle and success' is true (Saloutos 1964; Vlachos 1968; Georgakas 1987; Kourvetaris 1997; Moskos 1999; Christou 2001; Constantinou 2002).

The Greek-Americans capitalised on the possibilities that the United States offered for material affluence, educational advancement, social mobility and professional opportunity in an environment of – for the most part – democratic freedom and respect for their human and civil rights. Within this socio-political context the Greek-Americans progressively enhanced their vision and through hard work, patience, strength and spirit, reached their potential and accomplished much. If the acquisition of material goods and even the fame that comes with fortune and success was a product of hard work, capabilities and time, the development of a strong community – 'a fortress by which to protect and within which to cultivate and further develop his (sic) spiritual profile and identity' (Hatziemmanuel 1982: 182) – was certainly a methodical plan to preserve and protect ethnic heritage. For the first generation, the survival of ethnic heritage is undeniably linked to the spiritual well-being of the family. Ethnic ancestry, ingrained in the family in many forms (ultimately religion and language), is a task and an obligation that transforms the Church into an institution of ethno-cultural and religious perseverance (Christou 2001; Christou 2002).

The Greek and Greek-American press, television and radio programmes have also functioned, in their particular capacity, as transmitters of the 'Hellenic Orthodox' ethos and national consciousness in general. While the immigrant first generation relied heavily on satellite television and newspapers, subsequent generations are embracing the more 'globalised' medium of the Internet. It has been argued that current uses in media and technology signal the creation of new dimensions to Greek diasporic identity and imply stronger ties with the homeland thus creating new outlets for expressing ethnicity among those who already have some Greek ethnic consciousness (Panagakos 2003a; 2006a).

Organisations aimed at providing the 'Greek Orthodox' education to the youth for their proper guidance; that is, teaching the Greek language, Greek cultural history, religious beliefs and practices. A great deal of time and money (recorded as mostly coming from the working class of the Diaspora with little help from the government of Greece) has been invested in preparing those structures that aim at 'supporting the spiritual mission that is carried on within the community' (Hatziemmanuel 1982: 187).

At the present time we can point to three different Greek-American communities that have evolved during modern times: i) a predominantly post-World War II community composed of first-generation Greek immigrants and their families, ii) a mixed Greek-American community of early and late Greek immigrants and their off-spring, and iii) a Greek-American community composed of second-, third-, fourth- and subsequent generation American-born Greeks (Kourvetaris 1997). Precise statistical data do not exist on those Greek-Americans who do not consider themselves members of the Greek-American community, including those in mixed marriages and those who have converted to other religions or changed their last names. By and large, the members of the first two groups are urban, working- and lower-middle-class,

business owners (mostly restaurants), and some white-collar professionals. The third group is becoming increasingly suburban, primarily
middle- and upper-middle-class composed of professionals, entrepre-
neurs and scientists.

The first generation, in resisting acculturation, tended to be for some
time closed, ethnocentric and conservative. The second generation
were more preoccupied with assimilation and gaining social acceptabil-
ity and social status in US society than with seeking acceptance from
Greeks within the Greek ethnic community (Kourvetaris 1997). In contrast to the first generation that experienced 'culture shock', poverty,
prejudice and discrimination, the second generation surely had a number of advantages. In terms of findings and interpretations of the second-generation, Greek-American studies have illustrated a generational
continuity of both Greek Orthodox and Greek ethnic identity in the second generation (Scourby 1980; Constantakos 1982; Constantinou and
Harvey 1985; Demos 1988; Kourvetaris 1997). 'Greekness' and 'religiosity' are realigned and they move from an introverted identification
(esostrophic) to an extroverted identification (exostrophic) as we proceed from first to second generation on.

3.2   Patterns of settlement

3.2.1   Hostland practices: integration, assimilation, organisations

The depiction of immigration as a process of arrival and settlement is
frequent in the writings of US historians. The contrast between Oscar
Handlin's *Uprooted* (1951) and John Bodnar's *Transplanted* (1985) best
sums up the fundamental shift in American historical scholarship on
this. The US multicultural environment is a product of historical forces
that fostered assimilation and acculturation as much as pluralism and
diversity (i.e., from Glazer and Moynihan 1963 to Glazer and Moynihan 1975).

Within this shaky environment and amidst radical changes, the
Greeks adapted yet maintained ethnic ties. The topic of assimilation of
Greeks in the United States is studied by Vlachos (1968) through an
intensive analysis of assimilation of the Greek community of Anderson, Indiana. Although the author points to the lack or impossibility of
a single measure of assimilation as the basic limitation of the study, it
is nevertheless a compelling exploration that has produced important
findings in reflecting on the community's assimilation trajectory.

Institutional areas often examined as regards assimilation at both national and local levels in the host country are occupational mobility, formal associations, politics, education, language, religion and family. An
interrelationship exists between exposure in the host country and as-

similation, which is illustrated by the degree of social and cultural participation (hence structural and cultural assimilation[8]) of the Greek-Americans in the United States. I will briefly touch upon these components in the following sections, based on secondary source material. However, in later chapters the participants' life stories and narratives will centre upon these themes.

Historically, diasporas in the United States (Greeks, Jews, Italians, Irish, etc.) have been intensely loyal and dedicated to political causes in their countries of origin, often assuming a role of representative of their country abroad. Ethnic lobbies have tended to portray their devotion to the ancestral or symbolic homeland while maintaining allegiance to American values and strategic interests (Shain 1999).

The story of Greek-American politics is quite complex, culminating with a quite recent apology in 1999 to the Greek people during a visit by then US President Bill Clinton in Athens acknowledging that 'when the junta took over in 1967, the United States allowed its interests in prosecuting the Cold War to prevail over its interest, I should say its obligation, to support democracy, which was, after all, the cause for which we fought the Cold War. It is important to acknowledge that'[9]. On the other hand, Greeks (either abroad or in the homeland) tend to overemphasise the Greek presence in US politics (by the mid-1990s twelve Greek-Americans had been elected to the House of Representatives and three to the US Senate, several in cabinet positions), proudly referring to Greeks and Greek-Americans holding high public office (i. e., Spiro Agnew, Michael Dukakis), but do not dwell on the 'Americanness' of Greeks holding public office in Greece – those who were raised and educated in the US or are of Greek-American background.

By extension, there seems to be an interrelation between diasporic politics and the politicisation of diaspora[10]. Two competing paradigms have been used in interpreting the Greek-American experience and action in this respect: 'one views the Greek Americans as part of a homeland extension, an *homogenia*, a Hellenic diaspora. The other regards Greek Americans as entrants and then participants in American history' (Georgakas and Moskos 1991: 15). These are analytic models that also help explain the social history of Greek migrants in the United States. In both cases the issue of conflicting loyalties may be raised in that political sensitivities are accentuated by Greek-Americans' responsiveness to homeland political situations. This alerts us to the subject matter of the political component in identity construction, and how politics, inevitably, is an aspect of the identity debate that should be addressed. In the following chapters this will become clear in the returnees' accounts. A pivotal issue raised is that of an identity which is either ethnic or transplanted (or perhaps both, as 'hybridisation[11]' accounts suggest) and how profound the influence of culture – Greek and American – is in the dynamic of political consciousness. Highly complex, neither static nor concrete, the constellation of socio-political consciousness nurtures ties with both the homeland and the host-land[12]. This type of dual-loyalty/dual-identity arrangement is not a trade-off that undercuts interests; it is a relationship that permeates nearly all aspects of civic life. This, in a sense, is almost like a reciprocal power relationship between the dominant (United States) and the subordinate (Greece) homelands, where power is negotiated by the migrant-actor or, at times, the migrant-activist. Most acts, political or non-political, are motivated largely by a sense of honour, by the Greek *philo-timo*[13] or 'love of honour'. The Greeks of the diaspora politically are citizens of the country they reside in, but culturally they have some affinity with Greek customs and ethnicity (Kourvetaris 1997). In the tripartite relationship between hostland, homeland and the diaspora as the container within which political mobilisation and political activism takes place, the Greek diaspora was by and large unsuccessful in influencing US foreign policy (Constas and Platias 1993) but successful in promoting and strengthening ethnic identity and nationalism (Panagakos 1998). In this regard, the collective sense of political mobilisation realised through diaspora networks becomes a nexus of diaspora and ancestral homeland.

The role of ethnic networks has been an integral part of the Greek-American community. In addition to serving as socio-cultural and religious centres to assist with the adjustment of compatriots to the new surroundings, these organisations became active in charity, humanitarian aid and scholarship funding. The Greek-Americans show to this day incredible zeal and dedication to the causes and goals of their organisations, and commitment to philanthropy. Although the reasons for the establishment of these clubs and societies are pretty much in line with what was mentioned above, a geographical-spatial component that distinguishes it is that of regionalism-localism-provincialism as a motivating force to enter a specific club. That is, place of birth and origin became a methodical classification component – hence the creation of such clubs as the Laconians, the Cretans, the Arcadians, etc. Greek-American organisations are broadly divided into those that have a national agenda, volume and scope and those with regional and local ones[14]. It is widely accepted that the Church and Greek-American organisations have been instrumental in immigrant life. Yet they have not been conflict-free, and at times they have constituted an arena of competition and tension (Karpathakis 1994).

3.2.2 Homeland practices: family, language, religion

I have discussed elsewhere the role of the Greek family and the Greek community as networks of socio-cultural identification in the preservation of ethnicity, tradition and heritage (Christou 2002; 2003a). Within the context of family socialisation, members assume an active role as ethno-cultural transmitters, primarily toward young children who are the receptors and agents of such practices (Christou 2006b). The family is the life-long system of emotional and even economic support. It has also always played an important role in determining the status and security of older people, above all ageing parents (Costantakos 1993). In turn the children ought to 'obey', 'cherish' and 'practice' what has been 'preached'. The family thus is a cohesive unit, a totality made up of values that exemplify 'Greekness' and the 'Greek' way of life. The degree of intensity of how this may be 'imposed' or 'passed on' depends on the class, education level and generation of immigrant parents (Moskos 1999).

Historically, changes and compromises have occurred on family-related issues of great importance to ethnicity preservation, such as the acceptance of intermarriage. Saloutos declared that 'a son who married outside the group could become an outcast and be stigmatised, an ungrateful errant who is setting a bad example for others. The predicament of a daughter who deviated from the ethnic matrimonial norm of endogamy was viewed as something more *tragic*' (1964: 313-314; emphasis added). We are also enlightened by Callinicos' (1991) study of arranged marriage (proxenio) in the Greek-American community and by Kourvetaris' (1997) study of patterns of generational subculture and intermarriage of Greeks in the United States. As will become evident from the narratives in Chapter 6, women migrants, in their feminisation of return migration, define their relocation as an identity project in a gendered perspective that incorporates national representations. The idea of reunification with the ethnic community in the ancestral homeland and the symbolic ethnicisation of the return are refined by the conscious decision of the return in search of an identity that manifests itself within the religious, the national and the ethnic (Christou 2003b). Such multiple constructions are important markers in the way female migrants view themselves and this impacts on the way cultural production is articulated in the local, the global and the transnational context.

Meanwhile, Tavuchis' (1972) study of second-generation Greek-Americans in terms of family and mobility, intergenerational relations, patterns of interaction and mutual aid between respondents and parents draws on the family unit and kinship system as the locus of socio-psychological support. Gizelis reinforces this point: 'an extremely important factor which has stimulated the Greek-Americans' social and economic progress has been the consciousness of their identity as members of a group' (1974: 83). Several studies grounded in psychology also deal with the issue of ethnicity and family while some examine the Greek-American case (Safilios-Rothschild 1968; Primpas Welts 1982; Bilanakis, Madianos and Liakos 1995; Katakis 1999). The findings that these studies reach to some extent point to similar issues that were raised during the data collection stage of my research. This will be further examined in subsequent chapters on identity construction. Prior to that I will proceed to language, another integral component of identity formation.

The US federal, state, and local legislative acts and mandates on Bilingual Education affected Greek bilingual instructional programmes. The Greek bilingual programme was first established in 1974 and covered the needs of then recent arrivals from Greece. The initial scepticism and low support for these programmes by Greek parents were followed slowly by wider acceptance because of the persistence and success of the programmes' staff (Anemoyanis 1982).

Exactly how successful these programmes have been in the last three decades is beyond the scope of this chapter. Whether they provide positive academic and social experiences to the students and whether they have had positive results, are however interrelated to the primary agenda, which is to preserve and strengthen Greek-American self-image and self-worth (Anemoyanis 1982: 179); this is something that was also discussed during interviewing and will be a central theme in subsequent chapters. Language thus becomes the key to the world of culture from its usage as a system of symbols that allows members of the ethnic group to communicate with one another while fusing symbols with distinctive emotions.

Other studies have looked at ethnic language as a variable in subcultural continuity (Constantakos 1982) and a dominant theme of Greek-American ethnicity (Constantinou 1989). The findings of such studies – either exploratory or more deeply empirical – present the Greek language as significant in the ethnic identification process of the group and in the need for ethnicity maintenance and continuity. At an ideal or symbolic level (Gans 1979), language is a source of ethnicity that strengthens and serves as a boundary-maintenance formula.

Additionally, 'symbolic religiosity' has been developed as a parallel concept, conceived as consumption of religious symbols as a means of religious identification (Gans 1994). Religion, founded by humans, based on their timeless fascination with the sacred and the extraordinary, is a social institution that to this day addresses issues related to the meaning of life that nothing else (for most people) could fully satisfy or answer. Religious life in the diaspora underscores moral and emotional ties with compatriots; it provides comfort, purpose and spiritual awareness that enhance the struggle during such a major life transition thus offering the power of faith, which is hope. The influx of immigrants to the US from countries with mostly a single major religion accentuated the link between religion and national identity. Creed and nation often become intertwined when we refer for example to Anglo-Saxon Protestants, Italian and Irish Catholics, Russian Jews and Greek Orthodox.

The role of the Church in developing a Greek Orthodox American community is an evolving process that started with the first wave of Greek immigration to the United States and continues to this day (Patrinacos 1982; Karpathakis 1994). It is one of the key institutions immigrants and their children use to construct their ethnic and cultural identity (Constantinou 1989; Kourvetaris 1997; Moskos 1999). As Saloutos emphatically suggests, 'Loss of their Greek identity was a fear that haunted many immigrants before they reached this country, and continued to haunt them years after they arrived. This is what prompted them whenever they settled in certain areas in sufficient numbers to form Greek communities whose primary responsibility was to build churches and schools that would help ensure the perpetuation of their faith and nationality, their customs and traditions' (1973: 397). In the following chapters I will examine the role of religion in the identification processes of second-generation Greek-American return migrants. In the next section I will attempt to sketch the phenomenon of Greek return migration and relate it to the subject of my research.

3.3   Theorisation of return migration

Although it has been suggested that 'migration is a one-way trip, there is no "home" to go back to' (Hall 1987: 44), we are very much aware that historically migrants have returned to their country of origin or parental extraction. A large percentage of migrants have returned to their country of origin either soon after arrival or some years after migration[15]. Greek migrants have maintained regular contacts with family and friends, and many often visit Greece during the summer or major holidays. In an article dealing with Greek and Romanian immigrants as hyphenated Americans, James Patterson concludes that:

> The Greek Diaspora is a well-documented phenomenon; its ideal final phase is returning to the homeland, and when this happens, cultural connections between the homeland and the host country continue. ...my interviews with old-timers of both

cultures for the past two decades suggest more verbalization of
nostalgia for the mother country among Greeks, more return
visits, and more travel back and forth between Greece and North
America (1991: 159-160).

A good deal of new literature has emerged in the last few years on return migration[16]. Indeed, in some countries the phenomenon is becoming, according to Baganha and Peixoto, 'perhaps the most researched topic in recent emigration studies' (1997: 28). Yet many gaps
remain: 'Return migration is obviously an important phenomenon and
therefore, the lack of empirical work on the topic is surprising'
(Klinthäll 1999: 2) but its conceptual development appears blurred
while its analytical content remains hazy (cf. Cassarino 2004). I am in
full agreement with the view that return migration is a phenomenon
of unprecedented importance with major implications for both individuals as well as nation states. Return migration as a social, cultural,
economic and political phenomenon requires an extensive, comprehensive and critical analysis of all actors and trajectories involved and the
multiplicity of concepts related to it.
   A few projects have investigated Greek return migration from Sweden (Klinthäll 1998; 1999; 2003) and from Germany (listed in the next
section), primarily returnees from the post-war labour migration to
Northern Europe coming back to Greece in subsequent decades (King
1993; Fakiolas and King 1996). That literature fills the void to some extent, but many scholars have recently commented on the absence of
contemporary research concerning return migration and Greek-American return migration in particular. In fact, there is virtually no recent
literature on Greek-American return migration (Kondis 1997). The
only work on Greek-American return migration is Theodore Saloutos'
(1956) early and pioneering book *They Remember America: The Story of
the Repatriated Greek-Americans*, which deals with the return experience
of first-generation migrants. Richard Clogg's contribution to the study
of Greek History and the Greek Diaspora (1986; 1999; 2002) is also
notable, and the international recognition he has earned as a leading
authority on the history of modern Greece testifies to that; yet he still
bemoans the lack of attention paid to the study of the Greek Diaspora.
In his words, '*Xeniteia,* sojourning in foreign parts, the diaspora experience, call it what you will, has been so central to the history of the
Greek people in modern times that it merits much greater attention
than we historians have so far chosen to give it' (1999: 17). Panagakos'
(2003c) doctoral study is the only recent research project on second-
generation return migration to the ancestral homeland, and it examines the Greek-Canadian case through the life history narratives of
twenty-four women. Out of the twenty-four participants in Panagakos'

study, seven of the women counter-migrated to Canada, that is, approximately thirty percent of the sample, after having spent several years in Greece, eventually returned to Canada. In this study, the Greek Canadian women describe their experiences growing up in an immigrant community in Canada and their subsequent relocation to Greece in search of an authentic 'ideal' Greek lifestyle and 'ideal' spouse, both unattainable in their native Canada. This type of second-generation return constitutes a type of cultural migration that exposes underlying assumptions in relation to ethnic and gender identities in the diaspora (Panagakos 2003b: 80).

From just a few indications we realise what was mentioned previously, that return migration is an important yet neglected component of the migration process. Or, as King notes, 'return migration is the great unwritten chapter in the history of migration' (2000: 7).

Return migration is the core of this book. My research project is essentially conceptualised as a broader problematic that concerns the social construction of identities in relation to place during the course of return migration to the ancestral homeland. The theoretical and empirical study of notions of home and belonging draws attention to a framework of analysis of interaction between local, national and global cultural production in the representation of individual and collective identities. Narrative accounts illustrate subjectivity and provide insight into the return migration experience that often is not revealed by statistical data. Hence, the analysis of the empirical material in Chapters four, five and six will draw attention to the phenomenon as experienced by the participants in the attempt to clarify the abstract of subjectivity into a more concrete account of the human geography of return migration and identity construction.

This section aims at presenting the basics of return migration theories in order to relate these to issues of motivation, integration and settlement and in order to focus thereby on the 'micro-internalities' (individual pre- and post-return processes) as well as the 'macro-externalities' (collective and social effects) that illustrate how the *personal plan of action* is constructed. That is, how the conscious decision to return is perceived-planned-implemented in the cultural space created between *host* and *home*lands[17].

'Return migration', as the term suggests, is understood as the process of migrants' return to the country/place of origin, parental/ancestral extraction or to the 'symbolic homeland'. This implies a voluntary decision, but it may also be involuntary, forced on the migrant by either environmental/personal disaster or political action; in this case it is commonly referred to as 'repatriation'. Several terms have been used in the literature to refer to return migration, but they are not all synonymous terms: remigration, re-emigration, return flow, return move-

ment, reflex migration, retro-migration, back migration, counter migration, counter-current, counterflow, counterstream migration, second
time migration, U-turn migration and others. There seems to be an
abundance of terminology but no clear consensus on the contextual
usage of each thus creating much confusion[18]. The Greek word for return migration, παλιννόστηση (palinnostisi), means the return to the
homeland (nostos). 'Nostalgia, deriving from the Greek nostos and algos,
is literally the pain one feels in longing for home. However, confusion
exists as to who is classified as a return migrant. The Statistical Bureau
in Greece during the 1960s and 1970s defined a returning migrant as
one who had lived abroad for at least one year and who was intending
to stay in Greece for one year or more (King 2000). The Social
Sciences Centre in Greece in its first volume of Essays on Greek Migration (1967) briefly mentions the basic conclusions of a survey on return
migrants (mostly from Germany) conducted by the centre in cooperation with the Ministry of Labour and the Ministry of Coordination but
does not offer a typology of any sort.

Existing typologies advanced are based on i) economic distinctions,
development of host-home countries, ii) temporal variations, length of
time stay in the home country, iii) intentions of return and the implementation of such, and iv) the motivation of return (which can be sub-
divided into the reasons, i.e., religious, ideological, political, employment, marriage, etc. and rationalisation of acculturation, i.e., failure,
nostalgia, retirement, etc.)[19].

Fairly recent empirical investigations of return migration to Greece
(again mostly concerning return from Germany) have focused primarily on the economic variables of standard push-pull factors (Robolis,
Boules, Souri and Pasadis 1989; Robolis and Xideas 1990; Glytsos
1991). As such they follow previous surveys (Lianos 1975; Bernard and
Comitas 1978; Fakiolas 1980; Mousourou and Kollarou 1980; Papade-
metriou 1985; Unger 1986), with the exception of Bernard and Ashton-
Vouyoucalos (1976) who used life histories from fifteen migrants and
their families who had returned to Greece from Germany.

In further reflecting on my ethnographic exploration of second generation Greek-Americans and their settlement processes in the ethnic
ancestral homeland, I draw attention to this problem of terminology,
namely how to describe my participants in terms of their migration status because their relocation process is discursively and practically negotiated by the participants themselves. For pragmatic reasons, I call
them return migrants and their phenomenology return migration despite
the fact that they were not returning to the place where they were born
and from which they had earlier migrated. Instead they were returning
to the birthplace of their parents, the first-generation or primary migrants. Clearly this is a problematic usage of the term 'return migra-

tion' which needs further discussion. Indeed, one could say that, for this group of second-generation Greek-Americans, true return migration might be construed just as easily as a movement back from Greece to the place of their birth, the United States.

What is obvious is that my participants, the second generation *returning home*, challenge conventional and simplistic conceptualisations of international migration as a neat process leading from one country to another and then, for some at least, back again. In my research, the first generation did not return, but the second generation did. The situation potentially becomes more complicated when the first generation sometimes does return, accompanying their adult children or following them at a later stage. However, this discussion can easily become too contorted (and futile). Despite the conceptual elusiveness, I have held to the term 'return migration' to connote the second-generation Greek-Americans relocating to Greece for three basic reasons. First, as noted, is the pragmatism of the lack of a neat alternative and the clumsiness of having to repeatedly enter a caveat throughout the text that I acknowledge that the term does not adequately define what I am exploring. Second, I feel that, as employed by my analysis, the term does have hermeneutic validity since the participants did actually feel that they were *returning* to their 'home' – and this emerges powerfully from their narratives throughout the book. And thirdly, I need to point out that this is not a book primarily about return migration but about *identity* and about the potentially multi-sited, ambiguous and contested nature of *home*.

It is, nevertheless, intriguing that second-generation returnees have been so comprehensively ignored in the migration literature; perhaps this is unsurprising given that the general phenomenon of return remains under-researched and under-theorised in migration studies. The standard texts on migration (such as Rapport and Dawson 1998; Brettell and Hollifield 2000; Papastergiadis 2000) say nothing on second-generation return. Even the few texts which focus specifically on return migration say either nothing (Ghosh 2000) or very little (King 1986). Cohen (1997) acknowledges multi-generational returns in his *Global Diasporas* but only as part of a general analysis of diasporic migrations.

The most extended discussion of this thorny issue (though still very brief) is in King, Strachan and Mortimer (1983: 10-11; republished in King 1986: 6-7 in a slightly shorter version), where the term 'ancestral return' is used. In King's review, there are mentions of the French *pieds noirs*, the Portuguese *retornados* and the colonial Dutch repatriated from Indonesia as examples of 'forced' return involving second and subsequent generations whilst 'voluntary' ancestral return is discussed by King and by Cohen (1997) with reference to the 'return' of Jews to Israel. In this chapter I add several examples of recent research on return migration as outlined in footnote 16. Interestingly, Loretta Baldassar (2001), in her study *Visits Home: Migration experiences between Italy and Australia*, looks at first and second generation Italian-Australians, permanently living in Perth, Australia but having ancestral origins from San Fior, Italy and the transnational movements of these groups as 'return visits' in search for home and identity during those journeyings between the two countries. In Baldassar's study, 'home' is a constantly negotiated place for the migrants and the visits 'home' are constitutive of their identity. However, the focus here is on the 'visits' and not on permanent relocation to the ancestral homeland as this is how migrants perceive and plan their trips to Italy, that is, with a return ticket back to Australia.

As mentioned earlier, with the exception of Panagakos (2003c) on second-generation Greek-Canadian women, none of the previous examples specifically address the issue of the return-migrating adult second-generation who, like the Greek-American participants in my research, take the conscious decision to return in their early-adult years to their parents' home country and for whom no obvious term can be found. Amongst the lexicon of the return migration terms (remigration, reflex migration, retro-migration, counterstream, U-turn migration, back migration etc. – this list is from King, Strachan and Mortimer 1983: 8), none is particularly appropriate. The notion of 'ancestral return' comes a little closer, or perhaps one could coin a new term such as 'reverse migration' or even *progonostisi* (after *progonos* meaning 'ancestral' and *nostos*, longing for a *home*land).

Nonetheless, for practical purposes I use the term 'return migration' in the book as it is a relocation to an acknowledged homeland, and I specify throughout the analysis that this is a migration involving second-generation Greek-Americans who were born in the United States to Greek or Greek-American parents.

In the following sections I will outline the 'desired', the 'possible' and the 'realised' in terms of the integration processes of return. That, in conjunction with the conceived-constructed-implemented plan of return, will prepare the discussion of the *ideologies of home* as the articulation of *geographies of place*.

3.4 Motives of return, problems of integration: the desired and the possible in the country of origin

Strategies of return, insofar as they may be predetermined, organised and planned, are inextricably context-based. They materialise according to the specific socio-historic context and 'the coherence of the trajectories followed by returning emigrants is anchored in the actual locale, that is, in social conditions which exist there to receive, accommodate and integrate their "initiatives'" (Reis and Nave 1986: 35; quotations in the original).

For first-generation Greek-Americans, the homeland return is mostly a constant desire[20] of return to the 'lost native land', the 'old country' ways and to everything that was familiar and not foreign. 'I don't want to leave my bones here', referring to the United States, 'I want to visit my parents' grave and be buried there where the soil is sweet', refer- ring to Greece, are frequent refrains among first-generation Greek im- migrants in the United States, strongly asserting their 'emotional' com- mitment to an eventual homeland return. If we are to rationalise these desires in order to simplify the reasons behind them, we immediately think of the migrants as 'sojourners' who inevitably want, should and will return to their home country.

On the other hand, the second-generation return is a process that to an extent puzzles us, especially if the returning migrants decide to re- locate on their own, without their immediate families. Although the motives and strategies of return will be better examined in the next chapters through insights offered by the returnees' personal accounts, the basic categories that can be identified are related to plans and ex- pectations that are 1) personal/social (i.e., moving with a spouse or to meet a future spouse, relocating as a way to reunite with the extended family, climatic and life-style preferences, closer access to Europe for travel and vacation purposes, etc.); and 2) professional/educational (i.e., finding a better or more suitable job, having access to a different job market, attending college or university either as undergraduate, post- graduate or transfer student, etc.). All these motives, and some subcate- gories that will be discussed in relation to the narratives, are intercon- nected with processes of identification during settlement in the ances- tral homeland.

Finally, despite the returnees' expectations and strategic planning, problems[21] in integrating, complaints, dissatisfaction and disillusion- ment with the 'return reality' are vital components of the identification process. This type of 'struggle' highlights the interplay between 'mi- grant-actor' and 'homeland-structure' as well as the role of culture and ethnicity. The *return ideologies* construct *return geographies*: the return- ing migrant stories are stories of their newly constructed world[22].

3.5 Effects on the returnees, their families and the country of return

The motivation to abandon one's roots en route[23] to survival, even suc- cess, does not in any way diminish the trauma attached to the process.

The uprooting of people must be one of the most extraordinary dramas of life and history. Voluntary migration may in essence be forced if individuals desperately need to inhabit a new environment in refuge from political, economic, or other uncertain circumstances. We can immediately comprehend the psychological turmoil the migration-return adventure brings to individuals and families if we consider what King describes when he states:

> ... in many other 'emigration societies', the most important protagonist of emigration was the individual peasant who, in spite of being firmly anchored in the cultural traditions of his home community, was forced by economic circumstances to abandon the close-knit environment of his family and village and seek his betterment in an alien territory. The pain of departure from this womb-like Gemeinschaft (underlined in the original) naturally fixed his thoughts on an eventual, hopefully triumphant, return. (1988: 1; quotations in the original)

Even the 'rags to riches' saga encapsulates a multitude of turbulence throughout the journey. As Greeks often say, 'you go through forty waves'; that seems a pretty stormy trajectory. Or as Foner puts it, 'in story, film and family lore, turn-of-the-century immigrants are often recalled as noble sufferers and heroes who weathered hardships in Europe and a traumatic ocean crossing to make it to America. That is a hard act to follow' (2000: 34-35).

The consequences of emigration for the sending societies have been well-documented and the subject of much debate. On the other hand, the ideal effects of return migration would include the transfer of funds, investment of capital, valuable professional experience, qualifications and skills, in other words all forms of capital (human, financial, cultural) for the sake of development of the homeland.

In an effort to assist the Greek Diaspora during migration and return in resolving problems related to practical issues (insurance, taxation, education, medical coverage, employment, administrative paperwork etc.), the Greek government established the General Secretariat for Greeks abroad in 1983. The Secretariat's agenda (listed on the website www.ggae.gr; most pages are in Greek and some short paragraphs have been translated into English) is quite ambitious and comprehensive. However, the implementation of the suggested programmes that would help smooth the transition is very slow and remains, to this day, incomplete.

Alternatively, associations [i.e., 'The World Council of Hellenes Abroad' (SAE), 'American Hellenic Progressive Educational Association' (AHEPA), 'The Daughters of Penelope', 'American Women of Greece'

(AWOG), 'Alumni Association of American Universities', etc.] that are mostly non-profit and non-governmental organisations have assisted in filling some of those gaps. For the most part, however, Greek-American return migrants are not fully aware of various complex intricacies (i.e., bureaucratic procedures, army service, recognition of foreign degrees by the Greek Ministry of Education, etc.) and this can create additional anxiety and resentment that frustrate both the returnees and the process of settlement. We will see in the next chapters how the returnees have dealt and are still dealing with such complexities and what mechanisms they have been able to develop in order to try to cope – not always with full success.

3.6   Journeys, memories and praxis: space, place, cultural landscapes and the personal plan of action

For some, journeys are simply an escape from routine, fixed in time, fixed in their agenda. For others, life is a perpetual journey. Others shut the world out, and then there are those who openly let the world in. For the returning migrant, journeys of arrival and departure, recurrent goodbyes and new hellos are a link between the past and the present and a window to the future. The boundaries of subjectivity become permeable once a cultural space enters the journey and rewrites this new relationship, that of journey-memory-praxis. The 'personal plan of action' is the instrument by which the return migrant's *praxis* overrides the *cultural landscape* that once stood still in time. The journey of return becomes a bridge upon which the past is reconciled with the present and forms the future. This future is an amalgamation of cultural fields and spatial constructions that provide the symbolic landscape of home.

    To theorise about such journeys is to be mobile. To trace such theorisations is to approach home, in disagreement with Clifford who views 'theory as a product of displacement, comparison, a certain distance. To theorise, one leaves home' (1988: 177). Unlike Clifford I have understood the theoretical construction of the 'personal plan of action' – the conscious decision to implement the ancestral return as an articulation of the returnee's *ideologies* and *geographies* – as a project of home found, not home lost. Greece is a national space that the returnees can claim as their 'own'. In this creative experimentation of constructing national belongingness, identification processes are conducted through the rearrangement of their 'own' lives. The previously 'lived national space' of their country of birth, the United States, is the destination country of their parents' migratory plan, and in retrospect, one generation on, Greece becomes the destination country of the children's returning migratory plan, a 'living national space'. Between this 'lived' and 'living' national space and within the national place, identities are formed as 'homes' are found and futures are planned. However, in the journey toward 'idealised homecomings', obstacles emerge, barriers surface, dissatisfaction appears and thus, the impossibility of 'home' is also confronted and experienced. In the next three chapters I will trace the theorisation and the articulation of those 'homes', identities and futures.

4 Ideologies of home and geographies of place

In Chapters four, five and six, I use the life stories from my fieldwork study with second-generation Greek-American return migrants to address questions of *identity*, *home* and *belongingness*. As I pointed out in Chapter two, I needed a methodology that would not just focus on events and factual analysis but that would become a useful tool in seeking to understand the participants' relationships to their social worlds – the one they previously lived in and the one they have currently decided to live in – and their construction of self. This approach developed through the use of oral and written narratives that provided ways to access and then analyse the material about the returnees' lives and a method of 'throwing light' on their interpretation of self in society (Chanfrault-Duchet 1991; Mann 1998). To address this aim, oral and written techniques vocalised the stories. In this respect, the *storied life* transforms into a catalyst that initiates the reassessment of a *lived life* in the exploration of meanings directed by constructions of *culture*, *nation*, *ethnicity* and *place*, in their words, where the *ethnos* meets the *topos*. All the stories were constructed around a perception of *self*, contextualised in past and present constructions of *home* and leading, in response, to a re-evaluation of the future. Despite the stories revealing a variety of different personal experiences, the majority of viewpoints were similar and shared a basic storyline: the ancestral return was a *conscious decision* to relocate to the homeland where participants could feel their 'Greekness' to its fullest extent, experience first-hand the 'cultural stuff' that makes up such an existence, and settle in the *patrida* (ancestral homeland), the 'authentic' *topos* of their identification process.

The process by which the participants organised and offered an insight into their life events of migration and return migration is situated in a particular context at the given moment in time. No method of eliciting life stories can produce an 'authentic' product, and once this is acknowledged we can draw meaning from the personal perspective as such. As Mann affirms, 'if one of the aims of the life story analysis is to elucidate a personal view of self, enmeshed in, and making sense of, a life context, then all clues must be seized upon' (1998: 96). Indeed it is through interpretation that we can fully understand life stories and so we give special attention to the contexts that shape their creation (Kopijn 1998). In this way the interplay between the personal and the social is scrutinised while keeping in close perspective the flow of symbolic-social-political discourse. Return migration is as much a political event (the politics of return) as it is a socio-cultural (identity politics) and personal activity.

In this study I use the life stories of forty return migrants to examine whether second-generation returnees construct their return migration project as a search for identity and, if so, to investigate if this identity is constructed in relation to place as the manifestation of home and belongingness. The purpose of the study is to explain how and why return migrants negotiate and construct their identities in the ancestral homeland. The life stories and narratives serve to illuminate this experience. In this attempt I have been alerted by Ankersmit's claim that 'narrativism is a constructivism not of what the past might have been like, but of narrative interpretations of the past... narrative interpretations are theses, not hypotheses' (2001: 239-240). Thus, I approached the research inductively, both as an exploratory and explanatory study. I immersed myself in the data and searched for patterns, themes and constructs. I wanted to critically look at the returnees' trajectories as shaped by the context they lived in and at the participants themselves shaping their contexts: return migrants as 'active actors' and 'home-host' contexts as 'structures'.

During the analytical process I realised that I did not want to simply find filtering devices to deal with reducing the excess of information and overcoming the overwhelming task of managing the data. I wanted to use the 'heuristic potential' (Chanfrault-Duchet 1991: 79) of the life-story approach in order to overcome the natural temptation to use the material collected as an illustration of my research questions in a glib fashion, which would be rather easy but would undermine the 'hermeneutic potential' of the approach (meanings as understandings that emerge when 'thinking through' and 'with' others to exemplify intersubjectivity). The driving force, as Plummer says, is that 'we can see life stories working their way through a series of *circles: self, others, community, the whole society*' (2001: 243; italics in the original). The bridge between personal biography and cultural history connects the internal world to the external world, the subjective and the objective, while establishing boundaries of identities and collectivities as links across life phases and historical shifts in a culture (Plummer 2001).

To this end, another important feature of my research effort was to try to adhere to the potential of interdisciplinarity (Grele 1975; Portelli 1991) and overcome the temptation to borrow methodological tools from only one discipline. Reflecting on this, I felt fortunate and furious at the same time. Fortunate enough that my background in both the humanities and the social sciences had given me the tools I required but furious with my indecisiveness in the choice of the 'appropriate' one to use for my analysis. As I mentioned previously, I had rejected analyses that alluded solely to the 'heroic' representations of Greek-Americans, hence my initial hesitation and later stern resistance in not being trapped in a portrayal of 'heroic' characteristics in Greek-American return migration. I aimed at problematising notions of *nation, culture* and *ethnicity* in unveiling processes of *identification*. I strove to override assumptions of romanticised stories of migrants simply overcoming obstacles in a one-way path from struggle to success. I attempted to make critical cross-sectional observations that highlight action that negotiates, associates, and contests. So my focus was more on struggles. I attempted to make connections between migrants and 'home-host' constructs and to contextualise those experiences while framing the stories with theory and method. Consequently, individual and group dynamics (social, family, cultural, economic, political) that interacted to produce a 'personal plan of action' in the return trajectory would be clearly identified and explained. This, no doubt, could be no other than the matrix of identification.

The 'matrix of identification' at the same time reflected my decision on how I was to use the oral and written narratives as evidence evaluated, compared, analysed and interpreted. My aim was to create a writing document assessing meaning of personal and social constructions, through the facts and opinions given, by using the imaginative and narrative articulations toward a deeper historical consciousness of a critical human geography of return migration. My final decision of available forms of interpretation and analysis was a combination of using a 'thematic montage of extracts', 'narrative analysis' and 'reconstructive cross-analysis' (Thompson 2000: 270) in order to produce a multidimensional 'explanation' of second-generation Greek-American return migration.

In life history writing or research that employs life stories, there is a turn to comprehend the very act of writing as well, to understand the ways through which lives and realities are interwoven in the text. With this comes an awareness of the 'conditions that shape textuality'; according to Plummer (2001: 171), texts are 'readerly' (allowing the reader to make easy sense of the text) or they can be 'writerly' (allowing the writer a much freer play in the construction of the text). However, it is important to be careful not to lose sight of the richness of the data by becoming too obsessed over stylistics, aesthetics and poetics in the rhetoric and above all to be aware of not replacing the importance of narrative content with 'heuristic protocols and narratological frames' (Plummer 2001: 202). The degree of ease with which the reader understands the writing practice also sharpens understanding of the text and

deepens comprehension of meaning. As Plummer argues: 'Understanding these "new worlds of writing" helps us to critically rethink
some of our older and tired academic practices' (2001: 173). The above
critical observation is linked with the way I have been using the term
'geography' (from its Greek etymology) in relation to the narrative accounts: the return migrants are writing their own worlds. And they are
also, to quote the title of a book that reflects this migrant-centred narrative genre, 'writing across worlds' (King, Connell and White 1995) –
the worlds, and cultures, of Greece, the United States, and 'Greek-
America'.

As the life stories reflect partial, selective and at times fragmentary
consciousness of migrant subjectivities, the emergent process of 'self-
building' (identification processes) unfolds in a particular social context
of space and time whereupon the story is located. In that sense, 'exposing regional narratives and deconstructing them in a loose fashion is
important for understanding the process of identity construction
through the delineation of boundaries, of mappings and spatialities,
and of oral traditions inspired by local, regional, and national myths,
history, memory, and cultures' (Leontidou 2004: 595).

There is, of course, a difference between how individuals talk about
their lives and how they write about their lives. In both cases the life
stories (oral and written narratives) are used to illuminate lives and in
doing so are very powerful because they capture the multi-dimensional-
ity, richness and complexities of individual experiences, in particular
socio-cultural contexts (Lawrence-Lightfoot and Hoffman-Davis 1997).
Background data on the forty participants can be checked in the appendix.

4.1   The ancestral return: searching for a homeplace in the homeland

The use of 'ancestral return' as terminology to describe the process of
second-generation Greek-American return migration *inherently* points
to an attempt to (re)discover origins, roots and pathways of heritage. In
decoding the ancestral return, we also must point to the returnees' particular 'life-strategies', those decision-making processes that I have
termed the 'personal plan of action'. Individually as well as collectively,
the returnees are not 'fate driven' like heroines and heroes of a 'Greek
tragedy'; on the contrary, they are able to shape the reality of their lives
by pursuit of their life choices. Within the context of choices, although
the returnees appear to be 'heirs to the legend of heredity' and 'en-
trapped by the myth of homogeneity', they come to a Greece, the ancestral homeland, in search of an 'authentic' homeland but are then

confronted by a 'homeplace' that differs: it resonates with previous images of another 'homeplace', the United States. In this respect, views range from disappointment and alienation, feelings of being a 'stranger in my own country', to contentment and acceptance of familiar surroundings of melting pots and mosaics. Returning migrants process cultural landscapes as homeplaces that accentuate cultural belongingness. This should be analysed as an expression of agency that synthesises 'home-host' constructs in the negotiation of a home (dis)location.

The main themes that are identified in this section and that will be discussed by contexualising excerpts from the returning migrants' narratives are in reference to *cultural landscapes* in *topographies of nation*. This is the first encounter with the *ethnographies of ethnicity* that prepare for *cartographies of identity*. Specifically, cultural landscapes point to the intersection of *culture* and *nation*, thus presenting *local geographies of home*. Ethnographies of ethnicity point to the intersection of *ethnicity* and *nation*, thus drawing narrative maps of identifications through heritage in the homeland. Finally, by comprehending the returnees' representation of homeland as the ethnocultural construct of *homeplace*, we comprehend that *place is home*, and hence the next section will discuss constructions of *homeness* and *placeness*. This and the next section will analyse these meanings through narrative excerpts and engage in narrative analysis of the returnees' *logos* as we deconstruct their images and imaginings of the *topos*. Finally, this chapter will present the 'lived' and 'living' life of home in the national as narrated by stories of home *at home*.

Return migrants focus on culture, heritage, tradition and roots as a means to an end, the end being the end of a journey in search for a homeplace in the homeland. This is the 'essence' of the ancestral return, drawing close to where ancestors paved true meanings of 'Greekness'. As Clogg notes, 'it seems that "Greekness" is something that a person is born with and can no more easily be lost than it can be acquired by those not of Greek ancestry' (2002: 5). The ancestral homeland is the cultural landscape where return migrants come close to the origin of their ethnic and cultural selves. This is explained by *geographical* proximity to the ancestral place that reinforces self-actualisation through immersion in the spatialities enclosed in the ethnocultural boundaries. The 'cultural (and I might add, ethnic) stuff' is visualised, experienced and represented as a pathway to 'home' as a means to maximise ethnic belongingness. Cultural practices, cultural landscapes and ethnic symbols are all evoked to describe the connectedness with Greece as the ancestral homeland where history and tradition originated, flourished and continue to exist. These images, symbols and practices not only stimulate ethnic pride but also bring closure to a history of emptiness, absence, trauma and exile in 'foreign lands'. The an-

cestral homeland then becomes the terrain through which all those negatives have been re*placed* and regulated. Thus, the national habitat becomes a space of 'rehabilitation': the antidote to 'homesickness', the
poison that saturated the self in the life in 'foreign lands' is substituted
by 'oxygen', as Sophocles tells us further on. These are all powerful realisations of individuals who otherwise would consider a birthplace as a
birthright, and the right home those 'foreign lands'.

Some of these feelings of *rootedness* are captured in the following excerpts[1]:

> I am very strongly connected to Greece. This is something that
> comes from deep inside; it comes from deep within. In my idea of
> a homeland, culture is primary; it is the number one on my list of
> things that make me feel this way. My heritage is very important
> and so are my traditions. I feel close to my roots when I am in
> Greece. It was my destiny to come here and connect to my roots
> and it's the importance of the destiny I share with my people that
> matters above all. It's my family, I mean not just my immediate
> family and relatives, the people in my country are my family. I
> want to stay with my family; I want to stay with Greece my coun-
> try. My country and I will both become better when we are united.
> That's all I needed and wanted out of my life. (Achilles, male, 33
> years old)

> I feel so much at home here, it is a natural part of being myself,
> a Greek, in Greece. I would feel myself a stranger anywhere else.
> This is where my ancestors came from and this is where I return
> to. I can't emphasize enough how special it feels to come so close
> to your roots, your culture, your language and your people. I could
> never stop being a Greek, even in America, it is in my blood and
> my life but it feels great to be in a place I can call home. It gives
> me both the chills and warm feelings; it's touching and tremendous
> at the same time. This was a dream and now I can open my eyes
> and live my life in my forefathers land. (Patroklos, male, 37)

> For me with what is going on in the world today, I need to feel
> the security and comfort of being immersed in my culture and at-
> tached to my roots. I could only fully achieve this by moving to
> Greece. This was a well-thought of and well-planned decision, it
> was my decision, it was conscious and considered as the only life
> option for a complete and fulfilling life in the true country of my
> heritage. I would never feel at home anywhere else than in Greece.
> I could never adapt to another place devoid of my roots and heri-
> tage. I could never be happy anywhere else. My roots are here in

> *Greece. I belong to Greece and Greece is a part of me, the part*
> *that makes me whole. I have completed my ancestors' destiny and*
> *life cycle. I am finally here.* (Hector, male, 36)

According to the internalisations of *rootedness* elaborated by the participants, the second-generation Greek-American return migrants externa-
lise their feelings of being so rooted in Greek soil that exemplifies culture, heritage and tradition in the surroundings of the nation. This is a
shared experience indicated in the above statements. The emphasis on
organic links with Greece is characteristic of a *reterritorialisation* (Malkki 1992) of the Greek diaspora in the homeland surroundings, what
we might term a *counter-diasporic experience*. More on this will be discussed in Chapter six in relation to processes of negotiating and constructing *transhybrid* identities. However, it is necessary that any discussion of hybridity and diaspora in the articulation of identity be situated within the lived experience of history and the social relations of
everyday life so that the concepts are located geographically; otherwise,
this neglect can lead to theories and politics which disregard the everyday, grounded practices and economic relations in which identities and
narratives of race and nation unfold (Mitchell 1997: 533-534). The assertion of a conscious, planned and implemented 'rooted' return is expressed in relation to the (home)land as the fulfilment of belongingness. Relocation to the ancestral homeland, the 'true country of heritage', is perceived as part of the life cycle, destined to bring about
happiness and emotional completion to the migrants. It is a 'cultural
migration' (Panagakos 2003b: 80) envisioned as an idyllic lifestyle of
true 'Greekness' that seemingly 'empowers' migrants to take charge of
their destiny, their life and their future. In this sense achievement of
belongingness becomes the end goal in a series of strategies, that is,
through mobility the purpose is to attain stability in the acquisition of
an 'authentic' Greek identity.

Ethnic belongingness is sustained by acts of closure to culture, tradition and the ethnic past that become the returnees' motivation to a national present. Excerpts illustrate this type of agency, the action taken
by the returnees themselves upon return. The bridging of past and present, material and immaterial national constructions is a vital component of the rationalisation of return. As binaries of 'home-host', 'foreign-familiar', 'agony-nostalgia', 'suffocation-breathing' and 'strange
land-homeland' are clarified, the return decision is clear in terms of
the ancestral reunion. Cultural landscapes and ethnic symbols are
those national spaces that were discussed in Chapter two as 'sacred
spaces' because they contain a cultural core: the heritage of the ancient
past in the form of material and spiritual history. This is illustrated in
powerful images that participants visualise and the sensations they ex-

perience in awe of their internalisations of ethnic pride that emerge, whether they are gazing at the Acropolis or listening to Greek music. The objectification of Greek culture through lived experiences of ethnic symbols of pride, heritage and tradition transforms the struggles in private cultural space of cultural maintenance into an open and accessible site of cultural abundance in the public sphere (Christou 2003c). Hence, while cultural 'authenticity' in the diaspora space is inadvertently a site of continuous effort of attainment, the homeland return, where visual access and physical proximity to cultural monuments exists, the very vehicle of diminishing ethnic distance, has the transformative potential of the migrants' sense of self-actualisation. Returnees during everyday life experiences establish a sense of belonging that is anchored in their diasporic existence, that of a multi-locationality within and across territorial, cultural and psychic boundaries of the 'who I am' in the 'where I am' (Brah 1996; Christou 2003c). Belongingness as expressed through heritage and rootedness is experienced even during 'homecoming' visits, those short stays of a cultural 'pilgrimage' nature that sustain 'Greekness' in the diaspora:

> Even as a teenager or in my early twenties, I remember telling my parents that, even for short stays, being here we came in touch with our Greek culture, our Greek heritage. It's hard to even explain what Greek culture, Greek heritage is. I mean, I feel it's in my blood, and I know it, but the older I got, the more I felt closer to being Greek. Being here now is when I see the authentic way of doing that. Whether I am here in Athens or the village, my roots are here; they are in Greece, and I have thought about that. It's weird. Why is it that I feel that? Why is it that I feel so strong about being here and living in Greece? And it's just like I said, it's in my blood; it's the way I feel and think about being Greek. The specific time that I've been living here, I think it's the icing on the cake, the lid, whatever you want to call it; it actually fulfilled that emptiness I had living in the States. Even at the time I didn't know I had the need to have it filled, it was filled when I came here to live here, and it became part of who we are and who the Greeks are. I drive around and I see ... around Syntagma, around the Acropolis, around Monastiraki in complete awe of the fact that I am in Greece, Zeus' Temple, Plaka the ancient town, and I am sitting there thinking mesmerized, 'God, I am here in Greece living here'. (Pericles, male, 50)

The state of migrancy is not limited to sole mobility of persons but also involves the transposition of recollections and imaginations as well as collections of cultural objects and ways of life (Christou 2003c). The cultural consumption of objects, artefacts, products and practices facilitates proliferation of ethnic life. As regards the Greek-American community, in the sphere of popular entertainment as a mode of representation and identification, these notions become more explicit exactly because they are performed, flexible and fluid, as subjectivities offering comfort and enjoyment to the migrant community that indeed performs in this way in their everyday lives (Laliotou 2004: 134-135). Acoustically and visually, the same is understood in terms of national signifiers that stimulate pride and ethnic belongingness:

> The music for me was out of this world; I remember Theodora-kis' bouzouki, and I would burst into tears; it was out of this world. Not so much the lyrics for me, it was the music; it was the sound of the bouzouki, the sound of Theodorakis' music, Bithikotsis' voice, the voice, that crystal beautiful voice of some of the Greek singers, Bithikotsis, Dalaras, the music. Not so much the lyrics, I didn't pay that much attention to the lyrics; it's the music that speaks to me, not the lyrics. (Iphigenia, female, 50)

For the most part, Greek popular music (but also film and prose), especially in the 50s and 60s, captured through lyrics of bitterness, unhappiness, sadness and despair, the life in foreign lands. Second generation identification with the ancestral homeland relies on the ethnic reproduction of Greece through practice and indulgence in tradition and popular culture. As Panagakos confirms, 'the ability to "be Greek" through relations with the homeland can be used as a status symbol in which the individual is a bearer of "authentic" culture, not "hybridised" or "halfie" culture created in the diaspora' (2003b: 83). For the second generation, struggling to come to terms with their 'hyphenated' identities and from there to cope with their individual emotional, psychic and practical needs that are rarely autonomous, but for the most part are mediated through the family dynamics, the collective memory and group interactions, the very notion of the 'homeland', becomes a central indicator of 'Greekness'.

In line with this notion of 'ethnic territorial cultural belonging', Aspasia, on the other hand, goes deeper into the roots of her ancestors' regional origins. Her grandparents were of Pontic origin, 'ethnic'-Greek refugees from the Black Sea who settled in Greece. Her parents migrated to the United States but never forgot their Pontic origins and raised their children in that tradition. The Pontic tradition is a vivid component in Aspasia's life, which she hopes to pass on to her own children. Every time she listens to the music and watches the dances, she is drawn back in history, a history that is part and parcel of her past, her return decision and her present:

> I have devoted time and been involved with traditional dancing, I have been very much involved with traditional costumes, I like them a lot, I like seeing them, admiring them, I admire all those dances, the artwork produced, I feel very proud and I believe that our own self-development depends on that. Our development is very much dependent on the tradition we have. If I search myself very deep inside the first thing that comes out of inside me is that I am Pontic, that my roots are from very far back in history, further back than the immigrants, from people who started off from parts of Efxinos Pontos who went to Russia, who left from Russia and came to Greece to make a better living, those people were poor, they went through wars, they lived through difficult circumstances and they ended up in America to work, this immediately shows me how much they struggled, this automatically shows me how strong they are. From their dances only you can understand how strong they could be these people, from the rhythms that these dances have, because I have danced all the dances of Greece but I cannot refrain from saying that these are the most dynamic dances. More so with the feet, that is deep, deep, deep inside me that is true, meaning that how much more when I listen to the Pontic songs on the radio my skin gets goose bumps, I feel from my soul a different kind of feeling, my heart jumps. (Aspasia, female, 32)

Return migration is also a step toward familiar family paths taken as much as it is a step toward the national trajectory. It is a means of self-development, as Aspasia tells us, and a compass that redirects personal life toward national life. The ancestral return is justified, in part, by the sense of completeness it engenders by bringing participants closer to ancestry and thus fulfilling the journey of destiny. The participants feel strongly that they are heirs to a great heritage and adherents of a magnificent legend. The intensity of a 'sense of the past' is what guides the present and opens paths to a promising future. I would like to discuss this theme in two ways: on the surface as a form of 'nouveau nationalist intelligentsia' discourse and at a deeper level as a stimulant of 'critical comparative-analytic' voices of participants who are not solely locked into a 'great past' and the 'burden of antiquity' but can denounce the obsession with past glories (progonoplexia or what Clogg (2002) terms 'ancestoritis') and vocalise a critical review of modern Greece. The following excerpts move from constructions of a homeland worshipped to a homeland criticised. This evolves on two levels: from immaterial constructions (culture, tradition, ethnicity) to material constructions of everyday life (cultural landscapes, monuments) and from past *glories* (Ancient Greek civilisation) to present *inadequacies* (Modern Greek society). Second-generation Greek-American return migrants are receptors of the diasporic narrative as imagined and reproduced by the immigrant generations, but they are also consumers of modern 'Greekness' and as such, through everyday life experience can 'assess' the 'authenticity' of life in the ancestral homeland. Here, we come across two layers of diasporic life, one narrated (by the first generation) and lived in their country of origin (the United States) and another experienced and narrated (by the second generation) in the parents' country of origin (Greece). In the first instance, 'habitus, as the basis of daily practice, tends to be naturalized, taken for granted, or assimilated into the subconscious' (Panagakos 2003b: 85) while in the event of the homeland return, habitus (as it will become evident from the participants' narratives) becomes a transformative site of unexpected and unprecedented bitterness and disappointment. However, before we look at the exilic spaces of antagonism in the ancestral homeland, it is revealing to focus on those deeply embedded notions that fuel and sustain a sense of 'Greekness' in the second generation.

> Now, what does it mean being a Greek? It's having strong heritage, a strong history, and a very colorful and strong history, to have a basic population where everybody fought for the common good and maintaining its identity even though many conquerors passed this country. I think Greek history is something very important, and it's like reading the future in a way. Anybody who knows the real Greek history and doesn't just take the small parts just to use it really knows that Greeks from ancient times had the same values; they all had the same beliefs, and they all had their code of ethics. This has traveled throughout history and even reaches the modern Greek of today. There always was a strong family, always believed in communicating and keeping touch with people close to their family, relatives and all. I have a strong sense of ethnic pride. We are one of the few countries in the world that have that kind of history. Even though people from time to time say, 'well, it's not exactly what it is written out or put down on paper' but just going back three, four, five thousand years and to say that there was a civilization, there was a Greek civilization back then that was able to create so many things and make the world basically a richer place in terms of knowledge and findings. Well, who could not be proud of that? I learned early on where my roots were and everything; we were a

really tight family. I always felt more at ease with the Greek tradition than following the American. (Plato, male, 30)

The above is a characteristic argument of a particular national narrative
developed by most participants, namely, Greece's contribution to the
world as the cradle of western civilization. The argument draws attention to a pervasive sense of temporal and spatial global cultural and
scientific contribution of Greece and its historical continuity. The participant underlines such acts as routes toward excellence and emphasises the personal obligation and commitment that migrants (especially
the second generation) must have in discovering their roots.

Similar notions are apparent in such proclamations of Greece exemplified as the birthplace of modern Western civilisation:

> *I have pride in the gigantic accomplishments of the Hellenes. I*
> *have very strong bonds to the Hellenic civilization, to my roots.*
> (Sophocles, male, 28)

While Kassandra points to the fundamentals of why this sense of pride
has emerged, she explains that Greekness encompasses a sense of
pride based on the historical past of ancestral achievements as in-
scribed in the legacy of the traditional family unit of stability and comfort. Furthermore, the lived experience in the ancestral homeland provides access to the cultural, historical, artistic and other sources of ethnic consumption that Kassandra feels are all important forms of
valuing one's heritage. This type of validation reinforces ethnic pride.

> Very strong ties and roots, to the point that it could be very tir-
> ing, but I can't get away from that, and I think most Greek peo-
> ple feel that way; Greek-Americans, all that, they feel very
> strongly tied to their parents and brothers and sisters. Greek
> heritage is finding out about your background, history and rela-
> tives, associating with your relatives, finding out what they are
> all about, appreciating them for who they are. Living here has gi-
> ven me great insight regarding the culture, the history, the mu-
> sic, the food and the archaeology. Had I not lived here, I
> wouldn't appreciate my heritage as much; it is a good experi-
> ence. I think everybody who is Greek-American should come to
> Greece and live here for at least a certain amount of time. (Kas-
> sandra, female, 49)

On the other hand, in a Greece that has changed, is changing and will
no doubt continue to change, we witness the transformation from the
prototype of an 'authentic', 'unspoiled', 'pure' homeland[2] to a multicul-

tural and multifaith country. The 'shock' is quite extensive for those unwilling to accept the change of times (Ventoura 1994; Karydis 1996; Amitsis and Lazaridis 2001; Labrianidis and Lymberaki 2001; Marvakis, Parsanoglou and Pavlou 2001). When second-generation Greek-Americans embark on their journey of return migration, their imaginative journeys inflect ideas of 'home' and belonging in a space inhabited by family, relatives, Greek native compatriots where particular activities and relationships are warm and intimate and objects and practices are familiar. The memorialisation of 'home' in the terrain of belongingness is reflective of such feelings and relations that bring about a sense of comfort and security. 'Home' is a virtual place, a repository for memories of the lived spaces. It locates lived time and space, particularly intimate familial time and space (Mallet 2004: 63).

However, pleasant mnemonic recollections do not always coincide with contemporary pragmatic meanings of 'home'. As Mallet indicates, 'while memories of home are often nostalgic and sentimental, home is not simply recalled or experienced in positive ways' (2004: 64). It is possible that the familial, the comfortable and the secure become a space of inner tyranny, abstruse oppression and internal anguish. The disappointment and distress is quite clear in the narratives of participants who dwell on this new kind of 'culture shock' they are undergoing while trying to understand what has happened to a Greece they used to know. As presented in the narrative below, the homeland return is experienced almost as an 'exile' since immigration and the emerging multicultural picture rupture prior constructions of homogeneity in the homeland. Aspasia's reflections resonate with the general national Greek discourse that links immigrants (especially Albanians) with a rise in criminality.

Many changes, very big changes, extremely big changes! The Greece that I longed to return to is not the Greece I am living in now. The Greece I longed to return to was the Greece I knew back in the old days. The Greece where we would leave our balcony doors and front doors unlocked and wide open, where we would spread a little mattress on the balcony and sleep outdoors; we would leave the door wide open and there was nothing to fear, nothing to worry about; we knew all our neighbors. Now all this has changed. Greece has started to resemble America very much so insofar that there are other races here now and living here. Not that I am a racist; I have nothing against those people, but I liked it back then when Greece was Greece, and now Greece has started to change very much so. This new picture of migrants, the new picture of the life style, the way houses are built, the way we spend our time in fulfilling our obligations,

our responsibilities, all this anxiety, the stress of going out, of
buying, of trying to make it on time to have all this, I believe
that in the past it was more comfortable, that in the past life
was more comfortable; now it has changed. (Aspasia, female,
32)

There is a clear feeling that 'Greece had changed' and no longer resembles the place of their imaginings or of their parents' and grandparents'
reminiscences, or even of their own recollections and experiences of
'homecoming' visits. Here we are presented with the way in which the
comparison between expectation and reality is 'tainted' by a mixing of
the current urban setting with idealised memories of the ancestral
homeland. Instead, the ancestral homeland has surrendered to consumerist attitudes and materialistic values intermingled with high levels
of anxiety and stress. The distress that Aspasia experiences is attributed
to the presence of migrants as well as the 'modern' lifestyle of Greece.
  Even more dramatic is the following narrative from a young man
who reiterates his anger and frustration of alienation in the ancestral
homeland by describing why he feels like 'a stranger in his own land':

I want to feel and sense that I am Greek. To be Greek, however,
you can be Greek everywhere; you don't need to be in Greece to
be Greek. When I was in America, I felt Greek, and I was Greek.
Unfortunately, and I say this with deep disappointment and bitterness, at this moment, this specific time period in Greece, I
don't feel Greek. I feel like a stranger, like a foreigner in my
own country. Perhaps it's because of the migration policy that
exists today in the country. A lot of foreign migrants have come
to Greece, especially illegal migrants; you'll say, 'OK, I saw that
in America, too', but there you consider it a given; it's what I
said before about the changes. That drastic change brought
about a series of negative consequences and that is one of them.
We were not accustomed to this, us Greeks, neither as a state
nor as a society; it made a big impression on me. It seemed a
bit weird to me, a bit difficult. I didn't like it. I haven't accepted
it. I have not accepted it completely, and that is strange. In
America I was in the midst of all these ethnic groups and races,
all the nationalities of this world, and I didn't feel strange. And
here, where it's supposed to be the authentic country, my real
country in terms that I want to live here for the rest of my life
and I want to adjust better, I feel like a stranger; I feel like a foreigner. It has upset me. It has hurt me, and it has made me angry. I can say, yes, it has made me angry. It hasn't shocked me
because I expected it to happen at some point. It is a given, and

we couldn't have avoided it; either we like it or not, it would have happened. You know, these are things that some others impose on you because they are more powerful. It hasn't shocked me. It has upset me, I can say. It's anger. Perhaps it's fear transformed into anger and frustration. I don't feel the fear that intensely inside me; I feel the anger and the frustration, and those are my feelings. (Hercules, male, 27)

Participants' reaction to the presence of migrants in Greece is expressed with a negative standpoint, emphasised in an unconcealed and striking way as in the reaction of the previous respondent. The following extract from a retired teacher relates forceful negative reactions. This narrative recounts foremost the shifting student setting in some schools in Greece and then conveys additional general negative feelings towards immigrants in an emotive and striking way. The reaction reflects the 'drama' and 'trauma' of migration:

In our neighborhood there is an elementary school, and if you were there when there is a break, you would be shocked. I cried. Why did I cry? Because I heard Albanian-speaking children and went into the class, and I asked the teacher how many children were in the class. She has thirty children in the class. Out of the thirty children, three are Greek, twenty-seven are Albanian, Bulgarian, whatever they are, and I asked her, 'What is your most difficult problem?' because they don't speak Greek, and she said, 'My difficult problem is explaining to the foreigners because I can't go to the next topic until they know, and I keep those three Greeks behind' and that to me is not right; that is sad. I don't think that Greece is doing anything to preserve Greek and to address the issue; it disappoints me. I don't know what will happen in Greece ten years from now; I don't want to know. I think all this incoming immigration is a threat to national identity and religion. Oh yes, I think so, I really do. That saddens me. I'm trying to think, in America, I remember when I started teaching, we did the pledge of allegiance to the flag. When I stopped teaching, we stopped the salute to the flag because there were a lot of Puerto-Ricans at that time in the States and we couldn't have the Puerto-Rican children pledge allegiance to the flag. I'm afraid it's going to get like that. America is much bigger, but still when you go to America, you feel American; it's a melting pot still, lots of languages and stuff. But I think it's Greece's size that is going to change the Greeks. I don't see them yet doing anything to correct it, the government. They are still coming in; the borders are all open, and where I am, often I

see police cars rounding them up, putting them in these big
vans, and you hear them say, 'I'm coming back!' It's depressing.
I think that they should have stricter laws; they should be a bit
more careful. (Thalia, female, 68)

Commencing with Bakhtin's view, who sees society as a *decentered site
of polyphony* and *heterglossia* whose unity is always 'yet-to-be-attained'
(Nielsen 2002: 146), from the participants' narratives, it appears that
the city, as a *container of sociality* in a *postnational, postmodern and multicultural state*, is a collection of unitary but contrasting fragments of nor-
mative and (un)ethical substance, whose polyphonic perspective is not
dialogic, not inclusive, but *dehumanising, racist* and *exclusionary*, saturated by a *culture of fear* and *xenophobia*. Hence, the city of ancestral
homeland return, in this case, Athens, is a site of disarray and dismis-
siveness, as narrated by second-generation Greek-American return migrants who consciously relocated to their *ancestral homeland* in pursuit
of their own identity project of belongingness in locating their 'home'
but realised that this was instead an experience of *exile*. But on the
other hand, the diasporic voice and narrative, although having experienced a more 'cosmopolitan' lifeworld, is firmly anchored to the rootedness of the nation.

In *Flesh and Stone*, Richard Sennett has argued that urban spaces
take form largely from the ways people experience their own bodies.
Specifically, he argues that 'for people in a multi-cultural city to care
about one another, I believe we have to change the understanding we
have of our own bodies. We will never experience the difference of
others until we acknowledge the bodily insufficiencies in ourselves. Civic compassion issues from that physical awareness of lack in ourselves, not from sheer goodwill or political rectitude' (2002: 370). With
Sennett's framework in mind, in this section I would like to argue that
perceptions and acts of the migrant body in the spaces of the city it in-
habits reproduce *monologic performances of the self* and not *dialogic acts
of collective belongingness*, thus further dehumanising urban lifeworlds.
Hence, urban spaces are not just *containers* but also *producers* of *dehumanising lifeworlds*, rationalised as protective borders of social control
and protection. Furthermore, as Hardt and Negri ascertain in *Empire*,
'the behaviours of social integration and exclusion proper to rule are
thus increasingly interiorised within the subjects themselves. Power is
now exercised through machines that directly organize the brains (in
communication systems, information networks, etc.) and bodies (in
welfare systems, monitored activities, etc.) toward a state of autonomous alienation from the sense of life and the desire for creativity. The
society of control might thus be characterized by an intensification and
generalization of the normalizing apparatuses of disciplinarity that in-

ternally animate our common and daily practices, but in contrast to discipline, this control extends well outside the structured sites of social institutions through flexible and fluctuating networks' (2000: 41). Here, I would like to focus precisely on the 'interiorisation of exclusion within the subjects themselves' and the institutionalisation of exclusion in the city in everyday life through everyday practices. One of these everyday practices in everyday life in the city that emanates from a culture of fear and alienation is implemented through self-imposed borders. Specifically, this indicates the fear of the other, the criminalisation of the migrant other (Karydis 1996) when migrants encounter migrants.

But how does the very existence of the migrant other create a contested use of space in the homeland locale? How is difference negotiated in the ancestral homeland where the returnees imagine their relocation to a country of similarity? Hedetoft provides the following definition of the 'Other': 'An image of the Other is a non-motivated, moralistic, relational culture-sign; a stereotypical unit of perception organising the difference(s) between "Oneself" and a given "Otherness" by attributing characteristics to this Otherness that are suited to one's real or imagined interests. In such images, a notion (of wish or fear, repulsion or attraction) is substantiated and hence justified by being linked to some other area(s) of meaning – e.g. political notions of nationhood being legitimised with reference to natural, historical, or mythical concepts. Images of the Other impose a particular reading on the world and, in so doing, fictionalise it' (1995: 93). Moreover, the 'Other' can be mirrored against a 'postnational self' in the agonising search for belongingness and identification (Hedetoft and Hjort 2002) as a key component in national encounters between selves and others (Hedetoft 2003) but also within the narrativisation of a politics of multiple belonging (Hedetoft 2004). Thus, the narrativisation of the 'other' is a subjective, particular reading of a particular world, the urban diasporic state of migrancy in the ancestral homeland. The returnees translate images and encounters of the 'other' fictionalised through experiences of difference as a state of homelessness in the ancestral homeland. Here we can comprehend the way in which the comparison between expectation and reality is *contaminated* by a mixing of the current urban setting with idealised memories of life in the ancestral homeland. Furthermore, there appears to be an affirmation of a *racialised embodiment of the nation* and hence 'Greekness' as being exemplified 'contaminated' by other 'races'. Hence, the body is also the zone of nationness. The female body, as exemplified above in Aspasia's narrative, in the security and protection of the familiarity of the nation is without fear, but the body in the uncertainty and fear of the newly acquired multicultural context is vulnerable and threatened. The embodiment of exile in gendered bodies and the state of migrancy in the ancestral homeland resonates with an overall *culture of fear* stimulated by the presence of the 'other'. It is very interesting to see how new social spaces and cultural fields are constructed within the terrain of the return destination, which resembles more a point of departure rather than a place of arrival. The homeland return is experienced as 'exile' since previous constructions of homogeneity in the homeland are altered by the present multicultural picture. So we see that alternative homeland spaces create altered lives and ruptured expressions of the self.

Nevertheless, the ancestral return is the final destination of the journey in search of a homeplace in the homeland. Any intimacy with a homeplace requires an outspoken perspective on what makes it a place that is 'home'. The idea of home corresponds to comfort but that does not exclude criticism. A critical perspective may correspond to exclusion, the exclusion that returnees feel when they have processed (visually, mentally, emotionally, rationally) a new homeland version, a changed homeland. This is a testament to how much an imagined homeland differs from a pragmatic[3] homeland and how much visiting tales differ from returning testimonies. This realisation can offer a fresh perspective of how 'home-host' constructions may accentuate self-awareness and a newly discovered insight to one's life. What seems to happen is that the participants experience a kind of national and self-maturation, and in this trajectory they utilise steps of arrival and departure from the inbetweenness of the 'here-there' dilemma. These experiences aid in processes of identification. 'What doesn't kill us, surely makes us stronger' (and wiser, if I may add), as my participants exclaimed:

> It has been so positive, my experience here. I think I won the lottery because other people, they don't have the same experience of both worlds; they just know one thing. It's like school; you learn. This is what I feel; everyday here I learn. Truly, I can compare. I get both perspectives, and I get parts of both worlds, and that helps me become a better person. I truly believe that, and I know I have managed it; I just see it in myself. (Kalypso, female, 41)

> I think I wouldn't be the person I am today if I didn't know both worlds. I think I am privileged, very privileged, and everybody that has lived the same thing I have is very privileged, very privileged because we got to open up our minds and broaden our horizons. (Andromache, female, 34)

To sum up, the narratives in this section indicate that the return migrant emerges as a socially and politically sensitised figure on various levels of adjustment and social interaction during the return settlement. National ideologies and personal constructions of what constitutes 'Greekness' highlight a decisive demarcation of cultural representation and everyday life in the homeland return. The binary representations of 'home-host', 'foreign-familiar', 'agony-nostalgia', 'suffocation-breathing' and 'strange land-homeland' all express a *cultural anxiety* that takes shape in the form of anxious negotiations of the self as either more or less Greek (in terms of degree). But 'Greekness' as the ultimate plan of action, fulfilled during the homeland return, is tested by homeplace constructions of 'otherness' that create states of being of 'strangeness' for the return migrant. National discourses and cultural practices in the United States fortified the strength and cohesiveness of the Greek-American community and shielded its trust and dependence on family bonds, community cohesion, social and cultural capital, kinship, language and religion as powerful markers of ethnic and cultural maintenance. In this sense, the abundance of Greekness in the lives of migrants succeeded in transforming the second-generation Greek-American to a Greek. It will be interesting to explore in the following sections if the same second-generation Greek-American return migrant becomes more 'American' in Greece or if the previous still holds. In the next section I will address how *place* is conceived as *home* through deciphering constructions of placeness and homeness as relating to belongingness in the 'here and there'.

4.2   Place is home: constructions of placeness and homeness

Migrant constructions of placeness and homeness illustrate that the ethnic place is perceived but not necessarily experienced as home. Previously it was mentioned that alternative spaces create altered lives and ruptured identifications. Three alternative spaces emerge in the journeyings between 'home-host' contexts: the 'here', the 'there' and the 'here and there'. Although under specific circumstances I would agree with Clifford that 'homecomings, are, by definition, the negation of diaspora' (1997: 287), in the case of second-generation Greek-American return migrants I have to argue that the existence of this 'inbetweenness' of cultural space distinguishes them as a *diasporic* group, whom I mentioned in the previous section as undergoing a 'counter-diasporic' experience. Specific socio-spatial conditions impact on individuals and collectivities so that they are 'selectively restructured and re-routed according to *internal* and *external* dynamics' (Clifford 1997: 289; italics in the original). In this section I explore how those dynamics impact on returnees' constructions of placeness and homeness.

Firstly, in terms of the 'there', life in the United States intensely revolves around Greek culture, Greek Orthodox religion and the Church as well as traditions and ethnic practices to the point where it almost 'functions' as an incubator of 'Greekness'. Secondly, in terms of the 'here', ethnic life in Greece does not resemble ethnic life in the United States. Almost like a time lapse, life in the United States is described as frozen in time, resembling a Greece that used to be in the 1950s-70s when the first generation had migrated, transporting with them memories of a Greece never to be found again. Thirdly, in terms of the 'here and there', this is where 'home-host' constructions meet to produce negotiations and transitions of identification during the return settlement. This is not only a third category of spatial constructions of belongingness but also a third space in itself (Bhabha 1990). This is where the culture and ethnicity of a past meet the ambivalence of a present to form constructions of self for the future. The formation of such diasporic identities mirrors a cultural manifestation of a spatial and temporal production of how ethnicity is framed and enacted in the context of difference. Specific circumstances in particular moments in historical and real time during the homeland return in the intersection between the local and the global as well as sameness and difference challenge static preconceptions of 'Greekness'. Hence, the returning migrants discover 'in-between' spaces of 'homeness'. As Tsolidis states, 'inhabiting "in-between" spaces is more than ambivalence and non-belonging. It is also a space where inhabitants develop a particular type of power which grows out of having expertise with multiple ways of being. These multiple ways of being are not mutually exclusive but instead are articulated in response to particular place and time. It is in this sense that they can be constructed as transformative. In the context of globalization such fluid cultural identifications have great potential, particularly when recognized as functioning at a transnational level' (2003: 160).

Unequivocally, the narratives highlight the variations of dynamics in how 'home' is mediated through space. In terms of the first set of dynamics, of remembering 'there', narratives of life in the United States dwell on the agonising and almost desperate processes of safeguarding 'Greekness' while the mythic, idealised return to the ancestral roots and heritage becomes the achievement of a family legacy:

> *Although I have no complaints about my life in America, in all facets of my life it revolved around Greekness: the family, the church, the traditions, Greek school, Greek friends, Greek food and music and celebrations. My parents offered me all this and a great*

education, a wonderful life. My heritage gave me the strength, the vision, the energy, the dream. I certainly had the best of both worlds, a good American life with opportunities and a fulfilling Greek heritage. It was almost great, almost perfect if I didn't feel that split, that sense of being incomplete in a void that I had to fill. When I moved to Greece, it was difficult to adjust in the beginning, especially not having my support system around, my parents, my family, but then it felt like I had come home. I was always proud of my Greek roots and heritage but really experiencing it in the country of my forefathers was a legacy achieved. My family was always rooted in our Greekness and for me to be able to trace those roots was a lifetime dream that became full reality once I moved to Greece. (Achilles, male, 33)

Achilles' narrative is expressive of this idea of 'home' as homeland, the land of one's forebears as the fulfilment of an internal diasporic space. Although life in the United States is described as revolving around a profusion of 'Greekness', being a Greek-American is experienced as a condition of partition between two cultural worlds, one Greek and the other American. Most participants through their narratives portray their upbringing in the United States not as one experienced in a truly multicultural, multiracial and multifaith environment, community or neighbourhood but in a cluster of 'Greekness', a Greek 'bubble'. This Greek-American micro-environment, in a multifaceted system, preserved the socio-cultural and moral values of a (effectively rural) Greece of the 1950s and 1960s, the ideals and principles of the first generation. The narrativisation of ethnic imagining focuses on both culture as praxis in its sensory and ritual expression (Bauman 1999) as well as the mnemonic transposition of culture into the present (Christou 2003c).

My earliest memories are of a world which was Greek. From words that were Greek to worlds that were Greek. The smells of foods, the tastes, the sounds of words and music, the images of Greek movies, the images from my grandparents' storytelling. The images from Church celebrations and weddings and even funerals. The beauty of rituals, all that makes me feel at home in the Church, in my Greekness and Greece. Generations of passing the heritage from our origins with the same strength, nothing has faded away, we all honor our pasts because that is our future. It is the basis for everything we have learned and everything we have and will achieve. Our rich Hellenic heritage is not just memories; it's a reality of our lives. (Patroklos, male, 37)

In Chapter three I presented the central establishments that helped to maintain 'Greekness' in the diaspora life of the United States. Greek Orthodoxy and Greek ethnicity are to a degree intertwined but do not completely overlap since the family as an institution and its associated practices complements them. However, religion, ethnicity and culture are utilised to assign in-group similarities and to isolate the differences of others. The following narratives illuminate the importance of those institutions (family, religion, language) for second-generation Greek-Americans.

Artemis, a 32-year-old female participant, describes how the plethora of Greek values, ethics and tradition saturated her life and structured her life choices and personality:

> I would say 75 percent of my life was based around the Greek community. I went to a Greek-American school, church; we were in our youth society with just Greek kids from the village where we were from; my parents were in the adult society, and we would have fundraisers. It was understood that we would marry a Greek person. They never said it (the parents), but it was kind of the unwritten law. That's just the law. I never dated anybody that wasn't Greek. Family and the family being very Greek and old-fashioned made me a very conservative person. It shaped my actions in a certain way in marrying my husband and my choice of husband, choice of friends and all that. Religion, it made me, it gave me a certain train of thought. We were really ingrained in our Greekness. I don't think I could get a lot more Greek than I was already.

In this narrative, a female participant recalls her upbringing in the United States and emphasises the 'dominance' of 'Greekness' in all aspects of her public and private life. In many Greek households in the diaspora, a classic double standard exists where males are free to roam at will and females have strict curfews (Panagakos 2006b). But also in general, Greek migrant parents are usually very strict and conservative with girls whereas more flexible and lenient with boys. The theorisation of the cultural and moral values of 'honour and shame' is tied to the framing of how gender has been studied in the Greek and Mediterranean contexts of marriage and kinship (Cowan 1990; Dubisch 1995; Kirtsoglou 2004). According to the cultural code of honour, a woman's reputation is less threatened if she stays close to the house, avoids gossip and fulfils her role as mistress of the house while a man's honour is 'claimed' and 'evaluated' in the public realm (Dubisch in Kirtsoglou 2004: 20). On the basis of these values and as a direct consequence of the 'ethnic bubble' and the time warp mentioned previously that exists in diaspora communities, it becomes clear how and why 'ethnic family values' become the dominant norm in the lives of the second generation and even more so 'severely' reinforced in the case of Greek-American daughters. The core of ethnic ideology is praised, practiced and emulated by the participants, that is, the 'unwritten law' of marrying a Greek person, having Greek friends, following a Greek educational curriculum, attending Greek Orthodox church services and social events. Above all, Artemis proclaims, this 'ideology' has 'shaped' her actions, her thought and life choices.

Plato, a 30-year-old male participant, elaborates his perceptions of heritage, ethnic belongingness and cultural values that are all enhanced, preserved and transmitted by the family:

> When somebody thinks Greek, family values are the most important, religious values, I guess these are the things that are very strong abroad, especially with Greek communities abroad, and because these are the basic values that the Greek family has or the Greek society has. I think these are the things that make a Greek a Greek, basically: Strong family values, which I have not seen in any other ethnicity or ethnic group, and strong ties with religion. I learned early on where my roots were and everything; we were a really tight family. I always felt more at ease with the Greek tradition than following the American. Family to me, it felt more special and different, and it brings you basically closer to the family. I think that is what tradition is all about.

The firmness of family bonds is associated with the norms and values of a Greek ethnic ideology that incorporates strong religious adherence. The latter undertakes the role of institutionalised preservation and transmission of ethnicity and identity in diaspora life. Religious and ethnic-social activities reaffirm and strengthen the boundaries of the community and secure the 'ritualisation' of ethnic culture. This underscores the fact that 'ethnicity is best understood as a mode of narrativising the everyday life world in and through processes of boundary formation' (Brah 1996: 241). Medusa, a 21-year-old female participant, refers to the narrativisation of the everyday migrant lifeworld when she describes the Greek-American experience as the core of her 'Greekness' and the immediate source of identification:

> Being Greek-American has played a huge part in my life and being part of a big Greek community. The Greek Church, I think, is the center for not only the church, but also it is a center for social gatherings, stuff like that, and we are very into it. Holidays, you know, are very big, Easter and fasting, keeping the

roots. I think the most ultimate advantage to being raised Greek-American in the States was that I have in my opinion a very strong sense of identity; I am very proud in being Greek. I think that all the Greek-Americans hold on to this and praise it and try to pass it on to their children and to outsiders, the rest of the American community through Greek festivals and stuff like that. I am very proud of that, and there is a very strong sense of family and community within the Greek circle. So I have to say, that is one of the most positive aspects of being Greek. My ethnic and cultural backgrounds play a major role in my life, just my values, my traditions, like I said, I am very proud of my heritage to be able to hold on to, to be able to speak Greek. There is a strong sense of family and church life; you know the family participates in the church life.

The ethnic and cultural practice of 'Greekness' fuels identity; participants perceive it as a positive aspect of their lifeworlds and an obligation to sustain. Phaedra, a 27-year-old female participant, reminisces about her upbringing in the United States and confesses that she literally thought she was living in Greece because of the abundance of 'Greekness' in her life:

In my life the Greek culture and heritage plays a major role because my parents, even though we were born and grew up in America, they always made us believe that we were Greeks. So I always thought and knew that I was Greek. They always taught us; they taught us first how to speak Greek and then English, and we always used to go to the Church. The Orthodox Church was always very important, especially when we were younger, compared to now because we are older; we can always go by ourselves, but back then I especially remember it was very important to go to the Church to meet Greeks, Greek children. I remember, just before I was going to school, I thought I was living in Greece because my parents only used to have Greeks around: all the relatives were Greek, all their friends were Greek. It was like the Greeks 'us' and the Americans the 'others'. They never told me anything like 'You can't have American friends' or something like that, but it was always... I felt the difference between other people who were total Americans. Well, my parents, they made sure that we practice all our ethnic background. They made sure that we know about our background. We went to gatherings and social events because we were young, and we were in a different country, and they wanted to make sure that we knew who we were, who they were, and to learn about the

Greek heritage, which was difficult because we were there, but when we came to Greece, it wasn't that different. Over here, especially now that we came back, they are like any other Greek. We know that we are Greek; it's not something that we have to show any more, and it's easier than before.

From the life story narratives, it stands clear that identification in the diaspora is grounded in Greek heritage and tradition, manifested through adherence to cultural values, the Greek language, the Greek Orthodox religion and dedication to the family. Ethnic markers become reference points to define migrants in US society; as Phaedra points out, the demarcation is between 'the Greeks "us" and the Americans the "others"'. 'Greekness' as a point of identification cohesively binds migrants together and creates boundaries that distinguish them from the rest of the society. In addition to the importance of Greek culture, Greek Orthodox religion and Greek tradition to the individual life, participants also expressed how important it was to marry a Greek or Greek-American for family life and the upbringing of the children. Nephele, 32 years old, and Hera, 68 years old, have similar ideas on this issue. In both of the women's cases, there seems to be a rationalisation of strictly following family values, traditions and life plans with the inference of autonomous decision-making:

I was brought up with both languages and doing cultural activities in the United States and the Greek Church; that played a huge role in my life. Very much. I learned both languages; I went to Greek school as well; we had our Greek society, our Greek clubs; we learned Greek dances; we had our own parties; we did all of that, and I believe we tried to keep our tradition and heritage more than actual Greek people, I should say here or Greek citizens in general. I believe it has offered me a lot since I've been brought up with the Greek traditions and Mommy and Daddy saying it would be better to marry a Greek, to have the same religion, to speak the same languages, to have the same tradition, and in one aspect they were correct. If I tried to meet and marry someone from another ethnic group, not that I wouldn't love their ethnic group or them but we might have a problem with raising the children, dealing with certain problems, dealing with religion and stuff like that. Basically that is why I chose a Greek-American, not an American, a Greek, and we got married; it's much easier to raise the children to have the same religion, to have the same ethnic background and the same traditions. (Nephele, female, 32)

Well my mother always instilled the Greek culture in us. We grew up with the Church, Greek holidays, customs; she kept all this and made sure that all the children spoke Greek and we attended the Church and made us go to Greek school like six years. We all finished and learned how to read and write the Greek language fluently. Going to church and Sunday school, and she had a very close-knit family, and every Sunday they would get together: parties, dancing, everything was Greek. We really didn't grow up as Americans so I was really Greek even before I came here. I followed the Church, the traditions and the holidays. Yes, everything, everything, my mother made sure that we spoke Greek at home; she never spoke English to us. She always said, 'You will speak English at school. You learn that language outside of the house. Here, you must speak Greek', and I really appreciate that. I did the same with my son, too, and he is fluent, Greek and English; he reads and writes, very much. He went to Greek school up to the sixth grade, and when he came to Greece, he didn't have any problems with the language and the customs; he fit right in. He has Greek friends here. He is very pleased that we kept the Greek culture that we didn't forget it even though he grew up there. Greek heritage is very important to me. Very important, yes, and we try to instil it in our son so he doesn't forget his roots. My husband is from a Greek island, and he is very Greek even though he lived for 40 years in the States. We always speak Greek together; we never speak English. He has close family ties; he is also like my mom was. We do that with my son at home: we speak Greek, no English. It's very important. (Hera, female, 68)

Not only has women's migration slowly become part of the story of scattered lives, diasporic and hyphenated existences, but we have also come to comprehend that women's language about migratory experiences can be vastly different from men's understandings (Christou 2003b). Whereas men present the migration decision as autonomous, women view migration as a collective endeavour and represent the experience within the family context (Chamberlain 1997: 87-108). As the narratives indicate, we realise that women migrants in their 'feminisation' of return migration define their relocation as an identity construction in a gendered perspective that incorporates national representations. The ethnic community and the symbolic ethnicisation of the return is refined by the conscious decision of a 'motherland return[4]' in search of an identity that manifests itself within the religious, the national and the ethnic. These multiple constructions are important in the way female migrants view themselves and how this impacts the way cultural production is articulated on the local, the global and trans-national context. These particular orientations are important in how the homeland return is visualised, processed and understood. Gender and gender constructions also create multiple stories mediated by the intersection of national configurations with local experiences.

As I have discussed elsewhere (Christou 2003b), the female retur-nees, otherwise perceived as 'female birds of passage', in this case are also 'female nesting birds' and simultaneously exemplify their autono-mous decision-making perspective in the homeland return as one cor-related with:

1. The continuous interplay between the woman returnee as *active agent* and the national construction of 'motherland' as *structure.*
2. The *personal plan of action* of the diasporic journey of return to a na-tional homeland that exemplifies traditional cultural values as safe-guarding ethnic identity.
3. The spatial context of appraisal of nation as means to realise a *gen-dered self* as contextualised through emotional and rational processes of incorporation.

The socio-cultural processes involved in migrancy are significant out-lets of gender perspectives as well as the space of construction and ne-gotiation of gender identities. Furthermore, return migration is interre-lated to gendered identifications in how they are produced, reproduced, reinforced and challenged and the very process highlights the role of women in the migration cycle. It is important to incorporate women as active agents and to focus on the multivaried ways in which they are involved in the migratory project and process.

Recent feminist theory has underscored the role of women as active agents in constructing and articulating their own identities. Through their life experiences and the various discourses they intersect, female subjects are formed and reproduced (de Lauretis 1987). As Radcliffe suggests, 'the (self-) representation of gendered identity is evidenced by the interrelationships of place and history, their associational mean-ings, and gendered positionings in relation to these abstracts' (1993: 104). The female returnees, while engaging in traditional domestic and nurturing roles, at the same time reconfigure their gendered self and autonomous positioning by selecting to complete a 'motherland re-turn', the same way they selected their Greek spouses. Second genera-tion women inscribe cultural meanings to their 'marriage strategies' as constituted through transnational migration (Panagakos 2003b). Fe-male return migrants mobilise multiple socio-cultural geographies and spaces, meanings of spaces and spatial meanings; thus, the mobility of these women is a shifting in locations and identities (Christou 2003b). The reality of women's lives goes beyond simple dichotomies; it is a reality embedded in active engagement with subjecthood, identity and social transformations (Radcliffe 1993: 103). Family constitutes a fundamental principal of social space and organisation to the extent that social institutions and policies often exemplify family constructions and rhetoric (Christou 2002). The family is a major site of belonging and the source of other frameworks that assign meaning to groups through their aspirations and ideological rhetoric. The family unit is a central component of the female returnees' narratives of return. The place of family and placing the family in a terrain of belongingness is to assign stability to the family unit. The women's identification processes are shaped by the notion of 'national space', that place which illuminates specific ways that the family can conserve its unity and solidarity within the space of national unity, that is, ethnic and religious homogeneity, national solidarity and common values. Furthermore, there is a prioritisation of maintaining a 'Greek mentality' for the offspring and as such, practices of 'Greekness' are pivotal. These practices, thoroughly discussed previously (language, religion, family values, traditions), are actively passed down to the younger generations and they are a major component of a mother's project, what Tsolidis terms 'maternal Greekness' (2003: 154).

The second set of dynamics – focused on the 'here' of Greece – involves the contrasting differences the returning migrants discuss in terms of ethnic life in Greece. Important institutions such as family and religion that formed the core of ethnic life in the United States are perceived as weak and faded memories of the past in a Greece that is 'dangerously' modernising and secularising[5]. On the end of the spectrum of differences lies a space of alienation created by the anti-Americanism returnees have experienced in Greece. This is the most extreme set of issues faced during the settlement process. It generates torment and turmoil instead of the comfort sought in the homeland:

> Culture is something a part of me and not something I think about. We were raised a big part by culture, a huge part. Enormous is the Church; the Orthodox Church is the basis of everything, and everything else, the dancing, the singing, this and that, it all stems off from that. For me, let's say, number one is that for me. I enjoy the Greek culture a lot, the fun that everybody has, like going to the Greek *bouzoukia*, the dancing, like traditional dances. I think it's sad, another shock. Like in America, we have traditional Greek culture, and here it's not so much. It's like modern so that's a change right there as opposed to America and going to *bouzoukia tsifteteli* and stuff like that. Things like that... people are not so interested in stuff like that, like traditional dances and costumes and things like that. That's

another thing I grew up with, making costumes, doing stuff like that. (Medea, female, 22)

I am proud to be Greek, but I don't think I am as proud as I am when I am in America. I feel it much more, maybe because there are so many different ethnic backgrounds and, like, when we have the Greek parade, Greeks are so happy; they are so proud to be Greek. I mean I went to the Greek parade in the States a couple of years ago when I visited, and I haven't seen anything like it. People were screaming and jumping around when their island or the place they are from in Greece... when they would come down with the boat and say like the island's name or something like that, all the people would go crazy, jumping and screaming. Like here, I went to a few parades, and it's not the same, but I guess I can understand that because in America, there are so many different backgrounds, so many different parades. Much more Greek pride there. (Ariadne, female, 24)

Family is extremely important to me. Marriage also is up there. I think my feelings on the subject have been shaped by my Greek-American culture or background because I think there is a big difference between Greek culture and Greek-American culture. From what I see now, Greek-Americans are more family-oriented, and they want to keep the family structure, the community structure, and those are very important things to me, and that's how I grew up, knowing that there is a family structure, a family. I grew up knowing that family is very important, that our involvement in the community is very important. Here, it doesn't seem to be as important, as essential, from what I've seen. I could be wrong. I've been here only two years, but that is enough to see that marriage and family are not as important to people of my generation here in Greece, which kind of disturbs.... It doesn't disturb, but I am more, I don't want to say old-fashioned on the subject, but I'd like to have a family involvement in the community in the future or near future. (Hermione, female, 31)

For participants in their early twenties and thirties there appears to be a disappointment with the lack of 'performative ethnicity' in the ancestral homeland. The enthusiasm during national holiday parades, the making of national costumes, traditional entertainment and the sacredness of matrimony and religion are all performative expressions of 'symbolic ethnicity and symbolic religiosity' (Gans 1994) but also embodied enactments of 'banal nationalism' (Billig 1995). The participants point to the necessity of a visual representation and physical enactment of 'Greekness' in everyday life as a validation of ethnic self-actualisation. As such, they underline the lack of 'authentic' Greekness in many aspects of everyday life.

Thalia, a 68-year-old retired school teacher, speaks with much frustration about traditions being modified or discontinued. She has lived in Greece for 35 years and although she has come to terms with some of the changes, she is very critical about them. Furthermore, despite having the background 'prerequisites' such as Greek parentage and a Greek spouse, linguistic ability in Greek, having spent more than three decades living permanently in Greece, her narratives indicate lack of acceptance by Greek society. But, as she emphasises, to no extent does she regret her decision to move to her father's country. The lengthy narrative extracts that follow refer to the most powerful representations of ethnicity as she signals their decline in modern Greece:

> Tradition and roots are very important to me, and when Papandreou announced the civil marriage, I was really disappointed. Even the *podies*, I don't know if you know, Greek children went to school with blue and white coloured aprons. Well when that went away, it saddens me to see today the Greeks in Greece are pushing their traditions aside, and I think people like me are more Greek than the Greeks. And what really disappointed me is this October 28th Greek national holiday. I told my grandchildren, who are twelve, what the day was and the whole list of Metaxa and Mussolini, and then we were outside, and they have a friend who is nineteen, and he goes to public school, and when I asked him, 'Why aren't you in school today? What holiday is it?', he didn't know, and this shocked me. It really disappointed me, terrible. Being a Greek-American in Greece has a lot of drawbacks. The Greek people are not that ready to accept someone who is not really Greek. Even though I speak Greek, even though my dad was born in Greece, I am married to a Greek, I've been here 35 years, they have not accepted me at all. I have accepted how they feel about me, but the fact that I am so happy with my husband and my family and my children, I don't care, I really don't care.

> Family to me plays a very big role. The manners of the youth today... didn't they teach them anything in school? Well, I think school has to teach curriculum information. There are certain things that a family has to teach: when to wait your turn, don't speak when someone else is talking, all these things come from

the home, but here the way they use certain words, the way you see younger people dressed... Doesn't the mother see the way the girl walks out of the door? And then they come back at 7 o'clock in the morning, doesn't mother say, 'Where have you been?' I think that the Greek mother has given too much freedom to the kids. They don't want to take the time out to sit down and talk to these children. They give them a car to go out; they give them money to do something. To me material things are not what you give children. You have to give them love; you have to give them understanding, empathy, guidance, think of the other person. I don't think the Greek woman today raises their children the Greek way; she is too much interested in her card games and clothes. I think that the Greek-Americans are more conservative and more traditional, and yes I think so, and most times I think they are more Greek. When we got married in America, the Greek service was beautiful. All the years that I'm here, I've been to many weddings; I've never seen a wedding as beautiful as mine. It was so organized. The service was quiet; here, everyone hurdles around the couple; they are talking; they gossip. In many weddings, I have heard the priest say, 'Please stop talking!' I do believe that Greek-Americans are more Greek in many ways. Now this is hard, raising children this way, and I even had one of my kids tell me, 'Mom, you didn't do a good job with me', and I said, 'What did I do wrong'; 'you taught me to be polite, to open the car door for the girl. But you know when I open the car door for her, she tells me, 'What do think? I'm handicapped. I don't have hands of my own?", so I don't do it any more. I don't open the car door for the girl anymore'. It's difficult; it's difficult raising kids here.

I don't have any regrets even though some of the things I've said have been negative; you have to weigh the things. It would be very unfair for me to say that I'm not happy. I think I'm happier having lived here. I would have had..., just to see a beautiful day for me is something important. I would've missed that.

Thalia's reflections point to a struggling self in a state of ambivalence trying to counterbalance the 'natural beauty' of country and the 'naturalised' significance she places on historically instilled values of 'Greekness' that have eroded in contemporary Greece. She associates the preservation of traditional values with diasporic child rearing which has maintained cultural identifications in the United States and contrasts this with the change of maternal roles in Greece as responsible for the break down of Greek family values. However, the issue of the 'traditional' family has been predominant in the literature, and it is necessary not to ignore the changing aspects of families in Greece, in the United States and elsewhere (cf. Maratou-Alipranti 1999; Karpathakis 1999; Edwards 2004; Christou 2006b; Evergeti 2006). This is exactly the context of conflict and distress that emerges when returnees experience 'modernity' in Greece and are confronted by these altering spaces of social life in the ancestral homeland.

Spaces of confrontation and conflict also emerge when returnees come across occurrences of anti-Americanism in Greece. Andromache, a 34-year-old return migrant, has experienced instances of anti-Americanism along with cases of acceptance. This has placed her in an ambivalent space; sometimes she feels she belongs, other times she feels she does not. What these encounters have stimulated is a sense of 'awareness' that Andromache and other returnees have transformed into a plan of integration and vocation to give as much as they can to their homeland. She describes Greek-American returnees' as being marginalised by mainstream Greek society, and she urges all of them to become, in a sense, 'empowered' and active in combating this type of discrimination:

> I feel as if it will take time. The fact is that people here are very biased, extremely biased. My Greek is very good; they don't understand that I am Greek-American, so if I don't say anything, I am accepted. If I mention the fact that I am Greek-American, you see people take a step back. So that sort of makes you feel edgy sometimes, but then again you have other times when people hear it, and people have been taught differently most of their life actually, and these people tend to take a step forward towards you, and they are excited, and they think you have much more to offer, much more to contribute even to their lives and to their experiences. So it's... it depends on the people. So, sometimes I feel I belong, and sometimes I feel I don't belong. I feel I am much more aware. I realized how anti-Americanism happens. You know what I realized, that despite how many universities they go to, they don't question why is this or that or ok we don't agree with their foreign policy, ok do you agree with yours? because you don't even know what it is. I feel sorry for Greeks, and I feel sorry for Greek society because I realize, oh my God, they are brain-dead. People are just feeding you, even if that is television or radio stations or the media or any type of media or politicians, they just feed you anything, and you just gobble it down. They are not chewing it, and that's when I understood.... That's the first day I used that word, and that's one of the things that makes it hard here, the anti-Americanism in Greece. And

sometimes you just feel the need to stick together because how we felt in America, the need to stick together with other Greeks, here you just feel the need to stick together with other Greek-Americans because they are the ones that understand you. You are different; these people understand you. You had the same experiences; you lived the same way; you are tied to these people, and sometimes, you find yourself asking, 'Oh, does that mean that I am anti-social and that I have to be with people that are like me?' No, that's not it because you are bombarded with Greek every single day, with Americans you are not. It's just like something you would like to keep in touch with.

I will tell people good things and bad things about Greece, and I like meeting people who have had these same experiences with me or come and just need my help or anybody's help, and I am glad to help because it is important to have someone to help you realize certain things, not to be disappointed and discouraged from the beginning. You have to give it time; you have to give everything time. We all have to keep fighting; we all have to. And you know what it is so important? The fact that, I for one, I know I have met in the past two years over 100 return migrants; we have to have a voice; we have to get together; we have to do something. I mean I'm sure we could've done something all this time; we can't wait for other people. We have to fight them, not to be afraid. Greeks try to intimidate us; we are different. We are different, and it is a good thing that we are different. We finally have to do something; nobody cares about us. When I heard what you are doing, you know what, I had never felt happier. I hadn't even met you, and I just said, 'She is wonderful. Bravo! We have to help this girl, finally to stick together, to have a voice'. It's these little things, having people acknowledge our existence. It is very difficult; we should be visible. They have to know we are here, that we have feelings, that we have needs and that we have contributed so much to this country and we contribute every day. Every single day we contribute, either if that is from abroad or from the people that have come and are here and people have to start respecting that. They have to start acknowledging that. People here have to accept and respect that.

Andromache's extensive narrative describes mixed feelings and varied reactions when she 'reveals' her Greek-American background just as she holds both positive and negative impressions about living in Greece. She is very firm about developing coping strategies that extend beyond 'survival management' to stressing Greek-American presence in Greece, their visibility and contribution to the ancestral homeland. Andromache suggests that in order to deal with return migration negative experiences in accomplishing a successful adjustment, a combination of patience and action is to be implemented. However, this is not always true of all return migrants who find the initial encounter with anti-Americanism in Greece traumatic and hard to cope with.

Kalliope is 23 years old and an undergraduate student at an American university in Athens. She was surprised to experience anti-American sentiments at an 'American' academic environment, and that event has delayed her adjustment process, at times making her feel very uncomfortable:

> I feel that being American or half-American or raised in the States is not accepted at all. So still, when I go out and I meet new people that are Greek, I kind of shy away because I kind of know what they are going to say beforehand, and we had rude comments made to us before. And I thought that was something that would not happen, especially at an American college, but it's probably because of that I am very careful when I meet new people. It's still not as hard anymore. I speak the language much better now than when I first got here, but yes, I still find it kind of hard. I feel that I stand out even though I look... I know I look Greek, and it's not like I walk around with the American flag wrapped around me so people could know, but yes, I still feel like there's still something that... I don't feel like I fit in; they make me feel that way at times.

Medusa is 21 years old and an undergraduate at the same American university. Although she is not acquainted with Kalliope and is not aware of her experiences, she shares similar views about the issue:

> But I find it more difficult; there is here in Greece this anti-American sentiment, something that has a lot to do with Greek girls becoming friends with me. They have certain ideas about Americans, even Greek-Americans, that kind of puts a barrier. Greek guys tend to see American, Greek-American, girls as 'easy', stuff like that. Well, maybe that's not the case; I don't know. I was a little surprised. I thought I would come and be embraced; you know, our long-lost American friends that have Greek roots, but it wasn't so much that way. That was a little surprising. Just now in school I'm finding that people are just now starting to become friends with me because they checked me out for the past six months, three months, whatever, and you know realized that I was OK, I guess you could say, and became

friends with me. It was just that it was a little disappointing, but I think there were other factors like I said their anti-American sentiments, which is very ironic because even though they are anti-American, they do everything to become Americanized, and they have this thing, too. They watch Beverly Hills 90210, and they think we are all rich and snobby, and you know we have a better life, and we are coming over and trying to take over their territory kind of thing, so I can understand more where that is coming from, but I found that with my Greek-American friends, I am able to enjoy Greek life: go to *bouzoukia* and stuff like that but with the American way of thinking, and I don't know I found that kind of interesting. On the other hand, back in the States, all the Greeks form their own kind of Greek clique, and maybe it's the opposite; wherever you are, you stick with people of your own that have the same interests and backgrounds. And coming here to Athens, I am more with Greek-Americans, but I found it kind of interesting if I could be more with the Greek community, which I never felt wrongly, unjustifiably discriminated. I never felt discriminated, but then again I never felt being accepted.

And even over the summers, over the summers, I just feel that everyone here in Greece is always aiming to change and be first, the first cell phones and the newest fashion and clothes, and they are kind of losing, I feel, traditional values. And I want to say about Easter, this was my first Easter here in Greece and the *Anastasi* (the Resurrection of Jesus Christ) five minutes past midnight, the whole church had cleared out... nothing, they all left. They went to the *bouzoukia*, you know clubbing, some of them not even fasted, and I saw people going to church in obscene outfits. I thought they were ready to go clubbing, and you know back in the States, the Greek-Americans have more respect for certain things, you know, of the Greek culture. Not many people leave right after the *Anastasi*, maybe certain people with children or certain people with jobs. People, you know, dress more conservative with a lot more respect. I think with the Greek-Americans in the States, we miss Greece, and we've grown up with the old Greek values and hold on to them very tightly, and here in Greece I find they are floating off.

When Medusa relocated to Greece she anticipated that she would be welcomed into the community. However, instead of a warm reception she had to face contrasting behaviours from people her age. Medusa describes personal and intimate relationships in everyday encounters

in Greece with people her age as 'closed' as well as 'open' spaces of interaction. She indicates that it has been very difficult to develop friendships with women but that it has been easier to commence a romantic
relationship with men. Medusa's explanation for this points to a pre-
conceived idea that Greek men have about Greek-American women as
being more 'available' or 'easy' as she says for an intimate relationship.
Hence, Greek-American women are given an ascribed pre-constructed
sexualised identity. Moreover, Medusa mentions that in addition to a
general opposing feeling, Greeks have a distorted view of Greek-Americans lumping them all together in terms of socio-economic and class
status, that is, viewing Greek-Americans as wealthy, creating a sense of
envy and resentment on the part of the Greeks. Finally, Medusa underlines another contrasting aspect between Greek-Americans and Greeks,
one mentioned frequently by the participants, namely a conservative
traditional adherence to Greek values as being strong in the Greek-
American community while dissolving in Greece.

The third set of dynamics, as mentioned previously, is a third space
on its own, the 'here and there'. This is where negotiations occur after
the 'lived' past cultural space (United States) has intersected with the
'living' present ethnic place (Greece), and no matter the clash or contrast, a restored 'habitus' has emerged, negotiated and constructed by
the returning migrants as a final destination of the 'personal plan of
action'. Inadequacies have been assessed, gaps have been filled, differences have been negotiated and a homeplace has been constructed.
The homeplace is the third space where placeness and homeness have
resolved issues of alienation into matters of belongingness.

Aristophanes, a 23-year-old returnee, realised that his return migration project was a part of his self-maturation and self-identification process. During his settlement process, as he came closer to his roots
through interaction with seniors and their narrativisation of ancestry
and roots, Aristophanes gained confidence and this also enhanced his
sense of responsibility. This entire process led to a closer identification
with his 'Americanness' through exposure to 'Greekness':

> *The fact that my parents sold everything and decided that it was
> time to move to Greece all changed my life. Although every begin-
> ning is hard, as the Greek saying goes, I learned to appreciate the
> environment as well as my people. All my life I had nowhere to
> look for my own people until I went to Greece. I took time to
> learn the language and viewed this culture as my own. I had a
> difficulty finding friends, but I knew I belonged. I got to know my
> roots and met elders, whom are treated differently in Greece than
> in the United States. They told me stories about my ancestors and
> history first on. I matured and gained self-respect, and even be-*

came responsible and realized who I was. I came to the conclusion
that I am American, but I have Greek roots. Greece helped me
realize this love for country, and I feel first that I am American
and then Greek. Greece helped me acquire the knowledge necessary
to progress; America will help me put that knowledge to use.

One the other hand, Kalliope, a 23-year-old returnee, not only sees the
changes around her, she has eventually realised the changes in her attitude and behaviour, even appearance, as being more 'Greek':

My friends tell me that when I go back to the States every winter
and sometimes summers, they are like, 'You are so...'. Well, first
of all, they tell me that I've developed a slight accent speaking
English. I don't see that. Who is going to correct me? I'm
around Greek people all day. They say the way I dress is more
Mediterranean and Greek, more European they say. Yes, actually
I think also my sense of humor.... I'll laugh at things, and my
friends would be like, 'That wasn't funny', and the culture also...
there is a different sense of humor. Here, like there is in any
part of the world, that... and I'm more conservative now... in the
States like, now I see this. In the summers, when American
people come to the islands and stuff, you can always tell who is
American... like the loudest table in the room, and I've found
myself saying, 'Oh my God, they are American. God, they are so
loud and obnoxious', and I'm by myself saying that, and I'm
thinking, ' What I am saying? That's how I sounded four years
ago'. When I go to the States I am more conservative. It's here
because of the community; it is so tied together; everything is
on the hush-hush... like be careful when you go out, how you
dress, who you talk to, how you get around. I carry that with me
in the States where people don't gossip that much, especially
where I live, and I find myself more conservative and more
quiet. So I guess, without wanting to, I find myself having
picked up a lot of Greek... a lot.

So far, the personal narratives revolved around individual reflections
and strategies of adjustment in coping with daily life in Greece. Nephele, a 32-year-old returnee, is married to a Greek and raising two
young children in Greece. She has been through contestation and
reached a series of negotiations on a personal and family level:

I believe that since I am living here in Greece and I am married
and I have two children, I really, to tell you the truth, I don't
raise my children as Greek-Greeks; I raise them as Greek-Ameri-

cans. Not to say that raising them as a Greek-American or just Greek-Greek is better. Basically, it's because I have been raised that way, and I know... not that... not only I believe it is the correct way, it is the best way because I see many children here that are raised in the Greek mentality... either they are rude, they don't have much respect... not that my children have better respect than they would... but basically, I think I am teaching them the right way in order to have some respect in some aspects. I teach them about the Greek culture because I was taught about the Greek culture from my parents. We teach them the American language so they know both languages, the Greek and the English, and basically, I believe that this is myself; I am being the exact way I am here. Culture and Greek heritage, of course, it is very important. Before we had the older one here in Greece, we really didn't look into it that much before... of course in the States, I was very ethnic and traditional, going to Greek dances, doing everything Greek, spending time with my Greek friends. Ever since we had our son, I believe more of my Greek heritage has come out, wanting to teach them about October 28th, March 25th, all the important dates and to explain to them why we have this tradition, why we are like this. So I believe that I try to keep it as much as I can although some people here leave it as one question and they don't answer it at all. Probably many Greek-Americans will respond that here in Greece we try to bring our Greek-American self out more than we would in the States. In the States, we would say we are Greek, Greek, Greek. As soon as we come here, we put in that little American accent in, and we say, 'OK, we believe this, and no, this is also correct', but basically, I believe that I am both. I am Greek-American, and I state it many times; it may bother many people, but that's who I am; I can't change it.

Nephele explicates the dynamics that exist due to the multiple roles she is called to take on during her settlement in Greece stemming from her 'Greek-Americanness'. Her maternal role is deeply correlated with her sense of identity, that is, feeling and acting more Greek-American in Greece, a feature which, as she claims is fortified by living in Greece while in the United States the emphasis was always solely on the 'Greek' component of her sense of dual identity. This reflects on the fluid and changing role of ethnicity in the lives of migrants and how meanings of ethnicity and identity are transformed in relation to spatial and temporal conditions (social, cultural, political, historical). Ethnic origins are still salient in more subjective ways and a self-sub-consciousness about diverse ethnic origins finds expression in many areas of contemporary life. Changing features and self-understandings of ethnicity have important implications for how individuals think of themselves and how they interpret their experiences in relation to their ethnic points of origin. As Alba argues, 'ethnicity among whites (more precisely, non-Hispanic whites) in the United States is in the midst of a fundamental transformation...This transformation does not imply that ethnicity is less embedded in the structure of American society but rather that the ethnic distinctions that matter are undergoing a radical shift...In a sense, a new ethnic group is forming – one based on ancestry from *anywhere* on the European continent' (1990: 3; italics in the original). Alba's research confirms, to an extent, what the participants have described previously, specifically that ethnic distinctions remain associated with meaningful social differences and these distinctions are embedded in people's identifications and in the actions they take as a result. However, the narratives of second-generation Greek-Americans document the need to reconceptualise the ethnic content of identification as one also under transformation in the very context of its inception, to be exact, in the ancestral homeland.

Sappho, who is 23 years old, has reflected deeply on the issues revolving around her return migration. She basically summarises a plan of action that consists of an awareness and evaluation of both Greek and American societies, with her decision to return to Greece based on values sought and values found that culminates with the obligation to give back to the homeland (Greece) as much as she can offer. This idea is similar with what Andromache had mentioned earlier, the 'need to contribute to the homeland', an action that highlights the return migration venture with a type of special mission almost like a 'development assignment' that the returnees have to fulfil in order to complete their return project and justify their 'ethnic and cultural value' (or perhaps 'superiority' in comparison to the 'native' Greeks).

> Basically looking at culture and ethnicity in Greece, it is fading away, and I can't even imagine where it is going. Though when I first came to Greece, I could identify with Greeks, but it was a different identification because I knew a Greece that was during the 70s from my parents' stories and that's what I thought Greece was, and when I came, here it was a completely different picture. Due to political issues, government, economic, due to a lot of issues, even though I hadn't really had the picture myself of what Greece was before, I can compare and contrast, and I can see that there is a big difference... what Greece was 20-30 years ago. And culture is something very important for me; it identifies who you are in relation to other people and in relation to the world; it gives you a sense of belonging to something,

which is, I believe very much, it is a necessity for people to know that they belong somewhere to a specific culture. I am Greek, and I carry that heritage, the history, the past. I feel that I have a duty to carry that as a person living in a society where moral values and culture is decaying slowly. I feel that I have an obligation to carry that in a way and transmit that to my children, to my grandchildren... as far as that line may go. It's not the Greek traditions; it's not that, that you can get at your Greek festival in the Church; it's more than that: it's the books, the *Katzantzakis*, you know; it's listening to Theodorakis; it goes deeper than that, things that describe Greece in an era where it was in its highest culturally and politically; people were fighting for certain ideals. This was innately brought into me in a sense when even though I never lived in Greece before, I felt the need to fight for that, to keep that alive, because I was brought up feeling that it was so important.

It's the culture; it's everything because I was aware of the history and the philosophy, I am very into those subjects, of Greece, and I had a wide span of knowledge as far as those issues are concerned. Deeply reflecting, I would actually say that I am very happy as everything that I have learned in the past I can put into practice beyond everything that goes wrong in this society in Greece. I do have the opportunity to actually discuss issues that have concerned me. Growing up, it was very hard for me because of this very Greek environment. I never had the chance to discuss certain things that I would discuss in my family environment, and thus my thoughts were very isolated; I couldn't find anybody that I could truly identify with. Because I am very aware, philosophy and politics are very important to me. This is something which the Greek has and the American society lacks due to its history; it is very recent, due to political circumstances, and I believe that I am given a far greater chance here to expand and better myself as a person, to grow, because actually that is the point of what the ancient Greeks said, your *einai*, your inner being, to grow and better yourself so you can give back to the society which you live in, to better your society in the long run. This is something that being in Greece, it's given me that chance. The problem in the States is that these things, they are hard to find because of the isolation, because of a lot of problems. It's very hard to find somebody that you can interact and give and take in knowledge and experience. As I stated before, I do feel that I am Greek and this is my home because it's gone to a point, good and bad, I love them all so I know this is where

I can live and I can belong. In the States, there are things that
extremely irritated me, and I couldn't live with and that's the
problem with me; when I see that the situation cannot be changed due to ignorance or due to lack of knowledge, I go crazy,
and I guess I believe that in a way because this is my home, I
have a duty and an obligation to do something for it, so that's
why I am here I guess.

Again, the focus in this narrative is a reflective awareness of time and
space. On the one hand, there is an awareness of the time-lapse in
terms of the imaginative construction of Greece through parents' stories of a homeland in the 70s and the current temporal reassessment of
changes in lifestyles, values, ethics, morals, behaviours in contemporary Greece through the actual relocation and settlement. On the other
hand, there is an awareness of space and the cultural context of space
in both the United States and Greece and a reconsideration of belongingness and identification based on those values, ethics, morals, behaviours, lifestyles but also philosophy, politics and art (or the lack there-
of). On both levels of this introspective awareness, what stands out is
the emotional force of the need to 'be', to 'belong' and to 'bestow'.

As I have already mentioned in Chapter three, while reviewing
Greek-American studies, one of the most important contributions of
the Greek-American historian Theodore Saloutos, and the only one of
its kind thus far, is his study of the *Repatriated Greek-Americans* (1956)
with extensive fieldwork in both the United States and Greece. Convincingly he asserts, 'The experiences of Greek-Americans, as both immigrants and repatriates, brought humor, drama, tragedy, and success
into their lives. To these people, nothing stood out more vividly than
the emotional intensity with which the repatriates described what they
had experienced' (Saloutos 1956: 88). Through their stories Saloutos
presents the multiplicity of financial, professional, personal or social
problems that made their return to Greece both a 'challenge' and an
'adventure'. A sharp interplay between fortunes gained and misfor-
tunes encountered is a clear illustration of this theme. The participants
Saloutos interviewed, precisely half a century ago, all representatives of
the first generation of Greek immigrants, expressed intense disappointment and suffered unpleasant and disillusioning experiences upon return, especially when subjected to family ordeals of having to provide
financial aid to others and being rejected if the returnees were not willing to comply with such demands. Saloutos records a series of complaints ranging from lack of facilities and conveniences to deceptive
practices by locals; moreover, returnees were outcast or ridiculed for
dressing, speaking and behaving in a different manner. Some of the
subheadings Saloutos gives for his narratives are indicative of the retur-

nees' feelings of despair and frustration in their native country, for instance, '*I Left God's Country to Come to the Devil's*' (1956: 95). So,
although many feasts and celebrations preceded the much-anticipated
event of departure for Greece, with compatriots all gathered for the final farewell, it was often succeeded by misery and turmoil in the native
land.

The evidence of the narratives of the Greek-American returnees
whom I interviewed in Athens from 2001 to 2003, almost two generations after Saloutos' pioneering study, suggests cultural discrepancies
and differences do indeed still exist but to a lesser degree or rather on
diverse levels and varied perspectives than those recorded by Saloutos.
The differences outlined above highlight the returnees' struggle between 'how things are' (Modern Greece) and 'how we do things'
(Greek-Americans). This particular struggle is one of many encountered during identification processes in the ancestral 'home'.

4.3   Narrating the home in the national: stories of 'home' *at home*

In the final section of this chapter I address the conceptualisation of
home in the ancestral homeland through stories of *home* 'at home'. I
will present the five stories of Aristotle, Diomides, Iphigenia, Kalypso
and Pythia in order to give detailed personalised accounts of *ideologies
of home* and *geographies of place*.

I start with Aristotle, a 30-year-old returnee who relocated to Athens
in 2001. He managed to convince his then fiancée (now wife) to move
together and get married in Greece, with a traditional wedding cere-
mony in the ancestral homeland. Aristotle's parents had planned to
move with the couple and help them set up 'home' while his wife
would have to leave her family behind, like several other participants
had to. Aristotle emphasises that as far back as he remembers in his
childhood, his parents always longed for the return 'home'. Indeed he
was brought up with that idea, which also became his life plan:

> My family never had plans to stay there permanently. Never.
> From day one, they always talked about coming back. It is com-
> pletely different. Actually, that is one of the main reasons why
> we never bought a house there. It's not that logical, I guess, but
> with that type of thinking, we did not buy a house.

Although his life in the States was:

An isolating experience from the rest of the Greek community, but in general, it was a learning experience.

He prefers life in the homeland because he believes that:

Greek people are very hospitable but very cultural. I wouldn't say closed but very traditional compared to other ethnic backgrounds. And that's why you see, I believe, you still see a tighter family structure and things like that and a lot of traditions that still go on.

In finalising his return decision, Aristotle is very clear about his life choices:

I've always known that I wanted to come back. It's always been that way; I never doubted it. Here and there I had fears, you know, because when you live somewhere for your entire life, you get used to it, and you learn how things work, and, you know, it is a routine that everybody falls into. And it's also that safety margin when you build a safety zone where you are and where you work and the people you interact with and the friends you have... it's hard to get away from that zone and especially when moving to the other side of the planet. It's very difficult. Plus, like I said before, it's a very different culture. So even though I always wanted to, I feared it a little bit. Now that I am back, I know that I made the right decision even though I see a lot of things that are different from the US; actually, I see a lot of bad things from the US, negative things, but you know, every country has its negatives and positives. US has a lot of positives, but I think I made the right decision. I am happy that I am here; I am very happy that my wife came with me, and I guess I am happy because I am at home.

Aristotle defines his return as a search for home in the homeland:

I always felt that home was here, and it is weird; I never really felt like an American even though I was an American citizen, I have an American passport and everything. I never felt American. I always felt like a foreigner, but you always mingle in with other people. With Greeks you stay a little bit closer to your culture. It helps you know. I am proud to be Greek.

As for disappointments he has experienced during his return settlement, Aristotle also points to the 'changing' face of Greece, the 'Westernised-Americanised' face:

> I expect another picture from Greece, and I don't see that. I see the Greek government and the American, and I see Greece becoming like the US, very capitalistic, very individualistic and very commercial; I don't like that.

But Aristotle focuses more on the hard times he experienced in the US and justifies his return decision as the correct one:

> I had a rough time in the States as I was growing older. I went through a tough period where I almost spoke no Greek, and that had a negative effect on me. I started to forget Greek, and I started being with the American people there, which is of course good. It's not bad, but you forget your own background. So that was a tough time for me. I always had in my heart to come back; I don't know what it was. Greece always drew me back. Not like my brother, he chose to stay. I always wanted to come back, and I always felt that this was home. Although I love the US, I am very grateful to the US, you know, I see the US as my second home even though I lived there most of my life and most of my important years, until the age of 28, I still find Greece as home. I don't know why, and I think I made the right choice in coming back.

Diomides is a 34-year-old returnee who also moved to Greece in 2001 with his wife and son. Another similarity with the previous narrative is the fact that Diomides also had to convince his wife to relocate because her family had no intentions of returning to Greece. The same held for Diomides' family, but his reasons to return superseded the pain of moving away from the family since the relocation would bring him closer to a cultural and natural landscape of community, solidarity, natural beauty and a life of diminished stress. The latter was threatening his health and well-being:

> We found that life is so much slower and relaxing here. The States is a whole different country, different pace, fast pace. Life is very fast; it kind of wears you out. So, the thing is that I started feeling tired in the States. I am in my thirties now, and I don't have the energy I used to. Doctors also told me to slow down; I had some problems. So when I slowed down, I realized I was going with the flow: everyone goes fast, which over here

doesn't happen. I mean over there I would feel guilty if I would just sit and don't work whereas over here I have twelve weeks vacation and people even make me feel, oh, that's good, and I feel guilty, and in the States I would feel very guilty seeing everybody working and running like crazy and me sitting and doing nothing. It doesn't really make me feel good there, so that's one thing. Now, as far as life here, life is much slower: things you can enjoy, you go with a friend for a *frappe* (iced coffee), but in the States, just to get together you know might take two weeks of organization and phone calls and things like that. So life is much nicer in Greece. I came searching for the sea; I love the water. My aspiration for the time being is to enjoy the Aegean.

Diomides talks about his return decision not just in terms of a return to a natural landscape that helps to slow down the pace of life and reduce stress but also as a cultural landscape that cultivates feelings of familiarity and community:

Working in the States, you have a job, and you look forward to go to; working in the States is enjoyable. You work, go home, go to sleep and look forward for the weekend. Over here, it is different. In the States, number one thing is their job; I mean, number one is their family and after that their job. Again it is one extreme and the other. We came here looking for a better life. It was something that we would talk about, and then one day it became immediate reality..., to see what Greece is like and the people. We thought about it very immediately but also very carefully. Yes, we want our kid to learn Greek. It helps that it is Greece. I love this neighborhood in Greece. I love this neighborhood; it is beautiful and the water. And what I like is that I go to cafeterias and I see people I know, 'Hi, how are you', familiarity that community feeling, it is very hard to find in the States. You may live somewhere for 20 years and not really know your neighbors. There is no community there in the States. And I see these people in the States... What are you doing? You are missing the good part of Greece... being in a community.

Diomides also talks about the national space as an amalgamation of Balkan, eastern and western components. His 'personal plan of action' incorporates a critical perspective of evaluating 'what there is', acknowledging both good and bad parts and enjoying the good while ignoring the bad. In his assessment of 'how things are', he interjects a plan of 'how I will do things'. This type of agency underscores the construction of a mediated cultural space in everyday life:

> *I travel in Northern Greece and I see that Greece has a European side, an Eastern European side and a Middle Eastern side and I see all these three cultures trying to melt into together, they don't mix, it is interesting but there are discrepancies. We have a lot of Middle Eastern; we have the organization of Eastern Europe and some parts of Western Europe too. How can you put all these pieces together? I know I am better now, I see the things that are bad and the things that are good and I try to enjoy the good things and ignore the other things. When I went back visiting the States this year to see my family and my friends at the work place and I saw the professionalism I said God, I miss this but on the other hand looking at the people driving like crazy to go to work you know, rushing and all that, I realized the stress. It is not that fun like Greece it is fun.*

Iphigenia is a 50-year-old returnee who relocated to Athens on her own in 1977. Several years later her parents also returned to Greece hoping to 'convince' Iphigenia, who is still single and not interested in marrying, to get married. With an abundance of laughter, humouring the issue and the motives, she tells me:

> I had been in Greece for maybe 3 or 4 years when they decided to come back, and the first part of the reason they decided to come back, you won't believe this, they always wanted to see me married. OK, they felt that while I was here, I was wasting my time, and I wasn't looking to find a husband, and they decided if they come back and they are here to push me, I'll get married at some point. Well that plan fell through! Yes, that's parents for you, and some years later, they told me that they had changed their minds and they did not want to come back and that they came back for me, and when I think about it sometimes, I could kill them for that. As I said, they regretted it at some point. Actually, they told me that they didn't want to come back and that they came back for me. And what did they accomplish? I really don't know. I've told my father, I may not marry; I didn't have it in me.

Iphigenia talks about her life-long aspiration to relocate to Greece. She dwells on people and their attitude to life, the fact that they are full of 'life':

But it was always there, and we kept on saying in the United States, 'OK, one day, when we return to Greece, when we return to Greece'; we always felt that. I love Greece for a number of reasons. For a while, I didn't exactly know what exactly it was that I liked about Greece. Not that I know now. There were a lot of things I liked about Greeks, not the country so much but about the people. They are free-spirited. OK, they are loud. They make a lot of noise. They fight. They quarrel. I sort of like that. They are very friendly once you get to know them. OK, whereas in the States, it's exactly the opposite; people are very friendly in general, but sometimes they might not allow you to get in their inner world, their space. I understand both cultures very well.

Iphigenia talks about change but on the other side of the Atlantic. The United States and the place she called 'home' has changed, the people there have changed. Although she has faced ambivalence as regards where 'home' is, she has clarified points of uncertainty as to where the comfort and understanding of home lie. Similar to Diomides' 'personal plan of action', Iphigenia focuses on the good, maintains an awareness of the negative things in people, but ultimately retains the positive while aspiring to do the right thing, to contribute:

I don't remember now at what point I began to feel right at home in Greece and thinking of both the United States and Greece as my home. I feel like a misfit here, and I go back, and I feel like I misfit there, and it's because I don't look forward to going to the States as a home for me. It's because things are changing. It's the changes. America is changing. Where I grew up is not the same any more. It's a different city. It has become a beautiful more cosmopolitan city than the days back when I was there. My friends have changed. I have changed. When I returned to Greece, I had like most Greeks or Greek-Americans a superiority complex. I felt that I was superior to everyone here coming from a very advanced culture. Eventually, this has to do with open-mindedness, actually; I am a very open-minded person. I will accept everybody and everything, and I try to understand them. Eventually, I began to understand the Greeks because I like people and I like working here and I only see in people, that's my mother actually, only good points. I see the negative, but I just choose to ignore it, and I watch myself. I also watch people, for example, and if they are devious, I'll keep it in the back of my mind and think about it later if I see that they are trying to get in my way or if they are trying to create problems for me and then just work with whatever good ways and eventually they come around; it may take a while. But that's what keeps me going. If you start thinking negatively about people, about your life, about anything, then you've lost the game, you've lost the game. It deteriorates you. Enjoying your experiences, enjoying other people, enjoying being with other people, working with other people, working out problems, I don't know what else more is there in life, a collection of experiences; a collection of experiences. The better these experiences are, the better it is for you. You tend to feel fulfilled by doing good in your life. That's what I would like to be able to do... to look back and saying that I had a wonderful time, wonderful times and that I accomplished things and that I helped people. I like helping people and help them grow or develop.

Unlike other participants who sharply focus on the anti-American sentiments that may exist in Greece, Iphigenia translates those feelings into a love-hate schema where love of the 'American ways' prevails. She spent time getting to know Greeks and Greek behaviour:

I got to know Greeks quite well; no Greek is anti-American. That is a façade. Deep down, they admire the United States. There is a sort of love-hate relationship. They admire the United States for what it has done; they admire the United States because they all got relatives in the United States. Let's face it, I've got relatives, friends there of mine and relatives. Knowing Greeks, they are not anti-American, deep down they are not because there is this love, there is this admiration they have for the American culture, the American ways and the American system, the American Constitution, which they think is the best thing that has happened in the world, but I do know what happens in every small country that doesn't have that much power and control over what happens in the world. They have their envy, and whatever anti-Americanism we have here springs from that, the envy that Greece is not a powerful country and we are behind and low and almost all Greeks know that. There are a lot of things that the United States can be admired for, and I think it is envy deep down.

Kalypso is a 41-year-old returnee who moved to Greece in 1984. She is an only child and decided to move on her own; her parents relocated to Greece several years later. Kalypso knows many second-generation Greek-Americans who moved to Greece and stayed, unlike the parents who followed the children but could not adjust and left again. Kalypso feels that Greece was always 'home' for her, and she came searching for 'home'. Right after college she decided to move to Greece. She rejected job opportunities in the United States and preferred to work in Greece. The fact that her family had a tradition of 'homecoming' visits on an annual basis since she was a very young child actually had prepared her for relocation. There are many things that make her happy in Greece. Here she describes several of them:

> I would have Athens as a base because I always loved coming to Greece. Every summer since the age of 4 we were here, so I didn't feel like I was going to a foreign country; it felt like home so that's why I preferred working here. And I don't want to go back. Of course for vacation, yes, but not to live. I like the way they live here. it's not formal, you know, going to work, going for coffee, going to the sea. It's not that 9-5 and being at home and waking up again at the morning or going to a bar or something like that. So I think mainly I guess it was the coming back every summer where I felt this was home, not so much there because here it was vacation time; there it was work, so that's why I liked Greece better than America.

Kalypso has clearly rationalised the 'here and there' dichotomy into a creative process of bettering one's life and becoming a better person and ultimately a happier person with the stability that the sense of grounding to base, to how a 'home' feels like. She overemphasises the positive aspects of living in Greece, especially a carefree lifestyle, entertainment, the weather, access to natural beauty, the sea, the landscape, family, heritage, relatives and social relations. She prides herself on being the one who convinced her parents to return to their country of origin and feels content with having bridged discrepancies between the 'here' and 'there'. When she initially relocated, she was able to transfer from her post in the United States to an equivalent position in Greece but was laid off from her job two years later due to budget cuts. After losing the professional and financial stability that her previous employment offered, Kalypso had to enter a lower scale post in terms of responsibilities and salary in a totally different sector. Despite the anxiety that she experienced during her unemployment and the compromise she was forced to make in terms of her professional development, she did not express any regrets in relation to her decision to live permanently in Greece. Her lengthy account develops her trajectory:

> You must take in fact that Greece is Greece. It's not America and if you start comparing countries as one compares people, it's wrong. You are not going to get anywhere, so you just say, 'This is it. This is how Athens or Greece is', and you learn to ad-

just. If you don't like it, you leave, and so mainly, my character helped me, but coming back every summer helped because I got used to it right. No, I didn't regret it, and I don't really think that I could go back living the way I did in the US. I am out of that. Of course I want to go back to the States to visit; that's where I was born, and lots of my friends which I still keep in contact with but to live, no, no. And I don't regret it... Even though I didn't do what I wanted to do, even though my career was for two years, but I'm satisfied that I did it for two years, but other than that, I am very happy here, very very happy. Like, I am the one who brought my parents back here. I think they would stay 5, 6 more years there, but since I was back, I told them, 'Why don't you come back?' They wanted to, of course. In fact, when they went to the States, they said, 'OK, we'll work for two years and we will go back', and it was for many years, not two years, so it was a chance for them to come back with me.

I brought my parents here instead of them bringing me here; it was the other way around, the other way around. Geographically, Greece... I think it helped. Yes, you know where it is, the weather, so I really do think it helped. And of course lots of relatives... I'm sure most of us have relatives here, so that helped, but coming from the age of 4, you feel home... after you feel home so there wasn't a problem to adjust because I knew what I was getting into, so that really helped.

Greece is a country with history, so when a country has history, it has to offer a lot. What I like, I like the people because they are open. When they go to work, they don't consider they are going to work. After work, we go for coffee or go to the movies, even though it's not Saturday or Friday night, so that really, really changes things because in the States, Monday through Friday was work and home and nothing else. Only Saturday was, mainly Friday night and Saturday, this is what, you know you really really feel alive, and it's not like, 'Oh, Sunday is a really bad day because Monday is coming'. You don't feel that; at least I don't, especially where I work here. I come to see my friends, having coffee with them, discussing their problems, discussing what went good, what went bad, so that's what I didn't have in the US. I didn't have that. Another thing is the sea, which I always loved, the water, and I'm very close to it, and I didn't have that in the US. You see the progress whereas in the States, you don't see the progress because it's gotten to that point. Here you see the progress. I do think a person has to have an open mind, an open character and to accept what the country has to offer, just as we do with people, accept who they are and that's what I'm trying to do. I think I've accomplished it, with Greece, and that's why I've been here for such a long time.

You know you are from America; you think you know a lot. So when this starts to happen, you cool down. You say, 'Hey, people in Greece have not been abroad. They don't know how it is abroad'. So, you don't say, 'Oh, you do this here, and we do this there differently'. It is very very wrong. Once again, we are comparing two different people, two different countries, so you don't say, 'You know, in the States, this is better', 'It's not working here' or 'It's very wrong'. When I started doing that, when I first came here, I did that. It's natural, and you create enemies to a point, until they understand she was born there, she was raised there. But now, no, no, because I've changed me so that's something good that all this thing has brought upon me coming back to Greece and being from two different countries. You start to understand; you don't compare. That's a no-no, and you accept how the country is and how the people are, so that makes you a better person. Of course you are going to encounter a lesson; you are going to learn a lesson, but this is what helps all, I think, to become better people, so it's positive. Everything has been positive for me so far. I must tell you that I do feel at home. I see that as coming closer to my roots and my heritage.

I never felt that I was missing something here. It was very satisfying, and it still is very satisfying, very satisfying, I guess, in a way. Maybe I don't realize it. You know my background, culture, it really played a part in bringing me back. Maybe it does play a part why I feel so good here. I don't know. I really can't pinpoint that. I'd have to talk to other people and see if it's the same for them too, but I really think it's the base. I really do, I really do, and the more I'm here and the older I get, I think I really do realize this. I think it is.

It was an empowering and liberating experience. It was, it was all of what I expected. I was never disappointed, never, at all. If I had problems, they would just solve themselves so that made it a lot more easier for me to stay here. But it was what I dreamed of, what I felt it was going to be. It's like I had a dream, and I knew this is what it was going to be. Again I tell you my character must've helped; my flexibility must've helped because I do know a lot of people who have gone back but mostly the parents, not the children, not the second generation. I think that the first generation had problems adjusting to their country, and I've known kids whose parents have gone back, and they've stayed. They live here and their mom and dad back in the States, so I don't know what that is. I don't know.

For me, as I said, I didn't feel like I was going to a different country; it was home, every summer here right, so maybe I was an easy case. Everything was easier for me, much easier for me. If we take it differently, from someone raised in the United States had come here once or twice and decided to come, of course, that's a different story, but even in those cases, I've known people who've stayed and their parents have gone back. In general, positive, positive, positive. That's all I can say about it. It was a very.... I think I was.... I think I won the lottery, I think I won the lottery, you know, because other people, they don't have the same experience of both worlds; they just know one thing. It's like going to school and learning, you know, when you quit school no more, when you continue school, you learn, so this is what I feel. Everyday I learn. Truly, I learn, especially when I go back because you can compare, not compare, but you can get both perspectives and you can get parts of both worlds and that helps you become a better person. I truly believe that, and I know that I have managed it. I just see it in myself. But my base is and always will be Greece because the base is my Greekness, my culture and my heritage and my family.

Pythia is a 50-year-old returnee who moved to the ancestral homeland in the year 2000. Her return was a powerfully emotional journey to a place that has deeply affected her life and personality. Pythia is very vivid in her descriptions of the homeland, culture and belongingness. She is overwhelmed by how gratifying it is to finally accomplish the fulfilment of her parents' dream – who are now deceased and were never able to return to their country of origin. She is ecstatic at making the idea of Greece as home a reality, and her written narrative eloquently and powerfully develops the emotive aspects of longing and belonging:

> Since ancient times Greeks have left the ultramarine seas and bright skies of their native land to seek their fortunes abroad. No matter how far they may wander, however, Greeks, like their ancestor Odysseus, long for home. Short of death, the worst punishment an ancient polis 'city' could impose on its citizens was exile. Even today, Greeks tend to talk about sojourns in xenitia 'foreign

lands' as a kind of self-imposed exile. Ithaca 'home' beckons like a lighthouse in a storm, but most find that they cannot go home again. As a young immigrant child, I too experienced these feelings more often than I would like to remember. For a long time it seemed we lived in a haze. There was no existential problem about 'do I exist'. We didn't even know who our neighbors were. We go miles across town to visit our Greek relatives and friends. We were afraid to even say hello to the people next door to us. It's strange this place, America. The house permeated with Greek foods. My family was my first teacher of philosophy and psychology. But in America their minds and hearts were always heavy and worried. We retained all the Greek customs and traditions in our home. It was decorated with embroidery and lace handwork. Boubounieres, the small gifts given at Greek weddings and baptisms, graced the shelves. We would attend the mostly immigrant congregation of the Greek Orthodox Church in America. We just couldn't miss a Sunday. My father may have been a stranger in America, but he was still head of his family. He exerted a firm control over his wife and children and believed in the traditional roles of man, woman, and child. I felt the strict discipline in our life was part of the Greek tradition and accepted it, although not always happily. Father stopped saving to return to Greece because the demands and responsibilities of life in America didn't allow it. He also realized that his children were assimilating into American life. Father never went back to his beloved Greece. While growing into adulthood, I came to understand my father better. What seemed a stern and unfair behavior when I was a child was the very quality for which I now am grateful to him. He had given us only enough discipline to prepare us for self-control and courage to face life. Those 'Bahs', with which he used to shatter some of our fancies, were just his way of showing us the foolishness of sham and display. He wanted us to seek realities and not be deceived by pretence. He wanted us to be, act and remain Greek.

Only as I matured was I able to study the character of my people. Of course, I knew only the Greeks who had come to America. But among them were the idealistic and the mercenary, the honorable and dishonorable, the industrious and the idle, the successful and the unsuccessful, but I know the one thing they all shared was courage to leave our country, our home, our culture and travel half way across the world to a new life. Some of us were more successful than others in blending with the new civilization. Even so we each had something to add to the total flavor of America. But the longing for home would never dissipate. When I was seventeen years old my sister, mother and I returned to Greece for three months. A couple of years ago, over three decades later, I returned with my youngest son. As my son and I stood on the Acropolis and from there could survey the ancient city of Athens, I felt such peace, the kind of peace one feels only after arriving home. I thought how tiny Greece was, and yet what a history it has had. And how proud I am to be part of that history.

When arriving in Greece, whether by plane or ship, train or automobile, there is always a feeling of going home, although it may be a first visit. In one way or another, at some time or another, we have all been there, even if only in a dream. It is the familiarity of the Greek landscape that creates the immediate bond one feels with Greece on arrival. To watch the landscape of Greece, stark and unfamiliar as it may be, is to experience a rare sense of fulfilment and serenity. Scattered about the landscape of Greece are the monuments of its history, the oracles, the temples, the fortresses, and the churches. Greece is beautiful and varied enough to offer visitors a memorable journey without seeing a single ruin, but that would be unfortunate. Nothing explains contemporary Greece nor dramatizes our ties to it more than a visit to an ancient monument in its own setting. Touching the pieces of a shattered pillar, looking at a row of broken columns on a hillside, the mind seeks to restore what once was, and in that vision we glimpse how much of what we build, dream, create, believe and value is Greece. The birthplace of Western thought and culture is found in Athens in and around the Acropolis. Greeks are perfectly at ease with their position in life. We believe in destiny. My destiny and life dream was to return to Greece. Now I feel to rejoice in life, to find the world beautiful and delightful to live in, this is a mark of the Greek spirit. The joy of life is as evident in Greeks today as it was in our ancestors. Because of the people, I feel the rhythm of life seems to beat stronger and quicker in Greece than anywhere else. It is felt as soon as you leave the plane at an airport or disembark at a dock and watch passengers greeting relatives and friends who have come to meet them. The jostling, the shouting, the weeping and embracing are familiar from other airports and other harbors, but they are more intense in Greece. The strong beat of life is felt in the waterfront taverns and village squares as Greeks gather to talk, drink, sing, dance, and argue about everything from politics to the price of olives. It is felt in the streets, the sidewalk café, the balconies, the shops, the homes, and the schoolyards. It is evident even in church, where worshippers don't sit silently in pews but stand in knots in the unfurnished nave, chanting, whispering, shift-

ing restlessly, and sending an antiphony of sounds floating throughout the edifice along with the incense. Greeks disdain quiet and solitude. They find little joy in going out for a walk alone or scant pleasure in having dinner with one companion. Their happiness is not complete unless they can enjoy it surrounded by a parea, or a group of friends. Being with a good parea in Greece is like going to an event, having a party and joining a family reunion all at the same time. Greeks are perhaps the most gregarious people in the world and they find it easy to strike up conversations because they are not constrained by superfluous etiquette. For all those who love the light of reason and the joy of life, who strive for the best in themselves and who value truth and freedom, Greece is home. In speaking of Greek life I have emphasized the humble life, the lack of luxuries and the strong traditions, for I wanted to show how the spirit thrives on simple material surroundings and grows in abundance of love and history.

4.4   Summing up

In narrating the 'home' in the 'national', the five returnees quoted above have offered their stories of 'home' *at home*. For the participants, relocation involves a (dis)rupture of national temporalities and cultural spatialities. The relocation involves a (re)evaluation of relationships to both 'home' and 'host' countries. Ruptures occur when national constructions are complicated by the politics of a national space in the ethnic place. Various degrees of 'homeness' and 'placeness' are encountered as variegated voices appear throughout the narratives. Concerns and anxieties surrounding 'home-place' constructions shatter nostalgia; they evoke memories and strengthen longing for a national past. Thus, the returnees participate in a cultural discourse as both 'insiders' and 'outsiders'. The emergence of two distinct cultural systems (to their awe and surprise for most) *places* them as a 'diasporic group in the native land' where their experiences at times clash with Greek mainstream practices. This process may frustrate the returnees' settlement, but it illuminates their agency as it unveils personal change, transitional insights, self-development and maturation. Finally, the search for 'home' in the national landscape and the ethnic place is a constant moving between two 'homes' that resembles a 'transmigration' of return rather than a return migration once and for all. This is a central component of the newly constructed cultural world of the returnees; it will be further explained in the next chapter where the *ideologies of return* and *geographies of culture* are discussed. Furthermore, how this new ethnocultural space affects identification processes will be the core theme of Chapter six where the *ideologies of self* and *geographies of identity* are explored. Home is a useful analytical concept because it refers to those fluid spaces 'where one best knows oneself' (Rapport and Dawson 1998: 9) and thereby constitutes a platform to discuss identity. The search for identity involves movement, in body and mind, within and between spaces that are identified as 'home'.

In this chapter I have explored home as a space of social relations and of identification. In both these conceptual terrains, 'home' is not stripped from its social context. Instead it evokes images and imaginings of a nation as homeland, drawing ethnic collectivities within spaces of common religious and cultural backgrounds. Discourses and narratives of home express place as the locus of belongingness and stability in an era of movement. They localise migrants' struggles for being or becoming. Spaces of in-betweenness become places that alienate. Places of sameness become spaces of identification. Olwig argues that 'the upholding of an idealized, harmonious home, associated with specific values and social relations, may create a perfect place of identification for some, a prison for others. The interrelationship between a home as a conceptual space of identification and home as a nodal point in social relations is of great importance, and it presents a significant topic for follow-up work within this pioneering approach to identity and movement' (1998: 236). I find Olwig's argument extremely powerful and revealing of what my participants' narratives have communicated across conversations of *home, place* and *belonging*. The only divergence would be the discovery that even in their new world of stability, choice and return, harmony may not exist for all returned migrants. Perhaps the migrant's world is forever a world of turbulence (Papastergiadis 2000), despair (Ghosh 2000) and eternal internal turmoil (Christou 2006c). Perhaps the return migrant's new world is one that fluctuates between the blessings and curses of 'home-host' ambiguities, illusions and certainties. By looking at identification processes and the 'cultural stuff' evoked during those processes, we can delve into the intersubjectivities and dynamics between migrants as agents and homelands as structures. In this chapter, the returnees – some of them critical, others more accepting – illustrated their return decision in relation to a place where they could find 'home'. Home is at times 'sweet' and at others it is quite 'bitter', but the 'bitter-sweet' of this relationship is often precisely what clarifies the feeling of being 'at home'. This feeling is just one aspect of the 'self' at home. Before this stage (identification) is explored, I will examine *culture* in the return, the focus of the next chapter.

5 Ideologies of return and geographies of culture

As the narratives become a storied discourse of diasporic movement and a collection of 'moving stories'[1] we are confronted by a multiplicity of images and imaginings that have transformed into concrete experiences of the return migrant *agent* in the homeland *structure*. The intersection of self and nation prior to and during the return settlement and eventually throughout the post-adjustment period can be understood as a new spatial formation where identifications emerge, are questioned and are processed. This new space, as referred to previously, often called 'third space'[2] or 'hybrid space', is one formed, reformulated and understood by the returnees as a site of *arrival, homeness* and *belongingness*. Throughout the entire process of return-settlement-adjustment both the returnees and myself as researcher are spectators of these transformations and the products of personal metamorphosis during the migratory journey. As noted already this is a journey that starts in the country of birth and origin (the United States), passes through various states of *being* and *becoming*, and extends to the country of parental extraction, the ancestral homeland (Greece), as the illumination of *self* and *nation*. Hence, we are confronted by multiple journeys of multiple identifications. The country of birth and origin (US) initiates longing and nostalgia for the ancestral home, which stimulates, evokes and encourages the journey of self-awakening and the physical act of return. The evocation of the searching-self does not disturb or fragment the identification process; on the contrary, it complements the location of self as it simultaneously narrates the nation. The 'searching-self' trips are expressed as 'searching for roots' and are articulated by narratives of return. The landscapes of self are theorised as 'ethnoscapes'[3] or landscapes of national belonging.

In this chapter, the analysis of the narratives are once again conducted through the triadic relationship of:
1. returnee (return migrant-agent),
2. ancestral homeland (the nation as structure),
3. the return as a conscious act of identification (the symbolic interaction of both agency and structure).

And this relationship is understood on three levels that filter:

a. the narrative story of return,
b. the narrative themes emerging as voices of action and acts of agency, and finally,
c. the narrated self which illuminates and is enhanced by the nation as concept and image.

Throughout these stages we encounter the interplay of return and culture. This is demonstrated as both a return to culture and a cultural return. The meaning of belonging is both a stimulating factor and a factor of consideration. The consideration refers to how 'belonging' can be classified and defined and in what form it shapes returnees' lives.

A basic typology of belonging, if we can actually categorise such an abstract notion, is based on Hedetoft's four 'analytic sites' (2002: 2-4):
1. sources of belonging: locality and the familiar,
2. feelings of belonging: identification and memory,
3. ascriptions/constructions of belonging: nationalism and racism,
4. fluidities of belonging: globalism and cosmopolitanism.

In line with the theoretical framework I have set in my study and presented in detail throughout Chapter two, Hedetoft (2002) agrees that all four categories entail an element of 'construction'; they pass through mental processing, personal and collective experiences as well as the temporal and psychological filter of 'memory'. All these parameters shape migrant images and perceptions of belonging, which are 'unimaginable' or, perhaps better, 'unattainable' except in the context of a constructed national home. The following sections and narrative stories of the *patrida* in the ethnocultural space of return illustrate various patterns and configurations of these types of belongingness in the national home.

5.1   Home is the return: constructions of belongingness

Salman Rushdie's (1987) comment that we live in the century of the migrant points to what Peter Berger and his colleagues had argued rather earlier, namely that 'modern man (sic) has suffered from a deepening condition of *homelessness*: The correlate of the migratory character of his (sic) experience of society and of self has been what might be called a metaphysical loss of *home*' (1974: 77). The project of modernity is then 'to make oneself somehow at home in the maelstrom' (Berman 1983: 15), and the project of postmodernity, I would argue, is to redefine where the home is and to clarify how we feel 'at home' in the fluid spaces of the new, disorienting and permeable global contexts of the twenty-first century. But as Papastergiadis argues, 'Naming the project is one thing but knowing its trajectory is another...Modernity begins with the belief in both the journey away from and the permanence of home' (1998: 1). To clarify the polysemic and nuanced meanings of be-longingness, we should keep the following in focus:

> 'Belonging' is a concrete, innocent, almost pristine notion, clo-sely interwoven with and imbricated in the notion of 'home'. In fact, our home *is* where we belong, territorially and culturally, where 'our own' community is, where our family, friends and ac-quaintances reside, where we have our roots, and where we long to return to when we are elsewhere in the world. In this sense, belonging, (...) is a notion replete with concreteness, sensuality, organicist meanings and romantic images. It is a foundational, existential, 'thick' notion. In the ways that it circumscribes feel-ings of 'homeness', it is also a significant determinant of indivi-dual 'identity', that elusive but still real psychological state of feeling 'in sync with' oneself under given external conditions. Most importantly, 'home' and 'belonging', thus conceived, carry affective rather than cognitive meaning; the indicative and sim-plistic statement above, 'home is where we belong', really means 'home *is* where we *feel* we belong' (Hedetoft 2002: 5; quotations and italics in the original).

Home is about belongingness and this type of connectedness is about the 'fundamentals of culture and identity. And, as such, it is about sus-taining cultural boundaries and boundedness. To belong in this way is to protect exclusive, and therefore excluding, identities against those who are seen as "aliens" and "foreigners". The "other" is always con-tinuously a threat to the security and integrity of those who share a common home...In contemporary European culture, the longing for home is not an innocent utopia' (Morley and Robins 1993). These feel-ings of alienation and exclusion appeared in some of the returnees' voices heard in Chapter four. Fortunately, these are not the only voices that articulate the return to home. Some of the returnees are outraged by Greek xenophobic views and argue against fundamentalist beliefs or what Rushdie calls 'the absolutism of the Pure' (quoted in Morley and Robins 1993: 8).

Expressive of a diverse optic, returnees, although still often surprised at how much and to what degree their ancestral homeland has chan-ged, are nevertheless, more sympathetic towards the country's progres-sion towards a multicultural society, and most importantly, outraged at Greek xenophobia, racism and absolutist views of the essential 'purity' of the Greek ethnos. The following four excerpts epitomize this more positive and tolerant view (but at times indifferent or aware of potential negative issues involved), which is both filtered through their families' own experience of migration and mirrored against their personal encounters of multicultural urban experiences in the United States. Narratives that stand against absolutist and fundamentalist views state:

> It's a melting pot, as I say New York is; Athens is the same. Wherever you turn, you don't only see Greek people. Not only, you don't hear just Greek anymore, the way it used to be, but many times you open your door, and you hear another language, the way it is in the States. It doesn't bother me as much. One thing that does bother me is the way the Greek people talk about the different cultures that have immigrated here so far. They forget that themselves that once they immigrated and they went either to Australia, to Germany, they went to the States, and they were the same way immigrants today are, and they just wanted to make a better life for themselves, and that is one thing Greek society or the Greek government should try and remember and understand. (Nephele, female, 32)

> I'm not sure how I feel about it. On the one hand, it is nice. For me personally, in New York I was always used to different cultures, and it makes me feel more comfortable. I like it. On the other hand, sometimes I just don't feel like I am in Greece or in Athens I suppose. But it's not just Athens because even in the *eparchia* (provinces) where I visited, I don't feel like I am in Greece. I feel I am again in another multicultural place, but it doesn't bother me because I am used to having other cultures, and actually it makes me feel more comfortable having them around because I am used to it. (Hermione, female, 31)

> Greece has been transformed into a multicultural society. Yes, I've seen that. In Athens we have that a lot but even in Crete, especially in small villages, all you saw was Greek and Greek Orthodox, and now it's changing dramatically there. It's not problematic; it has its positive and its negative. But it's something that you can't stop. You can't tell people to stop coming to your country; we went to other countries. But I think in all groups, we have good people and bad people. No, it's not problematic; I think it's a good thing. Yes it is. I don't have problems with any cultures. (Phaedra, female, 27)

> It's a big change for Greece because Greece for so many years has been Greek and all of a sudden people came from Albania, from all over the world not just Albania, so I started to feel a lit-

tle like when I was back in the States. That's not bad; it's good
because Greece has so much to offer, and they can give out a
lot. This transformation from a homogenous to a multicultural
society for Greece, well, when this happens, it creates both many
problems and many positive things. I think Greece is right in
the middle; they are trying to get used to it, and it is very very
hard. I think they are doing a good job; they are doing a good
job, so I guess it's good, it's good. For me, it was a learning experience decades ago. Yes, for me it wasn't something different,
but for my Greek friends it's difficult. But I think it also helps
them to understand other people because we must not forget
that Greece... a lot of Greek people went abroad many years ago,
and yes, they have to understand people coming in so this gives
them a chance to understand. (Kalypso, female, 41)

From ancient to contemporary Greece, the homeland is a site of belonging and a stage of identification. Of course, classical Greece provides a wealth of literature that elaborates a strong awareness of cultural or ethnic difference, xenophobia and patriotic zeal (Pecora 2001).
Thucydides' *History of the Peloponnesian War* (431-413 BC) includes
Pericles' famous funeral oration for the Athenians who died in the first
year of the war. Evident is a fairly complex sense of patriotism that
combines pride in both the ethnic identity and the democratic form of
government of the Athenian city-state, the polis. As Pecora explains,
Pericles begins with the praise for 'our ancestors' who, 'generation to
generation', through their valour preserved and handed down the
homeland – though he also acknowledges that, having become an empire, Athens does not 'exclude foreigners from any opportunity of
learning or observing'. Significantly, he praises 'the form of government under which our greatness grew' as well as 'the national habits
out of which it sprang' (2001: 15). Several thousands of years later, return migration of the *homogeneia* to modern Greece shows that the
multiple complexities and paradoxes encountered during the return
unveil possibilities of being 'in exile' while 'at home'; they convey feelings of estrangement from the homeland that returnees longed to return to and reveal that at times their return is about being both part
and apart from their culture. These spaces of 'homeness' and 'alienation' unfold in relation to the cultural construction of the homeland as
persons feel that they belong to a community, a territory, or a state.
This way they are aware of who else belongs, who does not belong and
who is moderately tolerated.

    I would like to turn to those institutions that communicate and con-
struct belongingness and therefore 'home' in the return project: family
as a nexus of culture, memory as a source of national remembrance,

and a cluster of national spaces and signifiers that transmit belongingness. Put a little more cryptically, history told–history envisioned, language communicated–language as lifestyle. All these institutions exhibit a paramount quality: unconditional endurance to the spatio-temporal constructions of the returnees. Although aware and at times critical
about the modernising appearance and behaviour of the homeland, the
participants constantly 'participate' in the construction of their belongingness and the formation of their home. What underscores this belongingness is the sense of rootedness, the strong sentiments of belonging to a homeland that is a home because it exemplifies the notion
of one people: one family with common origins belonging together
and sharing together the past while building the future. The recourse
to the comfort and security of origins, rootedness, authenticity and a
'great past' alleviates feelings of isolation and alienation and substitutes
ambivalence with identification. To reiterate the basic premise of my
analysis, 'the first step down the road is to insist that place in whatever
guise is, like space and time a social construct. The only interesting
question that can be asked is: by what social process(es) is place constructed?' (Harvery 1993: 5). In trying to examine in more detail the
shifting relations between space and place, we need to particularly explain 'why it might be that the elaboration of place-bound identities
has become more rather than less important in a world of diminishing
spatial barriers to exchange, movement and communication' (Harvey
1993: 4). This will be fully explored in Chapter six where identification
is the focus of inquiry.

   To deconstruct what belongingness is and how this shapes feelings
of *home*, I would like to explore what I mentioned above as 'ethno-national' transmitters: family, language, religion. In Chapter three these
were discussed as 'homeland practices'. The narratives that follow illustrate not only the existence of these institutions in articulations of the
cultural worlds of the returnees but also their cultivation as constructs
of 'homely belongingness'. The importance of these institutions in life
in the diaspora is brought back and cultivated during the homeland return against the modernising context that the returnees encounter. In
the next section I will delve further into the 'ethno-cultural worlds' of
the returnees; their writing of new worlds which are primarily cultural
worlds. These cultural worlds involve:

1. the image of woman as mother as a reproductive source of ethno-
   national and religious values,
2. generational circuits as transmitters of values,
3. the 'unitive homing resolution' which is that component of the 'personal plan of action' activated by the returnees to justify the return
   plan as the only truly authentic and truthful process by which home
   is found. The intersubjectivity of the plan becomes the objectifica-

tion of the home; hence the return to 'home' is also narrated on the level of 'setting up house'. The material space of everyday life becomes a space of development and maturation. This illustrates returning migrants' agency in the search of home in the homeland.

The basic idea underlining the notion of 'action' is that it represents intentional behaviour. Actions are the activities that are represented as the result of purpose. An integral component of this 'intentional-purposeful' activity is the need to change situations that produce both intended and unintended consequences. The teleological aspect of such activities refers to the actors' intention of achieving a certain end by using certain means. The process of planning action formulates a series of events into a mould of coherent units. These are also units of social behaviour. Stable social constructions do not need glue or cement to capture intersubjectivity. Although there seems to be something esoteric and mysterious about these processes, they become very clear to the observer-researcher and the observed-researched when we first look at the return life stories holistically as narratives of agency and then tease out the 'ethnocultural spaces' constructed upon return to the homeland.

Part of what a narrator must make clear is why the *agents* concerned did what they did, which may require more explanations setting forth only what *they* believed or intended, not what was in fact true or what they ought to have intended. But it hardly seems necessary to conjure up a babel of 'voices' to make this point (Dray 2001: 165). The narratives are unequivocal about how 'at home' one is. The return is not only a search for home, but it is home in itself. Home in the United States was a permanent parental address they inhabited or now visit frequently or infrequently, or a 'place' they used to own or rent. Home is not synonymous with house. The material objects alone cannot translate into meanings and feelings of home. In the architectural construction of rooms of brick, mortar and cement there is plenty of room for the construction of cultural memory. We therefore encounter a real and imagined home in time and space. Home is employed as a destination in conjunction with a journey of return. In response to this, narratives reveal 'homey' feelings and thoughts that materialise into plans of where home is, as well as social constructions of home. Notions of being-at-home, creating or making home and the ideal home are usually conflated with or related to house, family, haven, self, gender, and journeying, which raises the question whether or not home is, '(a) place(s), (a) space(s), feeling(s), practices, and/or an active state of being in the world?' (Mallet 2004: 65).

Returnees appeal to the sense of 'community' as a justification of the return as home. This is a component of the 'personal plan of action', and I term this the 'unitive homing resolution': a plan to return to the ancestral homeland in search of roots and heritage, which simultaneously becomes both a comforting and a consumption plan of personal development. Hence, the returnees' trajectories for educational and professional advancement constitute both a practicable plan of return (it is able to be done) and a practical plan (they practise it during the return). This practice is multiple and connected to the return, a form of connectivity to the community and homeland: educational and professional practice, cultural habits, customs and traditions are also practiced. Conflict and criticism are apparent elements during the 'unitive homing resolution' because 'home-host' constructions are compared and contrasted.

However, in coming to Greece in search of their 'authentic' homeland, participants are confronted with a 'homeplace' that differs, in numerous respects, from their expectations and previous imaginations as it does not reverberate with previous images of homeland constructions, but interestingly, in many respects, it echoes aspects of their other homeplace, the United States. In either case, returnees are critical and dismissive of those life-style components they wanted to get away from as part of their 'personal plan of action'. Participants reflected on the 'McDonaldization' of Greece with the growth of fast-food culture, the crisis in family values and the increased divorce rate, consumerist attitudes and materialistic values and increases in crime and substance abuse. On the other hand, Greece was also found to differ from their expectations in other respects – for example, regarding corruption and employment prospects not previously experienced in the United States. Views range from disappointment and alienation to anger and frustration of the experience of how life truly is in its everyday reality in Greece.

> Working here is hard in the sense that sometimes, I'm even embarrassed to say I'm Greek; people here make me angry. They are blind; they are just blind. They make me outrageous. I'm really not fed up because I came here, but in the beginning I was thinking maybe it will change, but it's impossible. Over here, to start a business, you have to bribe half the population to start it. You have to pay for 'air' in this country as they say, and they think about themselves. They don't think about the future. That makes me frustrated. I mean, I'm proud to be Greek. I'll always be proud to be Greek, but thinking about modern day Greece, it makes me angry. I want to live here, but it's difficult. I'm not going to work for somebody for 500 dollars a month; I can make more money working at minimum wage at a fast food joint in America. There is no way. I'm going to work and try to

save up some money to buy land or something. I want to live here. I love this country, but it's kind of difficult to start from scratch here. You either got to have connections, or you got to have money. (...) I love to live here, but you can't start from scratch here so I have to work and hopefully do that one day. I believe we are the key to the future of Greece. I believe there is going to be a movement in the future where all the Greek-Americans are going to start moving back with the knowledge they have and the money and the capital, and they can put it to actually build Greece. Greece in my opinion in the future is going to be the Florida of Europe. It's got a great climate, beaches all around. Everywhere you go, there is a beach, except for the mountains. See that's another thing, it has mountains so you can also open up ski resorts. Greece has everything, everything and anything you want except the desert, which I don't think anybody would want. So I believe we are the key to Greece's future. (Lyssandros, male, 28)

My parents brought me up to be career-oriented. They always wanted me to have a professional career to aspire to high career goals. It was easier in the States to develop my career. Here it is a little bit harder because my field (...), and that is something that is impeding my career growth here because I am career-oriented, but it is harder here to develop your career and keep on. To go ahead professionally and develop is very difficult because many times, the fact that connections play a big role kind of gets in the way. I knew what I would have to encounter as far as public relations and services are going. I knew that in advance, how that would be; the only thing that worries me and concerns me is health care. I am used to how things run in the United States, and I am very comfortable with health care in the United States, and that's the only thing troubling me. (Hermione, female, 31)

All of the boys work with my husband. My husband has his own business in trade, and the last years when the boys started to work together, they worked on brand name imports from the international department, and they made all the sportswear but not for Greece, for Europe. There the boys had a wonderful time because they worked with men from the international department in Denmark, and they would speak English; the whole atmosphere was different, but four years ago Denmark said that Greece was too expensive, and they decided to move out of Greece. In so doing, my husband's work collapsed, so that's why the older one could not get adjusted to the Greek system and moved back. The second one has been looking very hard for the three past years, very hard, for something to trade with, but Greece is very expensive, and it's not easy at all. And the Greek people, Greek women are very, very difficult. It's not easy... It's not easy. But I can't go back... I can't go back. Even though I miss many things... I miss the organization. (...) That's a beautiful thing in America, and jobs you can find. Here it's not that easy, and the salaries are very low. I hate to tell you when my husband needed a salesman, I can't tell you how many PhD people came for a salesman job... It was heart breaking. Yes, it was heart breaking, the unemployment. Sometimes I wonder what my children would do if dad wasn't the family rock. I am very proud of them, but when the boys go out to the community and they have to work à la Greek, that's different; it's hard. (...) My other son went to an American university in Greece. He did well, but it's still Americanized his training. He is too honest. He is too much of a hard worker. He doesn't do *rousfeti* (corruption/nepotism) or anything like that. He is successful, but if he was in the States, he would be a lot more appreciated, and he would be a little more comfortable in his work. Now he has a lot of anxiety. (Thalia, female, 68)

So here we are here now, but the way we are really over here, as far as I am concerned, I live here, I work overseas, and I deal with companies in Northern Europe. A lot of difficulties. But the one thing that I could not imagine is the corruption, when it comes to government. That was a shock for me. And the people in the middle of the street, they just leave their cars. I come from the opposite kind of society: things are organized; they are efficient, and people are concerned. But my pride also, having to deal with the government, they treat you like dirt, and you lose your self-respect, your self-dignity. You either go crazy, or you have to accept it and adjust. (...) So in terms of business, I did some business here, a project, and I see, there is no responsibility in the market. There is some but I am generalizing, just talking about the biggest part. There is no responsibility and no respect. In the beginning, I took it personally. You have a business appointment, and they don't show up. They don't care. They treat you like trash. And then I realized that they do that to everybody. It's the rule. I've seen some in the business over here, management. They think they don't have to work. They have a big office, a secretary and sit there and do nothing. Lack of organization that causes that. I complain a lot; you'll hear me. (...) Another thing is the salaries; they are quite low, and on the other hand, I am thinking to myself, I mean, I've seen retired people that make so little a month. If the salaries don't go up, how are these people going to live? Then, over in the States what is good gets praised and gets pushed, and it goes higher. (...) Working in Greece is hell. Here there is no teamwork, just back-stabbing. And these are the major things. What bothers me is the corruption, and what I see is the police not enforcing anything; they are not trained. And if I sum up all these, I see that the one who got away with theft and everything, that's the smart one. The one who is ok in the business and everything, that's the one who is the idiot. That's what I see. There is more security in terms of job security, family security. Basic stuff is hard here. There are people in poverty here and then ship owners, so what is the deal? I see the corruption, and my income is 1/3 of that in the States. We basically had to get a smaller apartment and have one car; things are a bit in the air. I could live in a tiny apartment, but I want the same standard of living I was living in the States; I had a nice house there. We need a private school for our kid. Real estate in Athens is crazy. I see kids here, and I feel sorry for them. They study, and they hope to have a career, and they are not going anywhere. They don't care for the kids, to teach the kids. In the States they help you to create and go up. Here they just sit and do nothing. No encouragement, no learning. It is very hard for us to have a secure life. We had problems with buying just a small boat. Can you imagine what it is to buy property? But I love to live here. (Diomides, male, 34)

I sent my résumé out to a few companies that I would see advertisements that would fit my qualifications and got very discouraged when I didn't even get a response back from these companies. I only got more disillusioned realizing that even hiring practices here are corrupt. They put an ad in the paper, and even before the position has been published, the job has been filled by somebody's nephew or cousin. So, seeing that business here is like that, I realized I wasn't getting anywhere. That is what motivated me to decide just to leave it. (Pericles, male, 50)

The narratives are indicative of the struggle that exists between the 'what I want-what I am used to' and the 'what I found-what I cannot get used to'. The returnees' 'practible plan' is 'unpracticable' in the homeland. However, even at the level of anger and frustration, for the most part, the returning migrants claim that they have not regretted their decision to return. They continue to want to live a life in the homeland aware that it entails compromises. The very fact of this realisation emerging through the struggle of 'home-host' understandings, memories and practices is an interactive process between the 'migrant-actor' and the 'home-host' structure(s).

Bourdieu's *Outline of a Theory of Practice* (1977) is helpful in explaining the formation and transformation of structures containing practices as well as the strategic agents who conduct action. As a polemical disquisition on the question of human agency, the notion of habitus is central to Bourdieu's ethnographic study, and it entails a theory of embodiment (Cowan 1990). Strategic action (in the case of returnees, it is the 'homing unitive resolution' of the 'personal plan of action') affects as much as it is affected by their socio-cultural environment (habitus), and these processes creatively contribute to the direction of returnees' life projects. The narratives do not conceal structures or actions. Often, they highlight the returnees' negative feelings and deep frustrations, but more importantly they reveal perspectives of strategic action in the national place.

On the other hand we find narratives that articulate belongingness as the returnees' cultural constructions – achieved through marrying Greeks, speaking to elders and coming closer to tradition and roots while experiencing the safety and comfort that the collective sense of 'Greekness' brings. At the same time, the returnees are entering a new space of transition, a zone of (re)claimed belongingness in symbolic and personal spaces, living a life of homeness that shuts alienation and the 'alien nation' outside. This bridges the ordinary and the everyday with the imaginary and the symbolic construction of homeland in the day-to-day creative action of settlement. In conversations, the returnees qualified their belongingness, indicating the place of ancestry and the existence of a historical past generations back: a celebration and ritualisation of the nation. Nothing is cryptic or elliptical; the stories link present-day national space with the ethnic place of antiquity: local symbols, national icons, grand historical narratives, stories of a great past become great stories for a present return. A return to culture is a return to the cultural construction of belongingness. The 'homey' feeling of a community encapsulates the grand historical past and fulfils both the inner and outer void of inbetweenness: both the outside imaging and the inside imagining complement each other because they complete the aesthetic and sensory meanings of home. So, stopping by a store to shop or a café to relax and finding oneself surrounded by the community of friends and neighbours without any prior arrangements while having passed by several ancient ruins and ethno-religious monuments, all this is demonstrative of a belongingness that does not require effort.

I love this neighborhood in Greece. And what I like is that I go to cafeterias and I see people I know, 'Hi, how are you?'. Familiarity, that community feeling, it is very hard to find in the States. (...) Life is much slower; things you can enjoy. You go with a friend for a *frappe* (iced coffee). (Diomides, male, 34)

I do like living here for different reasons, but I haven't adjusted completely, I don't think. What I like about living here? What I really like about living here, I didn't have this in the States and that I really like is the fact that everybody in my neighborhood knows me: the supermarket, the guy at the bakery, everybody. I like being able to walk down the street, and everybody says hello to me. I like that closeness. I like that very close community thing that's going on. I don't know if it's fake or not, but I like that, I like that. I'm very comfortable actually right now. I'm very comfortable. (Kalliope, female, 23)

The narratives express an idealised version of a cohesive neighbourhood and community that connects residents with the bond of familiarity and intimacy. But in reality, is this description accurate and all-inclusive? Does everyday life in an Athenian neighbourhood reduce social isolation by building connections across divides of ethnicity and class? Does it include participatory activities of a community-building context that are welcoming, authentic and durable for all, including 'other' migrants by giving them a 'status' of membership in the community? This is hardly the case if we consider for example such narratives as the one from Thalia, the retired school teacher who desperately wants the 'other' migrants outside the 'cultural boundaries' of her neighbourhood. As Karakasidou accurately indicates, 'while Greece is still largely a culturally homogeneous country, Poles, Albanians, Bulgarians, Romanians, Russians, Kurds, Middle-Easterners, Africans, and people from as far as the Philippines, India and Sri Lanka mingle with the local population, especially in the urban 'melting pot' of Greece's big cities' (2002: 147; quotations in the original). But even in one of the previous narrative excerpts, Nephele effectively compares New York to Athens, describing the capital's human geography as a 'melting pot'. In this case, the notion of belongingness in the community context as articulated by some participants echoes identifications based on ethnic 'purity' and national 'authenticity' that will ground the return to one's roots. But even within the second-generation Greek-American group of returnees who have come to settle in Athens, in no sense can this collectivity be referred to as a 'community'. During the fieldwork as I closely observed the interactions between small clusters of groupings of friends and colleagues in private, public and professional settings, I could not ascertain a collective consciousness, a 'consistent' expression of an identity of 'Greekness' (or 'Greek-Americanness' and/or 'American-Greekness' for that matter), integration of members or frequent and close interaction within clearly demarcated boundaries that could be attributed to a community in the sociological sense. On the contrary, as the narratives are also indicative of this, heterogeneity of belongingness and identification tends to be pervasive and effectively limits an all-encompassing unified 'story' of settlement in relation to belonging. Nevertheless, frequent circulations of ethno-national labels that oscillate between culture as a shared tradition and physical access to such national ascriptions in the ancestral homeland are expressed as a reconciliation with the split and void of a previous diasporic existence.

The recurring theme of 'rootedness' is articulated in terms of bonds to ancestors, ancient ruins, cultural landscapes and traditions, often with explicit reference to the homeland territory and the soil in particular. The ancestral home becomes the terrain through which the negatives of life in the United States – from exile and nostalgia to the stressful battle of high paced life and not knowing one's neighbours – are re-*placed* and 'cured'. This 'healing' process is inextricably linked to participants' search for 'self' and 'home'. Hence, the 'homecoming' is a project of *being, becoming* and *belonging*; it is a project of identification and closure.

> Where my ancestors walked, I have the opportunity to walk to-day. Although I didn't know Athens that well, I started to commute to Athens from my trips here just a few days, and I walked by the Acropolis. I walked by Lycabettus. I saw all these museums, and I would take this with me. I would take this with me back and without being paid; EOT (Greek Organisation of Tourism) should have paid me. I was walking. I was doing propaganda for Greece: 'You have to go there', 'There are so many beautiful things', 'It's not just the islands', 'It's this and that', 'Go to Delfous', 'Go to Athens', 'Go to Thessaloniki'. (...) Last summer I said it at some point. It was summertime in Athens, in August. (...) I set off for the beach. I take my coffee; I take my crossword puzzle, and I go to the beach. I swim, and I am sitting there, and I have to go to work, so I am driving back on Vouliagmeni, and I see the palm trees, and I see the beach; I see the grass, and I see all these people, and the weather is so beautiful there. There is no humidity, and I say, 'I'm glad I am experiencing this', but I hadn't said before, I'm glad to be here, but now I said it. Now I say it all the time. (...) And all of a sudden I realized that the home is what I made for me. It was not my parents' home. Not that I don't feel that as home, but it was

me, my space. It was my circle. It was finally my life, and everything else was around it, my parents, my brother, my work, my
friends, but that was what home was, having everything around
me. It was here in Greece. (Andromache, female, 34)

These sentiments of belongingness are expressed in response to the
natural beauty of the ancestral homeland but translated through a subjective process of personal space and the negotiation of what home
means for each individual returnee. In stories of return where belongingness is a construction in the homeplace, an existential transcen-
dence from life to death and back to life is evoked as the reconciliation
of past with present, absence with fulfilment, trauma with healing and
alienation with home. Life and death are invoked to remind us that *xeniteia* (the sojourning in foreign lands) is the embodiment of a cultural
death[4]. In this respect we find accounts that reconcile the cultural
death with death in the migrant family, notions that are evocative and
apposite to the state of migrancy and the project of return.

Whether I am here in Athens or the *chorio* (village), my roots
are here. They are in Greece. (...) And ... every time I go there to
the village, a lot of people know me. I met a lot of people there.
I have a hard time relating to them, and that is what is funny
sometimes. They are all farmers, and there is really nothing in
common, so at times I feel I am out of place. Although I am
Greek and I feel Greek and the talking, but I don't understand
the *choriatiko* (village) accent and their way of thought. The first
year I was in the village and listening to these guys talking, I
couldn't understand a damned thing these guys were saying.
They were talking about their sheep and their chickens and their
fields and olive trees, things that had nothing to do with me and
my way of thinking or anything. But talking about other subjects, and I had the opportunity to talk with them at the *kafeneio*[5]
(coffee shop), I get along with everybody, and that is nice. Like I
said, they all know me. I have a hard time remembering everybody's name. I would only see them, up until now, once every
six months. I would meet somebody, and then six months later,
I would have to remember what their name is again, but I have
that problem in general with meeting people. But the roots, obviously, that is the reason. I'm going to the *chorio* because that is
my *chorio*. I wouldn't go to any other *chorio* anywhere else. I
think I am doing that for that reason because I wouldn't go to
any other village and set up home there and try to become part
of this new community. My father's family, my mom, my
mother's father, my mom's mom, we go back generations there,

so the cemetery is full of all my ancestors. So there is a sense of connection in terms of family. Yes, my father is there in the cemetery, so, yes, that's why I want to go back and live there. (Pericles, male, 50)

Pericles describes his plan to relocate to the regional place of origin, a small village where his family comes from, and he depicts this journey as setting up home where his roots are and becoming part of a new community that is more 'alien' than familiar. This homecoming act to a cultural microcosm of roots takes precedence over the multiple routes that one would have to cross in order to reconstruct 'ethnic life'. Life in the village for a second generation Greek-American who has had a dramatically different urbanised professional and social life-style involves entanglements with the difference of local-village Greek 'culture'. These interactions are contact zones more so of departure rather than arrival that produce critical personal spaces where identities are moulded through 'cultural action'. This type of cultural action is also apparent in the 'personal plan of action', that is, the return migratory project. For several participants their return migration also fulfilled their parents' dream of going back to the homeland. In the cases where the parents had deceased long before they could ever return permanently to Greece, their children's ancestral return had a component of a 'biblical covenant'. This 'metaphysical' aspect of the return highlights discussions of *land–soil* and *life in foreign lands–death in the homeland*. Danforth (1982), Rosaldo (1984) and Seremetakis (1991) provide important epistemological foundations of the anthropology of death while entering into the self-reflexivity debate in relation to the discussion of the death ritual in Greece. In rural Greece, elders visiting the cemetery to light candles in remembrance of the dead are often found either in a state of ecstasy or absolute silence, staring in solitude at the mountains or at the sea, lamenting *xenitia*. *Xenitia* is seen as the death of the living. As Seremetakis[6] illustrates:

> The road is one of the central signs of *xenitia*. Travel, journey, passage to a foreign land, and exile are central metaphors of death in rural Greece. They are perceived as *xenitia*, which *encompasses the condition of estrangement, the outside, the movement from the inside to the outside,* as well as *contact and exchange between foreign domains, objects, and agents. Xenitia* is a basic cognitive structure within which life and death are thought. *Xenitia* is reversible and situationally contingent. Inserting the logic or imagery of estrangement into any social situation, life event, or discourse immediately organizes the contingent into relations of the inside and outside, the same and the other. *Xenitia* then is a

foundational taxonomy, and its imagery informs dreaming, death rituals, kinship systems, marriage, geography, history, ethnicity, and politics (1991: 85; italics in the original).

In the first generation it is not unusual to wish death (when the time comes) in the homeland and not in foreign lands: 'I don't want to leave my bones here' (referring to the United States) and 'I want to visit my parents' grave and be buried there where the soil is sweet' (referring to Greece) are frequent desires among first-generation Greek immigrants in the United States, as I noted earlier. When speaking to first-generation Greek-American migrants about this plan to return at least before death takes them, they would simply explain to me that the soil in *xeniteia* had absorbed every last drop of their sweat and blood all those years of hardship and sacrifice and that they owed the *patrida* not just their *wretched flesh* but their *psyche* (soul). Apparent in these discussions was a feeling of guilt on their part for having left their homeland, describing their action quite harshly almost as betrayal of the highest of all their ethno-religious values, a treason. Their return (first-generation) was described as an opportunity to 'repent' for these past 'sins' and to seek 'forgiveness' for abandoning their families and loved ones many decades ago. In toasting to health and happiness for their children and grandchildren, the first-generation migrants would tearfully but emphatically add: 'Next year in the patrida, next year in Greece!'

5.2   The geography of return: writing the cultural world of returnees

The significance of individual consciousness and life experience is highlighted when we recognise the importance of the discursive frame of culture, the migrant and the community in their interactive space. Traditional social science has primarily proceeded to understand the social world from the top down, from society to individual, explaining individual action from social structures. In the context of ethnic and national cultures, assumptions that individuals are 'the nation writ small' (Cohen 1994: 157) must be balanced against the fact that 'individuals are more than their membership of and participation in collectivities, and, second, that collectivities are themselves the products of their individual members, so that ethnographic attention to individuals' consciousness of their membership is an appropriate way to understand the collectivity, rather than seeing it as constituted by an abstracted, if compelling logic' (Cohen 1994: 133). This section explores the *geographia* (the writing of one's world) of return, which is a cultural world in the homeland. We understand how *ideologies of return* connect to *geogra-*

phies of culture when we consider that 'importantly, moments of culture are moments of belonging and this is one very powerful way in which the seduction of national identities takes place offering a space, a "home" to individuals within the broadest time/space frame' (Radcliffe and Westwood 1996: 82).

Recently, a small body of feminist literature on nationalisms has emerged (Dhruvarajan and Vickers 2002), including feminist frameworks that theorise relationships between gender and nation (Yuval Davis and Anthias 1989; Yuval Davis 1997). In *Woman-Nation-State*, Yuval-Davis and Anthias identified five major ways that women have participated in national processes (1989: 7):

1. As biological reproducers of ethnic collectivities.
2. As reproducers of the boundaries of ethnic groups and nations.
3. As reproducers of collectives' ideologies and transmitters of their cultures.
4. As signifiers of ethnic and national differences – that is, how women dress or act are symbols in making, reproducing, and changing ethnic and national categories.
5. As participants in national military, economic, and political struggles.

Moreover, Yuval-Davis (1997) introduces the concepts 'nationed gender' and 'gendered nations' to break assumptions of universalism in both feminist accounts and general theories of nationalism. Gender relations are set in historical contexts that frame their content and expression: 'Women are not a homogeneous group. Our lives are affected by social, cultural, historical, political and geographic factors...People have to negotiate their own lives and decide which strategies are possible and/or feasible for them. Women are often deterred from defying traditions by loyalty to their families and their religious and ethnic communities, even when they aspire to a better life. Also immediate needs and concerns determine the strategies that they adopt' (Dhruvarajan and Vickers 2002: 294). This account is by no means exhaustive, but by raising critical questions concerning gender and identification in return migration, we can approach the complexity of the issues involved and think through them in order to comprehend these relationships. Although I discuss in Chapter six the gender component in relation to identification processes, in this section I would like to note the following: out of the 40 life stories gathered, none of the returnees had married what is commonly referred to in the Greek and Greek-American community as a *xeni* or *xeno* (foreigner). Some had attempted to date outside the Greek or Greek-American community, but, from what I was told, 'it did not work out'. From their personal experience of interethnic dating and cases in their own family environment they were aware of, the participants in my study emphasised that all such inter-ethnic relationships were disastrous. The following narratives explain in great detail why this is the case and why similarity of background in terms of ethnonational and religious aspects leads, according to participants, to a cohesive partnership:

> I absolutely hope to marry a Greek-American because I want my children to grow up with the same experiences and family and church environment that I had, and I think they'll love it just as much as I love it. (...) That is obviously my main focus. That is where I would like to see myself. I want my kids to come to the *chorio* (village) and see *giagia* (grandma) and *papou* (grandpa) and speak Greek. I know with each generation it gets harder, but I would like to hold on to that. My parents strongly encourage it, and they frown down upon me marrying outside the Greek or Greek-American community. I can give you an example. It's not my own but my brother's. He is very attached to the Greek community. He loves Greece. He speaks fluent Greek, and for a period he was dating a French girl, and they were completely in love. She claims he was the love of her life, and they were going towards marriage, and at the end unfortunately, I saw it all fall apart because of the clash of the two cultures. She was very connected to the French culture. She did not want to marry in the Greek Orthodox Church. She wanted the kids to speak French; my brother wanted the future kids to speak Greek, and in the end, she wanted to move to Montreal where there is a big French Canadian community... and at the end, the clash of the cultures didn't allow them to pursue their relationship. And I heard people say, 'Oh, well, if they were truly in love'... They were both devastated that it didn't work, but the truth is that it plays such a huge role in your life, such a huge role. And neither one of them could budge or let go of each other's backgrounds, and at the end, it caused a problem. I see my *nona*'s (godmother's) son that married an American girl of Irish background, but she didn't have such a strong tie to her background, so she was able to accept the Greek a little more, but still their kids now don't speak Greek. She doesn't take them to the church as much, and it has been a big disappointment not only to my godparents but to their son as well. I don't know. I have long discussions about it with friends and my brother. It's hard; it's very hard. Especially in the States, the Greek community, you hear your parents say there are many young Greeks and Greek-Americans, but it's still a very close-knit community. I don't know. I hope it works out. (Medusa, female, 21)

In this lengthy narrative, Medusa advances examples from her immediate family circle to defend the necessity to marry within the Greek or Greek-American community in order to preserve 'Greekness' as she passionately advocates that any other choice would create complications and loss of traditional values. Indisputably, it is the immigrant family in the first place that embarks on a systematic mission of preserving tradition while implementing a methodical parenting and socialisation plan of transmitting to the second generation the imperative of unquestioningly following the prescribed future of a traditional and 'authentic' Greek life-style in 'old-world' terms and conditions. In most cases, nothing else would be tolerated as the fate of the offspring is determined; any type of redirection or revolt could lead to 'eviction' from the family safety net. This type of immense pressure that the immigrant generation exerts on the second generation is rationalised by both generations as a gesture of love, protection and guidance by the wiser older generation and not as an intense strategy of regulating and manipulating the lives of the offspring. The reality of the situation is that 'the immigrant family with its strong bonds is not presented as the proverbial safe haven but as a chain and ball which keep the younger generation from reaching its full potential. This is especially true for the young women whose lives are even more regimented than those of their male peers' (Kotsaftis 2003: 132). Women occupy a precarious space in a patriarchal system, and it is assumed that they ought to dutifully guard prescribed roles without considering any alternatives. However, these issues will be further explored in the next chapter that looks into gendered identifications. In the interim, while the following narrative selections express female and male reflections on marriage strategies, there exists a prevalence of salient similarity of points of view:

> In my choice of husband, my family played an important role. My mom and dad always said you shouldn't marry a *xeno* (a foreigner). Like that movie, Greek no matter what, Greek because you will get lost, you lose your identity. Right, because when you have children, you have more problems. One parent wants the children to grow up with this religion, the other another, and you have lots of problems. My mother always said that you have to please marry a Greek, not even date somebody outside, because you are going to have a lot of problems. And it is true. I see a lot of problems in the mixed marriages; you lose your identity, and the children grow up, and they don't know what they are, and they have no religion, and they lose their religion so there is a confusion. So, my mother did instill that on us. They all married Greeks, all of them, and two of my sisters married from Greece directly. Yes, directly. The other a Greek-Ameri-

can, very nice. My older brother married from Greece, and that had to do a lot with my mother's insisting. Yes, she insisted. She always said don't go out with *xenoi* (foreigners) because there is no future... marry your own kind. (....) Make sure that the children continue to come back and forth so they keep the Greek thing, so they don't lose themselves. That's very important. (...) So that's what identity is all about: culture, language, religion. Not to lose yourself, to keep the Greek. We have a lot of friends in America. They brought up their children the American way. They let them marry whoever they want. They brought them foreigners, and then they divorced. They don't fit in. If you saw that film, then you understand. That's how the Greeks fit in, and they still do. (Hera, female, 70)

I think it is ethnicity that makes us decide, and I think it is pretty much needs of character that made me choose a Greek-American to marry and be with her. I like when a person is conservative, when a person is respectful, and when a person respects others. I don't like people who talk a lot; I don't like people who pretend. I guess you could say tradition and culture influence. Of course I chose my wife because she is Greek and it will be easier on us; she will understand more about who I am and certain things. I had a relationship before my wife. It was an American girl, and she was very nice. We had a good relationship, but at points, she couldn't really understand me and the way I think. There you could see the two different cultures. So, I guess that had an important role in choosing to marry a Greek, a Greek-American. The idea of having a Greek family plays a central role in my life. I think that family being close is very good; it builds stability; it really does. Now in our times you can never know what will happen; you can have the best family, a tied family, and people get divorced. (Aristotle, male, 30)

What is particularly striking in the previous set of extracts is the abundance of an extraordinarily hegemonic character of 'Greekness'. This is expressed as a kind of 'generational oppression' internalised in a particular way by the participants. It is also noteworthy to point out that these participants are of course a peculiarly 'biased' subset of Greek-Americans for the very fact of having return-migrated.

Although the return to the homeplace was discussed in the previous chapter, the returnees' cultural worlds also construct a 'third place'. When cross-cultural experiences of the 'home departure' (United States) intersect with those experienced in the 'home arrival' (Greece) and the 'here-there' is contested, then a 'third place' is constructed by the returnees' – the one they have decided to inhabit which is their own personal and cultural space. This is the realm where a 'double consciousness' (Gilroy 1993) emerges to fill the context of home in different habitats: the personal-professional in the national space and those incorporating transnational-cosmopolitan expressions. As Spivak argues, 'one must not either get nostalgic about or take away the cultural good of the native space' (1998: 59). We must be alerted to the meanings of home in those 'habitats', real and imaginary, because it is important to decipher the 'difference between things but also the connectivity of the space between them. Space is no longer seen as a neutral stage, but an active field constituted by dynamic forces' (Papastergiadis 1998: 71). The cultural fields and ethnic spaces that construct a meaningful home are representations of the returnees' public and private constructions of belongingness. In the following excerpts those meanings emerge as sites of struggle and spaces of reconciliation:

> I had a really difficult time in the beginning. Difficult time with the bureaucracy, you know how bureaucracy is, a lot of red tape. Difficulties getting the recognition of my degrees, getting my teaching permit; it took a long time. Running around and back and forth from one office to another, getting the wrong information from one office, getting different information from another office. It was really hectic. There were points when I felt like dumping everything and just leaving and going back. The adjustment was really hard. Very frustrating. It took me two years, and this is the honest truth. I was so frustrated, and if it wasn't for my job here, I would've gone back. My parents were still in the States. My brother was still there, and they didn't return until much later. (...) When I first moved back to Greece, Athens actually, I never lived in Athens before, we had only visited once as a kid, and I spent three-four days, my father had taken us when I was eight or nine so I didn't really know Athens and what it was like.... I was going to say that things began to change here in Greece, and I became more comfortable living here when I began to make friends. The friends that I made were people that I was working with, my colleagues here. (...) Whatever I got, I got because of a lot of hard work. I mean I adjust easily to various situations. It took me a while to adjust to Greece, but I adjusted. It took me a while to make friends, but I made eventually a lot of good friends because I like people and I have a lot of faith in people. I'm very careful about the friends that I make. I'm very careful about my associates, but the response that I had from people has been very positive. (Iphigenia, female, 50)

Iphigenia describes the obstacles she encountered when first moving to Greece, namely complications related to public administration services, the profusion of bureaucracy and the annoyance of red tape. The difficulties she experienced and the fact that she had to deal with them alone as her family was still in the United States almost hindered her plan of relocation. Although she frequently considered abandoning her life plan in Greece and moving back to the United States, she persevered, and when she created a new support network of friends who were mostly colleagues, she then started adjusting to life in Greece. The same is true for Kassandra who also expresses her frustration with the problems she had to face when she moved to Greece. Moreover, her aggravation escalates as she compares the 'here' and 'there' and the limitations of living in Greece:

> I had tremendous problems adjusting. Well, the fact that this country is totally disorganized. Coming from the States, everything is organized. Everything is easy, but when you go here to something like *Dimosio* (public sector), any kind of public whatever, you are hassled all the time. I mean every time you start out to go somewhere, you just don't know what to expect, and that is my biggest break. Everything is so difficult, to the simple things. People don't know how to drive, how to park. It is just totally different, totally, totally different. (...) I don't think that Greece has anything else to offer me anymore. I think I have constructed my personality. I have taken in whatever Greece has to offer, and right now I am just living here on a day to day basis. I really don't think that Greece is offering me anything, anything more than it has in the past. (...) I think I am more hyper than I was in New York and basically not as happy. I was happier in New York. More mellow and happier. My life was more constructed. I knew what I was doing. I had my routine. I had more friends. In a sense loose ends. It's difficult. I mean I wouldn't buy a car. These people don't know how to drive. It's such a turn-off. I don't know. I just feel like a fish out of water, and it's been three years now, and I still feel like a fish out of water, and I have a feeling that this time around, no matter what, I'm still going to feel like a fish out of water. As the years go by, I don't think I can get into the swing of things any more, not at this age. (...) Very different from working in the States. People here are very laid back of course as everybody knows; nothing is done right away. You just have to have patience because you can't fight the system and you can't change it. You can't try changing it. A lot of people that I interact with are luckily very polite, I find, which is a plus, so I feel good about that. I

feel good about my job, for the time being. I feel lucky to have a job, and I'll take it as long as it lasts, and if doesn't last, I'll take it from there. (Kassandra, female, 49)

In the cases of Iphigenia and Kassandra who are about the same age and happen to work in different but quite similar Greek-American professional settings as both previous narratives indicate, we find that the participants draw positive energy from their working lives more so than from their everyday life which seems less structured, lacking organisation and coherence. It seems that the professional Greek-American microcosm is almost a 'buffer zone' from the externalities of Greek society.

Ethno-cultural narratives also tell stories about gender roles in the 'politics of return' where 'politics' is the operative word and the operational structure that demarcates traditional roles. Greek husbands are supposed to be active in politics; their daily discourse is supposed to be political; after all, the ancient Greek philosopher Aristotle instructed that all 'men' are political beings:

> In general my family didn't have much political involvement. They might've had their political discussion on the table if someone would come over, but they never said that they want one political party over the other. With my husband, that's another story! He has his own political feeling, and he never tries to make me become one of him. That's one good thing, but he does express his opinion, and he does express it very much. (Nephele, female, 32)

> I had no direct involvement with politics in either country, and I am very disappointed with the political system here in Greece. I think politicians and people of power have more to offer and can offer more but they are not doing anything. I am very disappointed in them. I am supposed to go and vote, but I am so disappointed that nothing will change if I vote. I am tempted not to go, and my husband says I have to go because I am a civil servant and because of his job, we have to do what is expected of us as citizens. He is involved very much, but I have no interest in politics whatsoever. (Pandora, female, 43)

In the first instance we find that female participants have no interest whatsoever for public affairs and disengage from any practical involvement. However, these type of attitudes are not in any sense reminiscent of the 'honour and shame' ethnographic literature which was previously alluded to and which was particularly criticised for the portrayal of women as subordinate and passive in the active, gendered distinction between the domestic and public realms (cf. Cowan 1990; Dubisch 1995; Kirtsoglou 2004). Although the centrality of family, marriage and household as the site of domestic 'Greek' life is vividly reproduced in the narrativisation of self-realisation in diasporic life, the women mainly draw on the disappointment they feel in the inadequacy of politicians and the entire political system in Greece and hence translate their political apathy on the contrary as action. On the other hand, most male participants almost naturalise their political performativity as 'some kind of Greek man thing' emanating from the Hellenic spirit that questions everything even laws that perhaps may be imposed on them:

> I've always been drawn to that. In the US and Greece, I was political. I think it is some kind of Greek man thing. Yes, that's something that definitely defines a Greek, politics. That's all they talk about. What this guy does, what this guy shouldn't do, why the laws are like this and why these laws. I think this is the Greek spirit while people in the US are not really like that. People in the US are more accepting; they accept laws and go by it. A Greek won't do that. A Greek will question a law. Who the hell are you to impose this on me? Again the Greek spirit, the Greeks are highly individualist, and the Greeks do not want to be bossed around. They don't want anybody to boss them around. (Aristotle, male, 30)

> I have been involved in politics more in Greece than in the States. Of course at different times, different situations, I had a different mentality in politics. I would say I was above average in the States in terms of politics, being able to watch it and have an opinion about it and everything. In Greece due to the fact that almost everything is politics, I have been more involved in Greece than in the States; let's say that. I guess because in Greece politics does play such an important role in everyday life rather than the States where things are more organized and set out in a more long-term manner where here in Greece everything is short-term and everything changes from time to time. I guess you have to be more involved in Greece. You have to keep up, and you have to be more into things. The thing is that I've always liked history and politics so I've always studied and kept in touch with these issues. (Plato, male, 30)

In terms of everyday life, throughout my lengthy fieldwork I was invited by my participants to enter many intimate family spaces of their

Greek-American world. I was invited to major Greek holiday celebrations, birthday and nameday parties, weddings and baptisms, house-
warming gatherings and business openings, excursions to their summer cottages, Saturday dinners and Sunday brunches. In sum, as guest
and researcher, I observed those gatherings and the interactions that
took place. I was immersed in the 'sound-smell-image' representation,
production and reproduction of the returning migrants' cultural worlds
in visual and acoustic terms. Many of those encounters included interactions between the first, second and third generations as well as interactions with Greek-American migrants visiting the returnees and the
homeland.

Sensory absorbing captures the sense of a social setting that exists
within a space of representation and communication. This is not so
much an ambiguous experience as an embodied experience. The visual
representation of the experiences in the Greek-American return process highlights notions of performativity (Butler 1990; 1993) and roles.
Domestic spaces are also sites where identities are fluid and mobile,
openly experienced and performative rather than static and fixed. Even
within the closed spaces of the domestic home, there were open performances. The 'authentic' and 'real' identities were decentred and fragmented because certain core realities were rejected as false and oppressive: for example, the male returnees shared domestic chores and roles.
They helped out with the cooking and the children. This was a component of the 'politics of return' that was clearly negotiated in the return
space as primarily Greek parents-in-law fixed in traditional gender
roles did not always fully approve of 'American' behaviours responsible
for 'decaying morals'. Most couples confided instances of 'cultural
power struggles' and reassured me of being adamant of their principles
in leading their own lives and raising their children the way they saw
fit and appropriate:

> I believe that since I am living here in Greece and I am married
> and I have two children, really to tell you the truth, I don't raise
> my children as Greek-Greeks; I raise them as Greek-Americans.
> (Nephele, female, 32)

> My sister, she is very different than I am. She's not so close to
> her kids and her husband. She is more independent whereas I
> have to be there all the time and see what they are doing. I don't
> think I'm doing something wrong. She is more American; I
> guess that's how American people are. (Pandora, female, 43)

> Sometimes I question whether I did the right thing, but I know
> I did the right thing. They were educated beautifully. I did a

good job. I am very proud of them, but it's à la Greek-American when the boys go out to the community. Now this is hard, raising children this way. It's difficult raising kids here. But I did it my way with the three boys raising them here and now with my grandchildren. (Thalia, female, 68)

The categorisation of cultural worlds is also apparent in what type of parenting methods are implemented when returnees raise their children in the ancestral homeland. In the previous three excerpts we can distinguish between raising children in a Greek-American manner rather than a Greek-Greek or American way. Pandora's critical remarks on her sister's relationship with her husband and children as being 'Americanised' is indicative of a classification of (in)appropriate means of socialisation. What does this imply for the understanding of return migration and migrants' agency with regard to processes of identification in the ancestral homeland? Perceptions, feelings and views but most importantly experiences, representations and expressions of migrant behaviour in the ancestral homeland create a new socio-cultural cosmos with its own particularities. As social agents, returnees have the capacity to critically reflect upon this new world. How do returnees perceive themselves as 'agents of change' within their families and the new socio-cultural environment? Most significantly, how do experiences in the country where they were born and raised as well as experiences within two different cultural contexts impact on the way return migrants of the second generation shape their role as parents, and how are their relationships with the third generation shaped by the ancestral homeland? Answers to these types of questions require that returnees are viewed as both objects of 'cultural adjustment' and active subjects who themselves impact on the new cultural worlds they inhabit while adapting to them at the same time. While conforming in many instances to ideas of 'Greekness', returnees also act in the ancestral homeland setting, that is, they apply, reject or transform practices and eventually mediate identities while creating a new transnational space of identification. In their double agency, migrants and their actions in their encounters in the homeland may also contradict established cultural notions.

Apparently, Greek parents-in-law were not aware of what Thalia tells us in Chapter four in relation to Greek mothers and what return migrants mean when they mention in the same chapter that Greeks are more Americanised than Americans. Romantic notions of a bounded community are questioned and contrasted with the new cultural worlds of return. Multi-sited cultures emerge: public cultural spaces (Greece), private cultural spaces (Greek-Americans), and the dialectical relationship between the return migrants' cultural world and the homeland cultural world. Nonetheless, notions of 'pure', 'unspoiled' and 'authentic' cultures are questionable as 'hybridisation' takes place in all spaces of interaction. Return migration, especially, is all about relational processes. Such relational process must focus on the interconnectedness between actors and structures as the actors tell stories of how these processes affect them and how they situate themselves within sites of processes. Return migrant stories told and experienced are also narratives of hybridities and multiple possibilities. As I reflected on and critically examined those experiences, I was confronted by a matrix of culture and agency. As I probed into the socio-spatial constitution of home and belonging in return migrants' lives, I could not dismiss or neglect the 'meta-diasporic' context: diasporic lives[7], diasporic memories, generational interactions in the homeland socio-cultural environment and the returnees' imaginations into realisations formed this dynamic. Both an 'insider' and 'outsider' extrapolating the metaphoric and literal from those interactions, I became aware of how 'ethnocentric abstractions' were observable patterns of conscious behaviour in the homeland. The multicultural environment of the United States[8] had troubled some of the return migrants who presented their experiences as an 'exile discourse', alienated from their American birthplace as the idealised homeland return is so prevailing and such a triumphant conscious project of self-actualisation.

> The specific time that I've been living here, I think it's the icing on the cake, the lid, whatever you want to call it. It actually fulfilled that emptiness I had living in the States even at the time I didn't know I had the need to have it filled. It was filled when I came here to live here, and it became part of who we are and who the Greeks are. (Pericles, male, 50)

Others, even if they were not fully assimilated, had become integrated in that American environment. Memorialisation of pleasant surroundings and a comfortable life-style through recollections of everyday practices of familiarity and comforting routine is the narrative prism of a previous good life in a (non)diasporic context of family, friends, education, employment, achievements and amenities.

> I liked living in the United States since I was born there of course. I had my friends, my school, my work afterwards, of course, my family. I felt as though it was my home since I lived there for twenty-five years before of course I came to Greece. (Nephele, female, 32)

I enjoyed it very much, and I never thought I would be living in Greece now because I always thought that I would end up marrying in New York, getting a job in New York, finishing college in New York. The fact that I'm living in Greece right now, back then it would never cross my mind, never. I have very good memories. Both of my parents were very nice people, and we had a very warm relationship. I remember growing up in a really nice house with a yard, with comforts in the home. I have very good memories. (Pandora, female, 43)

During the homeland return they become aware of a newly acquired multicultural Greek environment and some of them are critical of immigration in Greece, even deeply troubled, as several accounts in the previous chapter illustrated. And yet, despite this, they were not averse to 'using' the labour of immigrants when it suited them, as in the field of domestic help. As I was told, never before did these return migrants have domestic service in the United States. In Greece, however, they were 'convinced' by family and friends that not only is it 'fashionable and required', but also people who do not have domestic service are rather 'strange' in a homeland of many 'strangers' who are here to 'serve'. Conversely, some second-generation Greek-American returnees reject this type of categorisation and rationalisation:

When I was in the States, I didn't have a maid. I had three and a half floors counting the basement, and I was doing it all myself. You complain. You get bored. You yell. You scream... but I never said, 'God, I hate this. I want to get out'. I mean, I knew that was my place. Here I have a cleaning lady, and she comes to the house every Tuesday and cleans for me, and I feel bad about it, and I try to save work so she doesn't have to do everything, and I tell people it's not where you live, it is how comfortable you are in a place and being yourself. (Artemis, female, 32)

Artemis declares that household duties and the domestication of her role in the private sphere of her life in the United States is 'her place'. She explains that a woman may complain, feel boredom and frustration in undertaking domestic tasks as part of her role but the essential understanding is that of acceptance and submissiveness to such an ascribed position as it becomes evident from her testimony. Interestingly, another participant also deviated from the mainstream practice and Greek views in relation to economic migrants and had the opposite opinion. She was appalled during a recent experience she had while using public transportation, and she explains her feelings:

I don't try to be that Greek. There are certain things that I have in me that are very important and because I want my children to do them, I have to do them too. I will get into an elevator and say '*geia sas*' (hello), and I don't care what they say. The other day I was in the bus, and I had to go to the doctor. I don't drive (in Greece), and I didn't want to take a cab, so I took the bus, and the bus was crowded, and next to me was sitting a *Philippinesa* (Philippino woman), and an older Greek woman gets on the bus. The *Philippinesa* gets up, the Greek older lady sits down, and I was waiting to hear something. I waited to hear a thank you. Nothing. She doesn't say thank you. The old lady didn't say anything. Well, I turned to the *Philippenesa* and said, 'For the Greek lady that you got up to give the seat for, I thank you', and she nodded her head, and she said: 'Oh, you made me feel good!' ...There are certain things, I don't know, it's in me. I won't give them up, and I don't want to give them up. I don't want my grandkids to see things like that. (Thalia, female, 68)

Again, it is captivating to note that this is the same retired teacher who shed tears of distress with the realisation that migrant school children (in the particular Greek school and classroom in her neighbourhood) outnumbered Greek school children. Yet, the same individual still maintains an attitude of politeness in a fleeting encounter with a migrant in a public bus, a particular type of behaviour acquired through habitual interpersonal routine practices of apologetic expressiveness in the United States when such instances as described above occur in everyday life. As a grandmother, Thalia also emphasises that this is something that she would prefer her grandchildren not to witness, hence it is presented as an instructional practice to the younger generations who are growing up in-between two cultural worlds.

As research has shown, kinship and gender identities in Greece are not fixed and stable: they are plural, as much as they are antagonistic, competing and continually redefined by social context (Loizos and Papataxiarchis 1991). The return migrant as a gendered and embodied subject in the ancestral homeland space becomes increasingly aware of notions of femininity and masculinity in an range of socio-cultural and spatio-temporal interactions. Through personal and intimate relationships the returnees confront performances of masculine and feminine 'Greekness' that challenge previously fixed notions they might have held in connection to gender identities and behaviours. These distinctions are realised through everyday experiential confrontations with native Greek men and women.

I find Greek girls very hard to trust, I don't know why, very very two faced, which may not be true, but that's the way I see it from my own experiences. (...) I don't want to marry a Greek guy. I don't want to marry a Greek guy. It's so weird ever since I started living here, I haven't even dated a guy in this society. I used to watch a lot of TV when I first got here, and that's probably why I picked up the language so well. All the Greek 'seras', the series that are on TV, every one of them has to do with people cheating on each other, 'kai oi pandremenoi echoun psyche'. All these shows have to do with this. There isn't a show ... comedy without that, and I'm sure, like these kids who are growing up watching shows like that, I don't know, the guys here have a complex in my opinion. I wouldn't want to marry a Greek guy. Greek-American, yes. Not a 100 percent Greek. I don't think I could handle that, cause I had, I still am in a relationship on and off with a Greek guy, and we just do not get along. He's from a different world; I'm from a different world, and we do not click like that. (...) I see a lot of Greek men smoke a lot. I don't know; these are negatives. Greek men don't have a lot of respect for women, a 100 percent I don't think so. I don't believe it. They talk down to Greek women. They go out with other women, and this is not just from my own experiences but from Greek-American friends of mine who have dated Greek-Greeks, no respect. The positive about American men, I don't know but from my own experiences, I think they treat you more like a friend. They treat you more like a buddy. They respect you more as a person. Greek men, I think, just want a housewife; I think they just want a housewife. But I only had one relationship since I got here. I can't talk about that issue further without referring to my own boyfriend. But it is the same like I said. That's how Greek men are here in Greece. (Kalliope, female, 23)

The ethnography of return in the participants' 'homes' became the reaffirmation of the spatiality of the 'homeplace' as the locus of socio-cultural relations of the family in the course of their everyday lives in the homeland. The *home* gatherings were emotive sources of a 'banal nationalism' (Billig 1995) highlighted by group interactions occurring spontaneously while accentuating generational dynamics in a context that 'gave voice' to the notion of home and the idea of homeness in 'togetherness'. Although I remained 'conscious' of my role as researcher and participant observer, my participants' and their families had invited over a friend and hence were all very carefree and natural in their 'home' setting. This was extremely helpful in unveiling both 'settledness' and 'rootedness' in conversation and action unfolding in the homeplace. The volatility of their diasporic lives was presented as being reconciled through the homeland return and the establishment of home in the national homeplace. While taking tremendous pride in their personal achievement and the achievements of Greek-Americans, they also exhibited intense nationalistic feelings and rigid generational boundaries. Having lived and travelled abroad widely, their cultural signifiers remained fierce without having blended with aspects of surrounding cultures. In this sense we also encounter cases of male figures, characteristically authoritarian, saturated in their *philotimo* (love of honour) and male sense of dominance and superiority over women; they revere their mothers who continue to control their lives and destinies even post-matrimony. Characteristically, Iphigenia vividly sketches these characteristics:

> I find them (Greek men)... The word that comes to mind is bully and domineering. I can't be told what to do. I like to be able to negotiate things with people, and I can only so far have this thing with my friends, girlfriends, and boy, male friends, not with a relationship. Not with a partner. I find them very domineering and possessive. Very traditional, too attached to their mothers. Obsessively so! Which is my worst problem. They may think that they hate their mothers or dislike their mothers, but they are so dependent on their mothers. Yes, dependent, so, the word that describes it is, in love with their mothers. Infatuated. And they expect their girlfriend or wife or whatever to be like their mother. A clone. To put up with their little quirks, and they are so much pretending. That's the problem with Greeks. And they are intimidated by independent, autonomous, powerful, successful women. (Iphigenia, female, 50)

'Togetherness' in family gatherings does not necessarily mean familial harmony. On the contrary, belongingness and sharing of 'national time-space' with parents, siblings, children and friends may encapsulate turbulent clashes and aggressive conflicts. Furthermore, such episodes exhibit a type of parental control to the degree of duress. Instances of parental coercion appear to be principally gender specific as women ought to display submissiveness to their parents' will as narrated previously, for example, in the choice of a spouse of Greek origin. Iphigenia again:

> Christmas and Easter, they would drag me, literally, to dances, weddings, and receptions. I remember a time that I fell down the stairs, and I broke my knee because I didn't want to go to this reception. I must've been 15 or 16 at the time. Can you be-

lieve that, doing that on purpose? I hated those receptions. I hated those weddings; there would always be a fight, someone, men you know how they are like, and I never understood over what. I never understood the quarrels and fights over wedding receptions. We had that constantly! Why is it that they do that? Christmas, Easter, birthdays, name days, weddings, baptisms, they start off very happy and very lively and enthusiastic, and then they start fighting, and then they don't speak for a couple of months until the next gathering. I never understood this, and it starts, and it spreads like wildfire throughout the night and the evening. I hated them all; I never wanted to go. I understood why my parents had to go because they were relatives, friends of theirs, etc., and they had to go, but I never understood that adult stuff as a teenager. I wanted to do my own thing. I didn't want to be dragged to weddings. And one of the things that now in a way regret, but I understand why I did it, because of peer pressure and the pressure I felt, but I think every teenager feels it, was to integrate. I cut myself off from the Greek community. I cut myself off from Greeks. I didn't want to see them. I didn't want to speak to them. For a while I didn't even speak Greek at all, apart from the usual stuff at my house: what are we going to eat, *kalimera* (good morning), *kalispera* (good evening), that sort of thing.

As Christensen, James and Jenks (2000) argue, disputes between family members over time and space in the home are inextricably linked to the tension underlying on the one hand the values attached to the rights, privileges and independence of family members and those on the other hand which promote family 'togetherness', for example reciprocity, mutual responsibility and family solidarity (148). Iphigenia repeatedly 'revolted' against such attempts at preserving 'Greekness' through familial solidarity and 'togetherness' that undermined her individuality and sense of freedom and autonomous decision-making capacity to select whether she would or would not like to attend those gatherings. It seems that events in the ethnic life are not always voluntarily chosen, especially in the case of children and teenagers but at times imposed and defined by ethnic signifiers – and by parents. In addition to Iphigenia's account, we realise that the homeland return is also perceived as a new space of personal freedom, creativity and choice. Whereas ethnic life in the United States resembles a pre-packaged deal that does not offer much room for the second generation to develop freely and make their own choices as well as their own mistakes, life in the homeland signifies a portion of personal independence made possible by movement. As illustrated previously, ethnic life in the United States revolves around the Church, which is the centre of 'Greekness'. Almost all of the returnees' parents and most of the first generation met their spouses at church. But even second-generation migrants met at church, for example, Thalia and her Greek husband or Medusa's parents:

> I met my husband at the Greek Orthodox Church. I was going to Hunter College at the time. He was at NYU and each school had a Greek club, and he was in his Greek club, and I was in mine. And one year the two schools decided to give a social in the Church on 74th street, and that's how we met, the Greek club of the universities in the Greek Church. It was funny. My husband finished the French school here, most fluent in Greek. He knew very little English, very little, and when I met him, he was from Greece, and he was speaking Greek to me, and I was ashamed of my Greek not being up to his standards. I was a French major at school; I really wanted to teach French, so I thought, 'Let's talk in French', so we were speaking in French at the time. (Thalia, female, 68)

> They (the parents) met through church, through the Greek Orthodox Church community. My dad became a teacher and eventually had my uncle as a student and through that made the connection. (Medusa, female, 21)

On the other hand, the homeland return as relocation to the national home signifies immersion in the culture. Ethnic life in the United States had a mission to preserve and safeguard ethnicity and identity. The ancestral return is by definition seemingly exempt from such cultural anxieties. However, narratives testify to the reverse situation: returnees are rather carefree and relaxed by virtue of having the weight lifted from pressure to constantly 'perform' an ethnic self:

> You can say that I found myself. I feel like I can understand why people may feel why they have found their sense of self here. Like I said before, it is more open. You feel like you can *exoterikefseis* (express) what you feel inside. (...) Look, one thing that I do know is that I do feel, I don't know if I make sense, I feel a little more like myself living here. I don't know if that makes sense. I don't know. But sometimes in the States, I don't know if it's because the social structure, the way it is set up there, or the culture but I did feel more constricted, restrained, I don't know, not from being Greek but actually saying what's on my mind, doing what I want to do. (...) But here I feel more ex-

troverted than I was in the States. Yes, it's true. No, it's strange, cause I think it's the way the social structure and the culture and just the freeness that everybody has that you just cannot help but go along with it. I think I always had an open mind. Here actually I think they make me feel that sometimes they are too open-minded. That makes me feel and want to do the opposite because they are a little too crazy. In a good way crazy, and it kind of pulls you along. (...) I'm not sure; personally I don't think that I've changed. People tell me that I've changed. For example, my family, they tell me I'm much more relaxed. I do more things than I used to do in the United States: I go out more, the climate is much warmer, and it calls for being outside more. In the United States, it was more work-home, work-home and sometimes social events. Here you go home, but then you always want to be outside, even different cultural events I see that I go to more. (Hermione, female, 31)

Surprisingly, homeland practices are so very much detached from intense 'ethnic performance' to the point where this is even criticised by returnees: for example, Lyssandros and Thalia mentioned in Chapter four that weddings are not traditional and Greeks in Greece are not as religious. Artemis and Medusa stressed that Greece is an ultra-modern society. Again, this is an important point: 'home-host' constructs intersect along with the 'personal plan of action' to produce altered identifications. Dynamics of 'migrant-actors' interact with 'home-host structures'; they are questioned and this deciphers shifting meanings of home, self and belonging. These processes are discussed in Chapter six in relation to social transformations, transitions within traditions and the construction of 'transhybrid' identities. But going back to everyday life in the ancestral homeland, Hermione previously mentioned that living in Greece is more unreserved, carefree, outgoing and unrestrained than living in the United States, which has made her feel more relaxed and open to experiences and outdoor entertainment as opposite to just a repetitive routine of going to work and then returning home only to distract the monotony with some sporadic social events. For participants like Hermione, the homeland return becomes a liberating experience of outdoor activities and cultural events during pleasant weather conditions in Greece and ultimately 'finding herself'.

Greeks in general always believed that the children are morally and religiously obligated to assist the parents throughout their life span but especially during old age, usually by living together and providing illness assistance, emotional and daily living support. In particular, studies of the Greek Diaspora emphasise the role of the family as a support system, not only for children but also for older generations while the responsibility of caring for ageing parents is paramount (Tsemberis, Psomiades and Karpathakis 1999; Evergeti 2006). Greek-Americans in particular believe that the sense of obligation toward parents is stronger among Greek-Americans although at the same time it is seen as declining by the third generation under the influence of acculturation forces (Costantakos 1993)[9].

> Xeniteia, yes, it was tough, really tough, and sometimes I actually feel guilty that I was enjoying myself and my parents were having a really rough time. (...) I guess my parents felt that they would be happier in their old age here in Greece, and it is something that I felt too. I saw it coming at some stage because if we had stayed in the United States, I would eventually have to put them in an old age home. You know how things are in the States. In Greece they had their home. Well in the States they had their home too, but it's different. I was really concerned about that. I worked in a nursing home for a few years, and I saw a lot of sad people. People who were neglected by their families and who were dumped there to rot. That was a really sad situation. I never wanted to see my parents end up in a nursing home. I always felt that they were right in saying that they would have a better life if they came back to Greece and spent their old age here, which they did. Coming back to their roots functioned as a safety net, most likely for most people in Greece. With us it was different; they had migrated. But when I was a nurse's aid, I worked there three years, the third year I was getting really fed up. I couldn't cope. I got too involved with these people, and the situation was so sad that it was getting to me. It was really getting to me. (Iphigenia, female, 50)

> My decision to come back was solely for my parents' sake. They were either going to come back to the States and live with me, or I was going to come and live here, and I decided to come here because I felt it would be a lot easier for them. I was going to try it, you know give it a try. Like I said, I am the only child, so there is no one else to take care of them, and now that they are getting older, it is one of those guilty, you know, the conscience thing, feeling guilty about leaving them on their own. (Kassandra, female, 49)

While Iphigenia explains the agony she felt over contemplating her parents' future during old age, having worked in a nursing home and having first-hand experience of a care facility and the type of institutionalised environment in which ageing people spend the end of their lives, Kassandra talks about her relocation to Greece exclusively in terms of her obligation to her aged parents who are in their nineties. Her parents' advanced age and the fact that Kassandra is an only child exacerbated her sense of guilt and the moral obligation she feels she has toward her mother and father. Nevertheless, this type of obligation is not perceived as an overwhelming burden despite the additional psychological as well as physical strain imposed or the changes in lifestyle one might have to make. On the contrary, duties and obligations to parents are prioritised, in most cases, over personal needs as they are strongly linked to an ethical code of familial responsibilities. This matrix of moral obligations to the family is instilled as a sense of duty to the children within a rigid ethnocultural force that binds the offspring to those obligations and subsequently to whatever course of action is demanded to fulfil them. Hence, the second generation is obliged to adhere to this tradition of care taking and to perform it for moral reasons. From early on, the offspring are told about the sacrifices that parents have made in order to provide their children with a better quality of life and opportunities for growth and development. For this reason, the offspring must never forget that 'every right implies a responsibility, every opportunity, an obligation and every possession, a duty'.

5.3   Narrating the return in the ethnocultural space: stories of the 'patrida' upon return

It would be more than appropriate in this section to note that the Greek epic poet, Homer, is frequently discussed as the originator of European narrative, referring to his two long narrative poems *The Iliad* and *The Odyssey* (Havelock 1986: 19). The latter of these is a canonical work exemplifying, among other notions, nostalgia, return, home and belongingness. Moreover, regional narratives on 'Europe' and its reborderings in different millennia have had a lasting significance in identity construction and spatialities around the Mediterranean and are evidence of the historically specific and constructed content of the boundaries of Europe but also of the power relations involved in changing spatialities (Leontidou 2004; 2005). Local narratives of the return migratory project contain their own cultural boundaries as they are shaped by socially and historically specific circumstances. These narratives are also indicative of power relations implicated in the participants' actions and relations in both public and private spaces. Hence, for a more holistic understanding of the ideology of return, it is important to focus on return migrants as human agents, as individuals in families and in communities rather than on return migration, the process, the mass movement or the numerical account (Potter, Conway and Phillips 2005), and this is achieved by examining participants' experiences and socio-spatial adjustments to their changing life circumstances.

In order to approach a more panoramic view of the return migratory project, it is pertinent to also focus on the 'rationalisation' of the adjustment, which includes those 'pull' factors in the homeland that possibly enticed the returnees into making a relocation decision and helped their settlement process. In addition to the cultural and natural context of the homeland (family, language, religion, landscape), there are other material support systems that created the starting point and then a bridge between emotional and practical needs. This includes the availability of such resources as employment and residence. Specifically, as regards this study, out of the forty participants, fifteen are homeowners, ten are living with parents or relatives and fifteen are renting (see appendix). Those who are renting preferred living on their own (while having available housing from their families) whereas the homeowners acquired housing as 'return gifts' or wedding gifts[10]. In any case, the returnees acknowledged this assistance with gratitude while recognising it as a stepping-stone in their adjustment process. Here are some relevant excerpts:

> I took my little suitcase, the little money I had saved and returned. OK, the conditions existed; there were houses and space offered to me where I could do some things because if I came and they didn't exist, then it would've been more difficult. That was the first aid; the first start was there. I didn't have to build it myself; I simply had to improve it from there on. (Aspasia, female, 32)

> The good point was that my parents had a house there (in Athens), so we knew that we had a place to live. When we came and we decided to live, we found a job right away. (Nephele, female, 32)

> To tell you the truth, I don't feel that I had any difficulties adjusting. I had an idea of how it was going to be. I knew how it was going to be. I knew the difficulties that I would face, and things have been going well for me: I found a job fairly quickly, I have a social circle established, which is very important, I had a place to live; it sounds perfect... (Hermione, female, 31)

The 'ethnocultural' space of return migration is an ambiguous term with a definite presence. Culture and ethnicity are symbolically known by most to be the manifestation of national holidays, dress, customs, cuisine, and linguistic characteristics, all in the frame of a 'banal na-tionalism' (Billig 1995) expressive in the banal realm of the everyday. Besides a largely passive role, culture also plays a crucial active role in the construction of social structures. Culture itself is a constantly self-renewing and self-perpetuating phenomenon, originating in and con-structed by the human geography of peoples and places. Despite its un-deniable existence, culture itself has not been consistently defined: 'dis-cussions about culture have been bedeviled by an inability for theorists to agree on a common definition, for it has remained a fluid term' (Edensor 2002: 12). I remain content not to have claimed any stasis from the fluid or any single definition for the *cultures of return* or the *return of culture*. In the fluid networking of everyday spaces, cultural meanings are first negotiated and then translated only to be trans-ported to a different realm, that of the ethnos. In the next chapter I in-tend to provide a grounding for those negotiations to be discussed and those translations to be elaborated by those who transmit messages of culture and self. Certainly, second-generation Greek-American return migrants are those who understand, shape and are shaped by their 'hy-phenated' existence. Returning migrants are above all 'active-actors' who perform and articulate identifications that highlight the ways in which culture is encoded and decoded and subject to 'preferred', 'nego-tiated' and 'contesting' meanings.

Within this framework, migration and return migration are both viewed as expressions of the cultural imaging of place, where the mi-grants' and returnees' evolving lives produce constructions and recon-structions of the extended social world, both in the home and the host country (Christou 2002). Individual migrants are recognised as socially situated, active, intentional agents who influence as much as they are influenced by the social context in which they are located. This per-spective follows Halfacree and Boyle's (1993) conceptualisation of mi-gration, which emphasises its situatedness within everyday life, and leads to a biographical approach. This approach seeks to unfold the meaning of migration and the migrant's identity and sense of place by exploring the migrant's life course. Findlay and Li go a step further in their methodological contribution and introduce the '*auto*'-biographical approach; here the researcher attempts to raise practical consciousness to the discursive realm in order to investigate how the growth of migra-tion intentions over time is related to the self-defined changing cultural contexts of the migrants' everyday life (1997: 35).

The stories about the *patrida* articulate the 'ethnocultural space of re-turn' and express deliberations that convey personal transformations of returning migrants who have multiple and shared social selves and are agents (active actors) in the wider socio-cultural context of their chan-ging place and positionality. Stories of the *patrida* also narrate return in the midst of fluidity, travel, memory, longing, inclusion or exclusion during situational, multiple and paradoxical al*locations* of identity.

There is a direct connection between the 'ethnocultural space' encountered and experienced with the one constructed by the returning migrants. The exploration of what constitutes 'home' and the cultural underpinnings of return migration bring identity questions to the fore. The strategies that returning migrants employ in their lives directly impact on the construction of their identities, primarily because they are in constant interaction with cultural agents and ethnic structures. Such orientations are 'filtered' through the lived and storied experience of narrating the 'homeplace'; they negotiate the ethnocultural spaces between lives lived (migrancy), lives told (oral narratives) and textual lives (written narratives) in what results as the documentation of identification. Within those three layers of how the ancestral return is expressed and depicted, we encounter voices that are parallel, similar or different but nevertheless revealing of *self* and *place*. Daily life is a multi-sited place of struggle, a site of the construction of 'home', and the ancestral homeland is the discursive place within which cultural frameworks (trans)form a sense of self and a sense of belonging. Return migration deploys a transitional area of creativity that involves the recognition of migrants' personal freedom and responsibility for their actions (with the risks, failures, losses but also gains that the process entails) and restraints seemingly imposed on them (the discovery of multiple forms of suffering, alienation and estrangement). The production of 'ethnocultural spaces' is in a way the most meaningful sense in which migrants can negotiate and form an identity as the result of their interactions.

The dynamics involved in such 'ethnocultural spaces' are clearly illuminated in Paul White's reflections on migration and return migration:

> To return may be to go back but it may equally be to start again: to seek but to lose. Return has both a temporal and a spatial dimension. For the individual returning to their 'own' past and place it is rarely fully satisfying: circumstances change, borders in all senses are altered, and identities change too. (...) In migration, above all topics, the levels of ambivalence, of plurality, of shifting identities and interpretations are perhaps greater than in many other aspects of life. The relationships between people and their contextual societies and places are intimate ones which are transformed by movement. Adjustment processes may never fully be completed: indeed, since we all continually refine our self-identities throughout our life-course it may be more truthful to say that migration intervenes in that process of renegotiation

as a lasting force, rather than as a single event (1995: 14-15; quotations in the original).

5.4   Summing up

Ethnographic and narrative accounts of culture and belonging during the homeland return contribute to social theories of home[11] by restating the importance of the social construction of the homeplace for return migrants in their negotiation of belongingness and identity. We do not encounter static notions of home and fixed identities, but, through dynamic spaces and fluid movements, a sense of belongingness is contested and constituted. Family tensions do not amplify constraints but offer spaces of choice for second-generation returning migrants. When parental control and power are exercised over returnees, they do not remain passive receptors. The returning migrants' everyday lives may at times appear fragmented, but they are overwhelmingly dynamic and not fate-driven. Emergent identifications testify to this. As Christensen, James and Jenks clearly explain, 'Identities are forged within a locational matrix of constraint, contested meaning, conventions of placing and avenues of possibilities. Spatial relations and the social relations they contain are essentially dynamic' (2000: 153).

Places become meaningful by the social relations and understandings that bind persons to them or alienate them (Massey 1994). Meaningful also are those questions posed about migrants' sense of belonging, alienation and identity formation in relation to place, understandings emanating from the narratives of migrants themselves (Lawson 1999). In addition to ambivalence created by multiple feelings emerging at the intersection of place and mobility, clarity about the role of social relations, and migrant perceptions of origins and destinations is possible: 'Affiliations with multiple places are cross-cut by relations of class, location, gender, age and "race", in which a sense of belonging is mediated through these power relations and positionings. Popular everyday expressions of relationships to place and national space are in themselves multiple, frequently contradictory and contested' (Radcliffe and Westwood 1996: 132).

In the next chapter I explore reconfigurations of the spaces created among 'home' and 'belonging' that form mediated identifications. The narratives of 'leaving home' and 'being at home' are journeys of place and belongingness; they are journeys of return. Ahmed suggests: 'It is such transnational journeys of subjects and others that invite us to consider what it means to be at home, to inhabit a particular place, and might call us to question the relationship between identity, belonging and home' (1999: 331). However, it is important to point out that ascriptions of membership in the homeland are negotiable as well within a socio-cultural context of 'home politics'. It seems that common ancestry, language and religion are not always enough to cultivate 'cultural' and 'ethnic' belongingness during the homeland return as the returnees' narratives of 'exile' and 'alienation' illustrate. Those narratives focusing on anti-American sentiments in the homeland direct us toward a meso-level understanding of a hyphenated identification negotiated on macro levels of 'home-host' constructs and micro levels of personal constructions. In the next chapter, tracing *ideologies of self* and *geographies of identity*, I deconstruct stories of the 'who I am' in the 'where I was', the 'where I am' and the 'where I am going'. Hence, the historicity of self is potentially a narrative of homeplace constructions.

Myth and constructions of connectedness are links in the homeland for returnees who construct collective and personal trajectories of homeness. As Pattie notes, 'Home', 'homeland', 'the old country' and 'diaspora' are at times overlapping, even antagonistic terms; they have different implications and point toward varying interpretations of experience as well as changing connections between place and culture (1994: 185). Experiences of the past are passed on as memory functions persistently to energise national cohesiveness and remembrance. Strong family bonds are emotive links between past and present while providing heavily rooted relationships for an ethnic future survival. The second generation is aware and grateful for the parents' sacrifices, grief and loss. The second generation is also relied upon to reinforce ethnic ties and ethnic belongingness. Return migration is additionally the application of such a heavy responsibility. It is simultaneously as much a legacy as it is a burden.

Andreas Papandreou had used enticing rhetoric with the phrase, 'Greece belongs to the Greeks' to counter Konstantinos Karamanlis' earlier rhetoric that 'Greece belongs to the West'[12]. Yet, most Greek-Americans dwell on such sayings as 'Greece eats her children' or 'Wherever I go, Greece hurts me' to recount the paradox of a home that hurts and a history that devours. If you deconstruct a paradox, you do not decipher its meaning; you dismantle its legend. The 'Greek Paradox' is often writ large in the narratives of returning migrants since return migration is an opportunity to (re)evaluate old and new paradoxes. The text *The Greek Paradox: Promise vs. Performance* (Allison and Nicolaidis 1997) encapsulates how such perspectives should be addressed in just a few lines of the book's dedication: 'This volume is dedicated to the leaders and citizens of Greece. May they seize the significant opportunities before them and inspire the spirit of democracy around the world not only by their history but by their performance'. I have addressed 'performativity' in the 'personal plan of action', the 'unitive homing resolution', as well as in relation to gender, culture and ethnicity. I have found James Faubion's (1993) *Modern Greek Lessons: A Primer in Historical Constructivism* an enormously enriching, original and important contribution that elegantly narrates Greece, Athens specifically, as a city on the 'margins of Europe', immersed in multiplicities and fragmentations, expressive of complexity and ambivalence in search of a 'modern identity'. Of course, the paradox is a struggle that evolves between a 'heroic past' and an 'ambivalent present', between Europe and the United States, between 'East' and 'West', between 'homogeneity' and 'heterogeneity', between 'individualism' and 'collectivism', as well as within other socio-cultural layers that serve as dynamics of collaboration or antagonism. Faubion, in his introduction, sketches the background of Yiorghos Papandreou[13], the son of Andreas Papandreou and Margaret Papandreou, an American woman who led the largest of Greece's feminist organisations (1993: 3-4). Faubion, present at a talk Papandreou gave on 3 October 1986 at the Athens offices of the American Educational Foundation to a small group of scholars and staff, states that the speaker could not have been more ideal: 'His English was impeccable; his temperament little inclined toward nationalist apologetics; his signature causes based for the past several years upon an articulate conviction in the virtues of social and cultural-fertilization' (1993: 3). Some of Papandreou's remarks are preoccupied with 'the Greek paradox' and his worries over how to 'get people to take things into their own hands' while explaining that he 'would have had difficulty returning to Greece from abroad had he not felt that the country could be changed' (Faubion 1993: 3-4).

Above all, what I want to hold here is a common vision that my participants expressed almost two decades after Papandreou's self-reflexive account: 'The nation's youth, the Greeks of the diaspora were "valuable" for their "critical perspective on society", for their attraction to and familiarity with "other ways of life", for their "marginality". He reiterated the point. It was precisely that "marginality", he said, that he hoped could be put in the service of the "transformation", of the "betterment" of Greece' (Faubion 1993: 4; quotations in the original). 'Belonging patterns', as we have seen from the narrative accounts, are split between spaces of 'home' and spaces of 'exile' in the *homeplace* that is the *patrida* (homeland). At the same time, the 'personal plan of action' for most returnees is an 'action plan' of contributing to the development of their homeland over and above the frustration and anger they experience. The simple idea of 'belonging' is constantly challenged by the realities of social life decisively shaped by global forces and local discourses. In an era of increasing exchange of information, ideas and people, 'ethnic belongingness' figures sharply as an urgent question on the contemporary global scene (Touraine 2000). Furthermore, how social science can construct a theoretical and morally defensible notion of belonging is another compelling question (Alleyne 2002) as well as the 'moral ambiguity of sources of identity based on belonging' (Lichten-berg 1999: 171). Guided by the discussion on *ideologies of self* and *geo-graphies of identity*, in the next chapter I seek to explore the processes that best capture the transformations and transitions of identification while identifying the contents and discontents of belongingness. In this process, I become 'immersed in joint action' (Ingold 1993) with the participants in the exploration of identification.

6 Ideologies of self and geographies of identity

In commencing this discussion on identification, I cannot resist indulging into the imagery of a recent film, released a few years ago, in 2002, which has been quite successful in both the United States and Europe, not to mention Greece. The film could be none other than *My Big Fat Greek Wedding*, the one that all my participants exclaimed in the midst of complete awe: 'You haven't seen it yet?!!!'; the one which I eventually got round to viewing accompanied by my field notes. I must admit that at the end I was the one in complete awe when listening to the dialogues or monologues and watching the wealth of other cultural communicative devices; I was convinced that my fieldwork had taken shape on the big screen! A common reaction when something said or written is so complex and incomprehensible is for Americans (and British) to say: 'It's all Greek to me!'. After all, the movie *My Big Fat Greek Wedding* is 'all Greek' to any viewer. However, since visual methodologies are not at the centre of the study, I will refrain from referencing the entire film[1] in this chapter, but let me mention one phrase to initiate the discussion on *ideologies of self* and *geographies of identities*: 'Don't make the past dictate who you are but let it make a part of who you will become'. This is what Toula, the protagonist in the film, is told by her brother Nick in the midst of her personal turmoil in trying to bring a *xeno* into the family as her future husband. But how much does the past dictate the 'self'? To what extent is the 'being' and 'becoming' of migrants tied to their cultural backgrounds? To what degree are those cultural dimensions symbolic, emotional, imaginary, social and political? In fact, they may all be threads of the fabric of everyday life and aspects of a daily routine that may be taken for granted.

Class, gender and ethnicity are the standard and useful analytical categories that situate second-generation return migrants, embodying them with diverse and varying personal biographies and social orientations. In such a framework, there are several collective dimensions that seem critical in comprehending identification patterns:

1. Family histories and timing of migration, as well as reasons for migration, and for personal and family settlement in the United States (class, gender)

2. Globalisation and its effects on both 'home' and 'host' countries (networks, organisations)
3. The transformation of Greece from a sending to a receiving country (immigration, ethnicity)
4. The events of September 11th, 2001 in the United States and their local and global impact (memory, global events)

While taking into consideration these collective dimensions, we must keep a balance between, on the one hand, personal constructions and the emotive power of narrative accounts and, on the other, national (re) configurations due to local or international global events. But, 'the fact that a narrative is the product of a creative process, a construct that articulates the past anew, does not by itself compromise its truth. ... What more is there to such understanding, after all, than our respective abilities to construct, recount, enact, embellish, share, and enjoy them?' (Norman 2002: 194).

In the following three sections of this chapter, I attempt to decipher the complexities of identity in correlation to the four collective dimensions outlined above and in response to the construction of place during the homeland return. In other words, I am interested in *locating* the multiple layers of how returnees vocalise and process the 'who I am' in the 'where I am' toward the 'what I might become'. In this way return migration can be understood as both an 'active' and a 'reactive' phenomenon insofar as returnees are both decision-makers and global actors.

Undoubtedly, identity questions – whether focusing on ethnicity, gender, or religion – are inherently complex for the researcher and usually anxiety-inducing for the researched. In psychological terms, for most people, identity is a rather metaphysical, abstract, mental notion tucked away in the subconscious and not to be meddled with:

> As questions, they are rarely asked by others or by the self. Self-interrogation is a rare thing. One typically does not ask oneself 'Who am I?' 'What am I?' except when thrust into acute self-consciousness during moments of transition brought about by such life events as threat of imminent death, acute illness, religious conversion, forced migration, marriage and divorce, natural disasters, or while in hospitals, transit lounges of international airports, hotels, concentration or refugee camps, and so on. Identity is put behind or underneath consciousness because of its taken-for-grantedness. It is ordinarily non-problematic, so one 'moves on with life' (Chee-kiong and Kwok-bun 2001; quotations in the original).

So I was not surprised when virtually all the participants in the study told me that they had never before considered what their 'identity' was, how they felt about it, how they defined it, how they understood their 'sense of self' throughout their lives. However, both conversational and written narratives were very revealing of the participants' constructions and negotiations of their identities. In the next section I will address identity in terms of these constructions and negotiations, probing also the inconsistencies, contradictions and self-revelations.

6.1 Constructing and negotiating identities

Narrative accounts of second-generation Greek-American return migrants are above all their life stories. This statement implies the significant connotation that life is a history, and as Bourdieu argues, 'a life is inseparably the sum of the events of the individual existence seen as a history and the narrative of that history' (2000: 297). The returnees' life paths and trajectories are mobility passages consisting of a beginning, versatile stages, crossroads of events, and relationships of the self and the other guided by self-actualisation plans and unplanned interactions. These processes contribute to the way constructions and negotiations are made in the return lives of migrants, by them and within the social context they inhabit as well as the one they originated from since the significance of mobility in their lives lies in the multiple layers of movement – geographical, social, cultural, economic and political. Thus, returnee narratives are about lives and processes engaged in spatial movements and their settlement in the homeland, the 'national place'. Narrative accounts situated in national historical time and space stimulate the constitution of meaning for returnees who depict their return migration in correlation with their personal identification: 'Since the past is not storied, historical narratives are not *found* or *discovered*; rather they are *invented*. In this sense, historical narratives are *constructions* – constructions that give a sequence of events, such as one might find notated in a historical chronicle or annal, a *meaning*. Historical narratives, in this regard, are also said to *constitute* meaning' (Carroll 2002: 249; italics in the original).

As part of the process of blurring of boundaries, Dubish believes that emotions (both the participants' and the researcher's) can be a valuable source of insight, insofar as they can be integrated with other kinds of data and thus 'serve as a "window" for the reader as well as a pathway to theoretical insights' (1995: 6; quotation marks in the original). However, at the same time, we encounter the problem of writing and dominance, especially since generalisation itself 'is inevitably the language of power' (Abu-Lughod 1991: 150). In this respect, Abu-Lughod advocates moving away from the concept of culture and moving toward what she terms 'ethnographies of the particular', which present more of the complexities of the fieldwork experience. Dubish addresses the problem of writing and dominance by proposing two solutions: 'One way is to extend the idea of writing metaphorically: "All cultures write". Thus other forms of cultural expression are placed on a par with writing. Another attempt to find a way out of the dominance conferred by writing is through "polyphonic" ethnographies, in which the "natives" are allowed greater latitude to "speak for themselves"' (1995: 142; quotation marks in the original). However, the researcher is still in control of the final text and the written product of the 'ethnography of the particular', as well as responsible for selecting the 'voices', and developing and contextualising the analysis.

In this chapter, where 'identity' figures so prominently, I have preceded and followed the narrative extracts and the written text (in addition to providing contextual or biographical information as previously) with commentaries on what I call 'the experiential reflective self'. This is a reflexive component of the researcher-researched relationship and an additional layer of subjectivity that framed my final meetings with the participants. Basically, this emerged during the last set of conversational narratives as the participants recapitulated on their 'sense of self' in relation to return migration; we could both discern, the participant and myself, how the research experience had interacted with their personal experience in crafting another 'performative space' of the identification process. This is understood in two ways: Firstly, by looking at oral narration in hermeneutical terms, that is, 'the interviewer is not understood as ferreting out data to be discovered only in the recesses of the informant's memory. Rather, the interviewer is actually creating a text *with* the informant. The interview is understood variously as a "social act", a "dialogue", and a "circular feedback" process in which the investigator and the informant continually influence one another' (Yans-McLaughlin 1990: 257; italics and quotation marks in the original). And, secondly, by the idea that not only the personal is political (Gluck and Patai 1991: 1), but most importantly, the personal is also theoretical (Okely 1992: 9). More specifically, in the section entitled, *Narrating the self upon finding the home: stories of 'who we are' in the 'where we are'*, I decipher those 'performative spaces' of identity by focusing more on the *experiential reflective self* as telling the story of the 'existential' (who I am) in the 'placial' (where I am) by means of a 'personal plan of action' (possibly future action as well).

In Chapter two, I explained the reasons why I did not wish to either categorise my research on identification processes and identity construction or impose specific identity prefixes (*national, ethnic, social, personal, self*). Nevertheless, I very much agree with Condor when he states that:

> A comprehensive analysis of national identity would have to take account of complex contextual variation. This would include variation due to the social location of individual subjects (in concrete social networks, family structures); geographical, historical and ideological variations in the significance and meaning of national identity, and the intersections of national identities with gender, generational, ethnic and class identities. Such analyses would have to consider context-specific norms in the expression of national identity...A full analysis of national self-identity would have to take account of the various ways in which identity may be symbolized (visually as well as verbally), and the possibility that, for the individual subject, national self-identification may exist at varying levels of consciousness (1996: 43).

The analysis of and discussion on second-generation Greek-American identity construction will allude to these issues in this and the next sections. Anthias has persuasively argued that 'Ethnicity, gender and class are grids for conceptualizing unity, difference and division, and involve social and political representations (rather than constituting concrete or permanent groups)' (2001: 377). Such social categories of ethnicity, gender and class relate to outcomes on both a material and symbolic level and thus should be taken into consideration as socio-cultural formations that contextualise identification processes.

6.1.1   Class, gender

Andrew Milner's *Class* (1999) provides an overview of the current attitudes to class in cultural studies and sociology, emphasising a strong reaffirmation of the concept's centrality in both disciplines. He reintroduces the debates over class and culture almost silenced by postmodernism, in an attempt to restore a focal presence of class in contemporary cultural studies. For, as Milner argues, 'if ever there was an academic discipline the intellectual origins of which were marked by class consciousness, then it was surely Cultural Studies' (1999: 3). Over two decades ago, Giddens still distinguished four different levels of 'class consciousness': 'class awareness', 'class identity', 'conflict consciousness' and 'revolutionary class consciousness' (1981: 111-113). It is not my intent here to provide a theoretical or historical account of the assertion or decline of class but rather to acknowledge social agency (Thompson 1963), social constructedness (Williams 1976), class cultures (Hall and Jefferson 1976) and class habitus (Bourdieu 1977)

while maintaining a reflexive 'awareness' of my own personal and family background, class and political consciousness in respect to my research setting and participants (Christou 2002; 2006b). Parallel to my
'experiential' understandings of 'class' were my earlier readings of
Marx, Poulantzas and Castoriadis, and I remain in full agreement with
Mann's view that societies are best understood as 'multiple overlapping
and interesting sociospatial networks of power' (1986: 1-2). Mann still
convinces when he asserts:

> In a world still characterized by capitalism...I find no sense in
> notions that 'class is dead'. But then classes have never had a
> full, pure and independent life. Class has been, first, a heuristic
> tool for the limited goal of positional measurement and, second,
> an actually limited and impure social actor, in a constant state of
> development and flux. Both roles will probably survive (1995: 53-
> 54).

The dominance of 'class' as the 'master identity' of the social – that category through which all other social identities are to be mediated –
has been challenged by the growth of various new social movements.
Du Gay, Evans and Redman (2000:1) mention 'feminisms', black
struggles and the ecological movement as a few of the most obvious
candidates. And yet, in a world that by no means is 'classless', I could
not abandon the category of class in this chapter since it figured prominently in all narrative accounts. My participants explicitly discussed
their family migration experience in terms of poverty, hardship, unequal opportunities, repression and misery in the homeland. Their family development, through difficult circumstances and rough living
conditions, but above all as a result of hard work and vision, had in
some cases minor and in others substantial 'class shifts'. The participants were very vivid and at times emotional about their family's 'humble beginnings'. In this respect we realise that 'biographies, as metaphors of self, also function as metaphors for history as it is commonly
understood by the narrators. When immigrants express different vi-
sions of past time and of their own relationship to it, they are projecting these personal and political beliefs upon the past' (Yans-McLaughlin 1990: 272). In accord with this I would argue that past recollections
constructed by returnees in narratives of 'a collective sense of the past'
reflect both their subjectivity and the historical realities of their cultural
constructions. The recollection of memories serves as a reconstruction
of identities (Christou 2003c). The second-generation returnees' own
narrations of themselves and their families as 'active-actors' in the past
in relation to migrancy and the diasporic experience, for example, correspond with the activism identified with Greeks during historical peri-

ods of repression and struggle, poverty and hardship, political and social upheaval. There is a constancy between how the second generation
conceptualises the glories of their ancestors' pasts and even their families' pasts with the narratives they offer about roots and heritage as
pull factors in their return migration. On the other hand, the experience per se of the homeland return as illustrated through the narratives of adjustment in the previous chapters has created differentiated
understandings.

For the first generation, crossing the Atlantic was a step towards a
'new Atlantis', meaning that they would reach their full potential by
maximising their personal and financial status while holding tight to
the plan of return to the homeland, successful and wealthy. Migration
most of the time was perceived as a temporary move. The United
States represented the *Promised Land* and the key to achieve all that
they promised themselves and their families. In a extremely vivid manner, Papanikolas describes the trail of emigration also reflective of specific gender roles: 'From this land, with its ancient lore and lost greatness, the boys and men prepared to leave with anxiety, fear, and excite-
ment, but always with the certainty of return. Families mortgaged their
ancestral land at usurious rates to provide passage for the great number of these nearly illiterate sons. They were to work for their sisters'
dowries, lift their parents out of penury, and return. *Ksenitia* was the
word for foreign lands' (2002: 52; italics in the original). The lengthy
extract that follows from Pythia's written narrative exemplifies the economic, social and cultural context of life in foreign lands:

> *The magic word of my parents' childhood was America. It was the*
> *land of dreams and gold and opportunity. (...) Parents watched*
> *their sons and relatives vanish into the mysterious western land*
> *with mingled joy, fear, and pride. With their vague ideas of geo-*
> *graphy people often asked an emigrant bound for New York to car-*
> *ry messages to their relatives in Capetown or Buenos Aires. The*
> *coming of a letter from America was an event, and friends stood*
> *around to see whether it was fat with money. They would wish the*
> *receiver 'good spending' and expect a glass of wine or ouzo to*
> *drink to the health of the writer. When a relative was returning*
> *for a visit, virtually the whole town would walk the mile or so to*
> *the train station to welcome him. Undoubtedly my relatives had to*
> *struggle to establish themselves but they never discouraged us with*
> *details of these early struggles, or the severe climate of America, or*
> *of their social isolation as 'mere foreigners'. My father owned a*
> *fish market and fresh produce business in his native village. To*
> *him, the seemingly endless counters contained all the fish in the*
> *world's lakes, and the sweetest fruit ever to be found. When his*

business waned, he and my mother decided to come to the United States. Glowing reports of life in the New World from my relatives in America convinced them that only in America could they find prosperity. They sold all their worldly possessions and made plans through an agent to travel by train through Europe to France. From there they would board a ship that would take them to America. Their memories are somewhat vague and difficult for them to put into words. (...) I felt the sadness in my father. He acted like a man defeated, a man who was giving up his life so that his children might have a greater opportunity in life than he had. I shared in his pain; he did not want to leave home. For a long time it seemed they lived in a haze in the States. They knew not a word of English, but soon began to learn the language (...) and began also to understand the meaning of all the insults and prejudice hurled at them. We were the 'greaseballs' in the neighborhood and we were going to make the property values go down. I believe that the intense suffering, confusion and anxiety that immigrants experience from name-calling and racial or ethnic epithets is difficult to fully understand unless one has actually been the object of such abuse. It is a pain that penetrates the soul. They came to America with nothing! Absolutely nothing except the clothes on their backs. And for a long time we didn't know where our meals were coming from. Father and mother both worked and worked and worked, night and day. My mother working outside of the home changed me forever. It was possibly the most difficult adjustment for me to make. Now I know that my parents' example of hard work and sacrifice contributed enormously to my personal work ethic. They taught us about work, and they taught us about responsibility. We didn't sit around. We had something to do. We were part of a family. Father went to work at my uncle's restaurant. My grandfather established the business many years ago. (...) I think that Greeks prospered so well in the restaurant business because it coincides with their natural proclivities. In their country they attach great importance to matters of diet and appear to be a nation of natural born cooks. In spite of our hardships my family was fortunate in having relatives there who gave us comfort and companionship. My parents found working in America entirely different than what they had experienced in Greece. They worked as hard or harder than in Greece. But there their minds were always heavy and worried. My mother for example worked at the Clothing Company twelve sometimes fourteen-hour days, but she never complained. She worked with a group of Italian women who couldn't speak English, so in order for her to be able to communicate with them, she learned their language, Italian. I can remember waking

up every morning to a warm house, because my parents would get
up at four o'clock to shovel coal in the furnace. They brought with
them to our new life the secret of happiness and never lost their
power to work with a smile. (Pythia, female, 50)

Despite the hardships and the pain as described above in an evocative
manner, for most first-generation Greek-American migrants, the United States kept one part of the bargain and fulfilled those promises as
the land of freedom and opportunity, the abundance of all that the
homeland was lacking at the time. This of course involved a cost, very
high at times, beyond the physical exhaustion and personal sacrifice,
the deep psychological trauma of the children who had to endure the
absence of their working parents along with their sadness and concerns but also the sense of social rejection that incidents of racism and
xenophobia produce. The ultimate aspiration was of course to obtain
prosperity and thus reduce economic strain and life complications. Perhaps that was one of the reasons why the returnees' families and
friends took bets on their return back to the States:

In '97 I decided enough with the States and decided to come
here, sold everything, and in 1998 it became a reality, and I
came to live here. To me now for the last five years, this literally
has been home. It's not just a place somewhere to spend summer; it is a place where I really feel I belong, now at this stage
of my life, although now I'm thinking of moving to the village.
(...) It feels permanent (...) within the first six months, feeling
totally comfortable here, and they (my friends) can't understand.
All my friends in the States were taking bets that I wouldn't last
more than a year; I think I should've made the bet! (Pericles,
male, 50)

The first days for me were incredible because I kept seeing old
acquaintances, old friends, vacation time; everybody was coming
to see me. Everybody found out that I was moving to Greece. I
was by myself; I was free and single. I didn't have any difficulties in adjusting. I am the type of person who in general doesn't
have problems in adjusting. I believe I adjust easily wherever I
go, immediately. I very much liked this new beginning despite
coming from America; everybody kept betting that I would return back in three months. I proved to them that twelve years
have gone by and I only go back on vacation! I have rejected
such an idea, and I would never go back to America. That
thought is not in my mind. (Aspasia, female, 32)

Apparent in these narratives is a strong sense of perseverance in actualising the plan of return and determination in making their return project a successful one. Just as previous generations of Greek migrants persisted with diligence in transforming personal hardship into personal success, intrinsically linked to the development of an ethnic and cultural legacy of achievements, the second generation is conscientiously (perhaps even subconsciously) committed to fulfilling their families' idealisation of a triumphant return to the ancestral homeland. As illustrated by the returnees, their parents' 'struggles' and 'sacrifices' are primarily the reason why (nearly) all participants seem to belong to the urban middle class. Some exceptions of working-class participants do exist and as mentioned earlier, detailed social background information can be found in the appendix. In any case, the social experience of migranthood has to inevitably also focus on class as participants underscore the vision of prosperity and financial security interconnected with the burden of a life of migrancy.

In terms of the class discussion developed earlier, the returnees narrated in great detail their parents' humble beginnings and economic hardships that led to migration. On one level, beyond the sense of pride that the offspring may feel for the parents, it is almost like a heavy load transported with profound emotional force that creates intense guilt on the part of those children who have taken upon themselves the role of 'curator' of the cultural transit from 'host' to 'home' countries. Characteristically, some of these highlight in vast detail these issues and feature elements of generational dynamics in the preservation of 'family values' during the attainment of personal accomplishments that break through class barriers. The following narratives are lengthy accounts of such family struggles in the achievement of success, where family is the unit of solidarity and the grounds for endurance:

> My father left the island while he was a young boy. His only aim at that time was to escape poverty and do something different. For that time, the United States was the land of opportunity for him, like many other Greeks. (...) At the beginning he was a cook in a transatlantic boat. He stayed as a cook for two years until the day that he decided to take the big step and search for better luck in New York. The first years he worked as a cook in a number of different Greek restaurants. He spent 10 years working for somebody else. Then he came back to the island for bride hunting. His dream was to find someone from his own place. The next year he got married with my mother, and both moved back in the States. Meanwhile, my father went in partnership with mother's cousin. They decided to go into business together, and they opened a deli. (Kallisto, female, 21)

My family migrated to the United States for both economic and
political reasons. I grew up in a series of little towns. (...) We
moved three times. (...) And then my father lost his job, and we
were forced to move in a smaller house, (...) And after that, we
moved to another place inside the town, inside the town which
was actually a cheap place to live. It was across from a junkyard;
on the one side, there was a tire place, and on the other side,
there was a fabric store, and I basically grew up there. We lived
there for 8 years, and I think it is there where I formed my identity. (...) Basically, when we say rural, it was a really hick town.
We had a guy across the street who raised turkeys and kept a
half German Shepard, half wolf on the leash. It was hick. My
mother was born and raised in New York City, and because of
that, she really had problems adjusting to that kind of environment. Behind our house, there was a pasture with cows and hay
bells and a road leading up to a big dock and the mountains.
(...) It was really an idyllic pastoral setting, but of course it was
backward and hick, extraordinarily hick. Horseheads sounds like
a very hick name, and I suppose it is, but Horseheads is not that
hick. It's right next to Elmira. A lot of people know about Elmira
College. Mark Twain lived in Elmira. The name stems from 17th
century (...) 1778, or something like that. There is a long story
behind the name. It's not really hick. It is a suburban environment. We did, however, live in the poorest and most ramshackle
area within Horseheads, on old Ithaca Road which led to Ithaca,
of course, which was kind of fun. The urban experience that I
had was as a child, basically in San Francisco in a suburb. (...)
Erin was hick, Horseheads, it was suburban poverty. We never
went on welfare because my family doesn't believe in welfare,
but I think we should have. We went through a period where we
made I think 6.5 thousand over the course of a year. It was really
amazing just where the level of poverty is possible in suburban
America. The level of poverty in suburban America is just amazing. Other than that, my urban experiences were mostly positive:
I like cities; I like libraries; I like universities. (Sophocles, male,
28)

Sophocles is a prime example of the fact that some of the participants
had experienced poverty during their childhood years in the United
States. However, through their parents' path of struggle and vision that
led to success, the second generation enjoyed a rather comfortable life
in their early adolescence, and as the demographic information listed
in the appendix indicates, nearly all participants seem to belong to the
urban middle class with some slight variations of lower to upper mid-

dle class in terms of current living conditions. A similar variation exists in relation to their professional trajectories that may or may not correspond to their previous training and experience as the participants classify themselves as 'highly skilled' and make this judgement about skills not only on their years of education or level of remuneration but primarily based on the value of the skills they have attained through their specific professional qualifications acquired in the United States. Consequently, when the returnees express intense dissatisfaction, frustration and a sense of disempowerment and stagnation with their employment situation in Greece in feeling undermined, unacknowledged, overworked, underpaid and disrespected in their working lives, they correlate these experiences with their sense of self (Christou 2006a).

As I already explained in Chapter two, a number of authors point to the importance of biography to the construction of identity, the justification of previous action, and the continuity of the self into the future (Harré 1983: 213-14; Gergen and Davis 1985: 259-63; Giddens 1991: 47-55). To demonstrate precisely this, excerpts of women's narratives follow. The *Personal Narratives Group* argues that the dynamics of gender emerge particularly clearly in the personal narratives of women: 'women's personal narratives are...stories of how women negotiate their "exceptional" gender status both in their daily lives and over the course of a lifetime. They assume that one can understand the life only if one takes into account gender roles and gender expectations' (1989: 4-5).

In their particular 'feminisation' of return migration, women migrants define their relocation as a gendered identity construction that incorporates national representations. The ethnic community and the symbolic ethnicisation of the return are refined by the conscious decision of a 'motherland' return in search of an identity that manifests itself within the religious, the national and the ethnic. These multiple constructions are important in the way female migrants view themselves and how this impacts on the way cultural production is articulated within the local, the global and transnational contexts (Christou 2003b). These particular orientations are important in how the homeland return is visualised, processed and understood.

Recent feminist theory has underscored the role of women as active agents in constructing and articulating their own identities. Through their life experiences and the various discourses they intersect with, female subjects are formed and reproduced (de Lauretis 1987). As Radcliffe suggests, 'the (self-) representation of gendered identity is evidenced by the interrelationships of place and history, their associational meanings, and gendered positionings in relation to these abstracts' (1993: 104). The female returnees, while engaging in traditional domestic and nurturing roles, at the same time reconfigure their gender-self and autonomous positioning by choosing to complete a motherland[2] return. Female return migrants mobilise multiple socio-cultural geographies and spaces. The mobility of these women is a shifting in locations and identities. The reality of women's lives goes beyond simple dichotomies; it is a reality embedded in active engagement with subjecthood, identity and social transformations (Radcliffe 1993: 103).

Women's self-agency is contingent upon their individual capacity to produce meanings and to organise their activities as self-conscious expressions of daily and life practices. This is a 'personalisation' process that materialises with the 'personal plan of action', in the case of this study, the return migration project. Close attention should be paid to the ways gender and ethnicity are embedded and concurrently produced in representations of identity and how these are articulated and circulated (Christou 2006a). Gender processes have been regarded as important in understanding how nationhood and belongingness are retained and reconstituted, particularly through the role of women as ethnic actors (Yuval-Davis and Anthias 1989; Yuval-Davis 1997).

The women portray themselves as good mothers, good wives, good sisters and as honourable and obedient daughters. When asked to describe themselves in connection to their family, kin and personal relations, they produced identity narrations consistent with ascribed gender and family roles. Education, work and careers also figured prominently in the discourse, all central for them as female returnees and Greek-American women. Typical responses included characteristics and behaviours which exemplified two differing poles of attitude: compliance and conformity along with academic aspiration, a strong work ethic, career ambition and drive to succeed professionally. To be precise, their sense of self, being and becoming is correlated with self-sufficiency, autonomy, independent decision-making and the implementation of such goals but which also emphasises 'traditional' female roles as an obligation of pursuit and practice. According to the life path taught and promoted in the Greek-American family environment, the girls are first and foremost good daughters and good sisters. The family surrounding the girls, relatives included, all urge the cultivation of characteristics that will later on produce good wives, good daughters-in-law and good mothers: obedient, respectful, gentle, virtuous and hard workers. National constructs of ethnic practices, religion and language are all very important; they are taught and practiced from an early age. The narratives that follow all illustrate the above constructions, focusing particularly on those aspects of return narration that are *gendered* and illuminate female participants' varying 'roles' as women return migrants, wives, mothers, daughters and sisters:

When my son reached the age of twelve, my husband and I
decided that maybe that was an important turning point; either
we leave then and come here and my son would really get more
of a Greek education here, or it might be too late if we stayed
there because when you bring the children later, when they are
older, they may have difficulties in adjusting. So we left when
he went to the 7th grade here, and he finished high school here,
and he adjusted very well here. He met his friends here, and we
never regretted it. (...) Well, I fit into every aspect of life here
where there is family, and they have the holidays, we go, and we
invite them. They keep the traditions and the name days and
that, the Church, especially, my husband is very religious we
never miss a Sunday mass and the holidays. We go to his island
with his family, Easter especially. At night we attend church,
and I would say, I mean, that I fit in. I don't have any problem,
and that has to do of course with my upbringing, with my
mother and father; they used to do the same thing. Everything
that I saw in my own house, I continue it now for my own son
so he grows up that way too... Be close with his family. He has
cousins here and relatives that we are in touch, and there is a lot
of back and forth. They come over; we are not cut-off from
them, and I do the same on my side. I go to the island every
year and see them. I enjoy that. In fact my sister, who is also
second-generation, bought a beautiful home there, and they
come every year, certain holidays, and she was born in the
States, but she married a Greek fellow from that island, the
same town my mom was from, and she makes sure that her
children continue to come back and forth so they keep the
Greek thing... so they don't lose themselves. That's very important. (...) So that's what identity is all about: culture, language,
religion. Not to lose yourself, to keep the Greek. We have a lot of
friends in America. They brought up their children the American way. They let them marry whoever they want. They brought
them foreigners, and then they divorced. They don't fit in. You
saw that film. That's how the Greeks fit in, and they still do. (...)
When I started looking to get married, I wanted someone from
Europe, someone from Greece. I didn't like the American life-
style. I didn't like that. I prefer European and Greek. (Hera, female, 70)

Furthermore, the female cultures of support are not devoid of generational differences and contradiction, even rivalry. The performances of
such household power negotiations construct new spaces of heterogeneous gender identities. Pandora explores her maturation struggles

while growing up in the United States and, upon return, her relations with her two sisters and her mother. She projects herself as a hero child, parenting her parents and raising her younger sisters:

> I don't remember myself having a hard time. But this translating... I took it upon myself. I was translating for my parents, for years onwards for my parents. My father had to look for a job I would be the one going with him. My father used to work in construction so I remember accompanying him to the union these workers had, and I would translate. My mother, she was working for a factory. She was making dresses or shirts or something. She herself had problems communicating, so I was the one, if you can imagine a little girl going to second grade, going to all these places having to explain things. What else can I say? Ever since then, I am the one in the family who is going to take care of anything that is important, like going to the various offices, taking care of anything that we need to buy...contracts, and things like that; I am the one who does all these things. My mother she doesn't do anything, neither do any of my sisters. I have the leadership responsibilities. I don't know, ever since I was in second grade. I don't know. I don't know. What is that, my husband gets really angry with this attitude because he thinks that they are taking advantage of me. (...) We spoke Greek at home. It wasn't that intense because my parents would work all the time and my sister and I were mostly on our own... taking care of ourselves because my father was working the night shift and my mother was working all day in the factory, and when she got home and she was too tired even to do the housework, so my sister and I would play board games together, do the housework. We also had two dogs, so we were more or less on our own. Only when they were around, we would speak Greek... (...) My mother, she wanted my younger sister to be married as soon as possible because as I told you, my father got killed, and it was her and my sister, and she didn't want to feel the responsibility, so the moment she found out that my sister was going out with a Greek, she made it a point to call his mother and to tell her that the kids have to get married that way... She just wanted to get rid of the responsibility, and that's how my sister ended up with three kids; she got married at eighteen, and you know that's not what I was dreaming for my sister. I wanted her to go to college, and I remember setting up a secret meeting with my future brother-in-law, and I told him to leave my sister alone because she wants to go to college and things like that, and after she finishes, you can marry her; you

can do whatever you like, and he still tells me, 'You never should've done that. You never should've poked your nose in our business'. That was a mother's job, and my mother wouldn't do that, what was proper for her, so I felt I had to do it. It made no difference because I didn't have nobody on my side to help me. My other sister didn't care; she was indifferent, and my mother wanted to marry the little girl off, so she was eighteen, and at nineteen she had the one boy, and now three kids later, she wants to go back to college, but it is impossible with three kids. That's the problem. (...) I am very close with my sisters. Very much, more with the little one than the other one. I am very close to my younger sister; at times I feel she is my daughter or something because when she was born I was fifteen years old, and my mother used to work all the time, and I remember taking care of her, changing her diapers, feeding her... It was like having a baby, bringing up a baby.

The female returnees have clearly processed the religious and national aspects of their identity in a conscious manner. Even in the case where female returnees experienced a hegemonic, oppressive, conservative, domineering, authoritarian, repressive and strict upbringing in the United States through their parents' anguished attempts to protect traditionalistic roles, the return migratory project was not constructed as a plan of 'liberation' or 'empowerment' but rather was internalised as a plan of belongingness and identification. In these cases, we have examples of a conscious hybridisation[3], which is a part of the entire process of adjustment in the return project, their 'self-identification'. This is a process of redefinition, a self-defining strategy that is forged in a context of dialogue with structures of the nation-state. The women participating in the study have learned to self-identify as women living in the ancestral homeland, at times a different culture, and therefore had to negotiate their roles but have all found it to a certain degree an experience of self-actualisation.

The female returnees stressed the 'essence' of their identity by emphasising multiple roles: 'I am mother, I am wife, I am woman, I am here (in my motherland)'. By negotiating roles and constructing performativity[4], we can observe the unfolding of identification processes. The women's narratives in discussing identity, memory and the construction of selfhood work substantially within the framework of performativity. This situatedness is concerned primarily with how female returnees from the United States to Greece construct narratives of the migratory past in the summation of post-migratory identity. It is a common practice of selfhood that 'people tell others who they are, but even more important, they tell themselves and then try to act as though they are who they say they are' (Holland, Lachicotte, Skinner and Cain 1998: 3). The women, through their stories, are producing understandings of themselves that are improvised from the cultural resources they have. In narrating the social situations they encounter, they represent dilemmas about their past and present actions. These are stories 'of', 'about' and 'for' themselves and their cultural worlds.

As Bromley argues, 'It is crucial that the migrant should be able to find space to construct an identity that can accommodate what he or she once was and is now supposed to be: an identity that is somewhere in-between' (2000: 66). This in-betweenness is what Hestia had to confront in her return journey, along with clarifying what her gendered self is:

One of the reasons that I agreed to come here was because of the values. I saw that US values were deteriorating and, I mean, also in here. I realized that, too, but somehow you feel that you can hold on to that. There are a lot of older people. There is a big population that is old, and there is a tradition, and I like that. I like that you know where you are coming from. I guess in the US, I didn't feel that. It's not bad to get to know other cultures; it's just that if you start mixing with them, you forget who you are. So, in Greece, with the way of life, you just don't forget that. (...) I think I already have an identity, but it may change the way I do things... in the US, I would've always be working, and I think there is something else here, or I pay more attention to family, where in the US, well we did, but it's not the same thing. They are more tied here. In the US, we are tied, too, but it is a different feeling. And everybody here speaks the same language; I like that. In the US, you couldn't find that easily. I guess it will shape me, somehow, hopefully better... When I was in the US, I was like, 'I'm Greek'. I didn't want to view myself as an American; I wanted to stay Greek. So you are always going back and forth. Deep down inside, you are Greek: you were born Greek; you were baptized; your parents taught you a certain way. I think culture also plays a certain role. (...) Well before, it was luck that I found I wasn't looking for a Greek. I told myself I am better off starting to hang out with more Greeks because you always lose yourself. My only decision to come to Greece was because I met my husband and we decided to get married and we wanted to move back to Greece. That was the main reason, the only reason. It took me about I guess six months to decide. I knew, and I discussed it with my parents. They met him and all was OK, and they agreed. Everybody liked him, and I moved here. (...) I feel I rather stay at home and build a family and do what my mother couldn't do. I have the option. I can stay home, and I can work, and I would rather build a family. I mean, if I have to, I will work. (...) It's hard in the US because there are people from all parts of the world, and I had a relationship that was not Greek, and I was not happy with that. I left it because it's hard to mix the two together and I wasn't happy with it and I wanted to follow my mom's, my parents' way and baptize the children a certain way and you have the holidays and all that, being religious, this religion thing. That's how I put Greece together. (...) One of the reasons in the US that I started working for a Greek company was for that reason, because I wanted to get back into the Greek community that I had lost, so I am in the process of doing that. (...) I don't know, I feel more Greek I guess. I started to learn all the name days; I never knew that before. It's very important here; they celebrate every other week someone's name day or a big holiday like May 1st. I didn't know that in the US. Religious, that was the main thing for me about being Greek. They are very religious, and they keep up...Easter and all that. It is very important. I feel that people here are more with their families; they take care of each other. Well that's how we are here. We were like that in the US, but they are different here.

The conscious decision to return to the 'motherland' is often articulated as a planned process of belonging. The terminology of 'losing' one's sense of 'Greekness' in the United States and 'finding' oneself in the ancestral homeland is quite repetitive in most narratives. This expresses self-awareness and a decisive personal plan of action planned ahead. Women returnees are in 'place'[5] as they construct and translate spatial constructs of nation and gender. In a very stimulating article, 'It's All in the Family: Intersections of Gender, Race, and Nation', Patricia Hill Collins decides, rather than examining gender, race, class and nation as distinctive social hierarchies, to utilise intersectionality as the means to examine how they mutually construct one another. She explores 'how the traditional family ideal functions as a privileged exemplar of intersectionality' and demonstrates 'specific connections between family as a gendered system of social organization, racial ideas and practices, as constructions of US national identity' (2000: 156). Family constitutes a fundamental principal of social space and organisation to the extent that social institutions and policies often exemplify family constructions and rhetoric.

The family is a major site of belonging and the source of other frameworks that assign meaning to groups through their aspirations and ideological oratory (Christou 2006b). The family unit is a central component of the female returnees' narratives of return. The *place* of family, and *placing* the family in a terrain of belongingness, assigns stability to the family unit. The women's identification processes are shaped by the notion of 'national space', that place which illuminates specific ways that the family can conserve its centrality and harmony within the space of national unity, that is, ethnic cohesion and religious homogeneity, national solidarity and common values. Hence collectivity and the sense of collective security underline the gendered return to a motherland where the 'mothering' of the land complements the mothers' journeying. Return migrants, the 'new nationals', are generating new versions of local spaces that produce cultural geographies of global spaces. The cultural consequences of displacement and dislocation through conscious relocation via return migration implies the relocation of hybridised cultural baggage and transformative roles. By emphasising their agency and shifting roles, such diasporic cultural production generates new spaces of motion and movement. Multiple cultural and ethnic sites[6] of convergence are mobilised through gendered interpretations of otherwise stable notions in search for stability. The production of interim spaces are those that need to be addressed because the narratives for a newly discovered belonging are the narratives of a nation in remaking, remarking and disembarking from a Greece that can no longer be found except in dusty shelves and grey memories, as discussed in Chapters four and five. This is what is meant when we discuss geographies of identities that refer to contested spatial dimensions of multiple processes of identity formation and affiliation to place (Radcliffe and Westwood 1996; Christou 2002).

The collective memory of national constructs creates, fuels and sustains a return-place not only of 're-membering' but also a home-place, a motherland construction where gendered lives of past and present inhabit the return space as signifying actors (Christou 2003c). The projected meaning of gendered definitions of becoming and being are national identifications, imperatives of ethnicity and gender that interact for a mutual construction of a gendered self (Christou 2003a). The self is simultaneously ethnicised and gendered while the return migratory project is a process that maintains a terrain of belonging (Christou 2003b). Multilocationality can exist in fixed places; the gendering process of identity that I have attempted to present in this section highlights the importance of considering both identity and home as a linked process always undergoing plural formations and transformations. It is possible for identity to be conceived as a point of arrival and more importantly as a point of departure, and this is illustrated by the in-betweenness of migrant identities (Christou 2006c). The gendering of diaspora can thus be understood on the heuristic level of analysis that considers the women as self-defined within their own 'diaspora community' and beyond transnational networks that extend across national borders. I find myself in complete agreement with Nelson in hoping that 'geographers stand to make important contributions to debates about the situatedness of the subject and the doing of identity... geographers can think through how to spatialize and historicize the creation and recreation of identity' (1999: 348-349). A starting point for a cartography of identity could be to map how individuals and/or collective subjects 'do identity' (identification performance) in relation to various discursive processes (e.g., class, race, gender and sexuality), to other subjects, and to layers of institutions and practices located concretely in time and space.

6.1.2 Networks, organisations

Recently, among the extensive commentary on globalisation and the decline of the nation-state, another discussion of a new postmodern era of politics as a post-national one has emerged (Hobsbawm 1990; Smith 1990; Bauman 1993). Moreover, in contrast with a bipolar vision of migrants as either sojourners or settlers with an identity that reflects either the place of birth or the host country, it is now apparent that migration is profoundly and fundamentally a transnational phenomenon (Mitchell 1997). So, instead of an 'either/or' understanding of movement and identity, it is necessary to look at how the 'sense of self' of contemporary migrants is most often characterised by a counteractive, hybrid identity.

Various ethnographies of transnationalism emphasise the subjective perspectives of migrancy and identity, demonstrating that identification is not bounded to a single geographic locality, but at the same time foregrounding the parochialism of transnational groups: migrants draw tighter bonds and boundaries around themselves, whether as ethnic groups, families, or citizens of a home country (McKeown 2001). However, geographic dispersal includes movement of social and cultural constructions. Transnational links are communicative social and ethnic networks and additional means by which identities are shaped. These types of relationships underscore how place is a social production and how local, national and international spaces are dynamic contexts in this process: 'The interlinking of scales between local, national and international communities destabilizes the static notions of place and shows that places and regions are not naturally bounded entities but rather are always in the process of being made – constituted in and through specific particularisms, and...through multiple understandings of "culture" and "nation"' (Mitchell 1997: 111; quotations in the original).

Theoretically oriented empirical studies of immigration that examine networks from a variety of frameworks have marked an energetic trajectory within migration studies in the past decade and have built bridges between the humanities and the social sciences (Christou 2004b). Networks have been examined and advanced as conceptual frameworks to investigate larger themes. To this end, old concepts have been analytically reshaped and new notions applied. It is not my intention here to provide a detailed literature review of such developments. Rather, I will commit to sketching the framework I have used, developed through a critical review of major conceptual perspectives and studies.

In broad terms, I would distinguish two major approaches in theoretical readings and empirical insights on networks that may be useful in migration research and, hence, in return migration research: 1) *societal constructions* of social networks that focus on the collectivity as understood through a social prism of 'home-host' categories and constructed within the collective sense of place and identity, and 2) *migrant constructions* of social networks that focus on the individual as 'active-actor' who shapes and is shaped by a 'politics of identity' within hybridised notions of belongingness. These broad distinctions integrate both structure and agency in the construction and comprehension of social networks in cases of return migration. The 'meso-level' approach helps to appreciate how structurationist perspectives may illuminate meta-migration formulations. In this sense, it becomes apparent that agents penetrate structures as much as structures saturate agents. Social and political fields may be used to explore how structures operate in the sense of everyday being and becoming. Thus a concrete argument can be advanced in relation to the formation of returning migrants' social networks: returnees' experiences and trajectories are highly embedded within socio-cultural constraints and possibilities that emerge either in opposition or in response to the local and national spaces and places of sending and receiving contexts that shape these networks. Social networks are stimulated by and stimulate national discourse. The importance of the local in understanding the translocal and the transnational cannot be emphasised enough. Methodologically, such explanations must distance themselves from individualist positions that attempt to explain social phenomena in terms of rational calculations made by solely self-interested individuals and from theoretical explanations that view social interaction as a social exchange modelled solely on economic actions, motivated by rewards and profits. Alternatively, collective action, social norms (i.e., trust, altruism, reciprocity, obligation, moral and ideological commitment) and the cultural politics of spatial constructions are necessary elements of a meso-level approach that goes beyond the structure/agency dichotomy. This approach must take into consideration place as 'an historically contingent process' (Pred 1985: 338) and the 'becoming of place as interwoven with individual biographies' (Pred quoted in Cloke, Philo and Sadler 1991: 117).

Paying attention to social interactions and social networks in the mundane and ordinary conversations of everyday life opens up new dialogues of how to conceptualise and analytically unveil the multiplicity of voices that articulate the social, the ethnic and the cultural in the national. Such explorations precipitate the *problematique* of social networks and return migration and serve as an alternative theoretical framework in so far as networks can be used as an exploratory tool in qualitative research in migration studies (Christou 2004b).

The analysis can be visualised as a schema that is composed of three distinct but overlapping circles: networks of migration (United States), networks of return migration (Greece), networks of the returnee/migrant. In this simple format, three basic constructions are interrelated as they interact: the 'home', the 'host' and the 'migrant'. The home could be the United States, but it could also be Greece. For the 'host' the same holds true. The 'migrant', forever a traveller and a sojourner, is as much a returnee as a migrant within, between and across 'home-host' constructs. The focal point is that migrants and returnees are connected; they establish, negotiate and produce distinct networks, which they also reconstruct, alter and reformulate as new spatio-temporal contexts permeate and impact on those relationships. Before I present those interrelationships and networks encountered in my research, I must emphasise once more the role of ethnic networks as an integral part of the Greek-American community in the diaspora, which I already presented in Chapter three. While the role of personal contact and interaction with members of the group is characterised as indispensable in the maintenance of ties and thus of ethnic identification (Christou 2001), satellite technology and new technologies such as the Internet and the use of electronic communication play a role not only in strengthening contacts (Constantinou 2002; Christou 2004b) but most importantly in constructing new patterns of networks and in shaping the content of those networks.

The term *networks*, as used in my study, refers not only to the 'official', that is, organised system or activity that forms a society, association or organisation within the Greek-American community, but also to the 'unofficial', that is, those that do not necessarily require a membership screening, application and fee, those that may take place in private spaces in addition to public spaces, and which may not necessarily require physical contact – that is, they could be virtual communities, and therefore anonymity could also be preserved. There could be a clear agenda of action or simply action that could be decoded as an ultimate agenda. This ultimate agenda interpreted throughout the fieldwork research constitutes those variables that negotiate, contest, question and construct the 'ethnic' component of the network group.

Norms of trust, obligation, and reciprocity are the crux of networks and are established through membership in social networks (Portes 1995; Light and Gold 2000; Marger 2001). Social networks influence ethnic groups in both 'home' and 'host' contexts. Such networks may influence immigration decisions, settlement patterns, and social incorporation (Elliot 1997). They provide support systems, assistance, information and psychological security, if not financial. All this, of course, is well known and widely researched. I want to focus, however, on return migrant networks and the substance behind 'official' and 'unofficial' networks that develop during the return settlement process. The 'official' networks have been presented in Chapter three. Here, I would like to discuss the 'unofficial' ones. A prime example is the use of cyber networks that have a communicative, social and ethnic component. The basic observations worth focusing on can be summarised as follows:

Although 'actor-network theory' (Callon 1986a, 1986b; Latour 1987, 1988; Law 1988, 1991) found its place in the sociology of science and technology, it can be useful in that it resembles Erving Goffman's (1969) symbolic interactionist answer that human beings have bodies but also inner lives; social agents are never located in bodies alone, but rather an actor is a patterned network of heterogeneous relations, hence the term actor-network – an actor is always a network as well. This poses a challenging path of inquiry between the pragmatic or imagined 'homogeneity' of ethnic groups that act also as 'ethnic' networks and the 'heterogeneity' of voices and practices shaped by a continuum of relations among the migrant-actor and the 'home-host' constructs. In this respect, 'actor-network theory' treats structures as sites of struggle, in common with several other contemporary social theories: Elias' theory of 'figuration' (1978), Giddens' notion of 'structuration' (1984) and Bourdieu's concept of 'habitus' (1989).

Secondly, there is the assertion by social scientists and philosophers who sustain that virtual networking is solely a representation of a synthetic world artificially created by technology. More specifically, they claim that in these groups, 'there is the invocation of community, but not the production of a society. There is a "groupmind", but not a social encounter....This is another synthetic world, and here, too, history is frozen' (Robins 1995: 150). This poses another challenging question insofar as 'history' is not frozen but constructed, negotiated and actively contested in the spatial context of networks.

Finally, we can point to the sociality of enclaved social spaces constructed in opposition to place and the recent views on the sociality of the numerous 'parallel' social tribes[7] that never fully meet each other.

Interaction between different actors where structures are questioned or defended no longer takes 'place' in 'authentic' surroundings. This can be meaningfully deciphered when we explore the spatio-temporal construction of public and private notions of space and interaction. Furthermore, new media information and communication technologies (ICTs) should not be taken at face value by diaspora consumers since access to media varies due to significantly differentiated experiences that diaspora members have based on their gender, generation, age and class (Panagakos 2006a).

Here, I would like to argue that the emergence of 'official' forms of return migrant networks constitutes reproductions of national representations. At the same time, these networks have by their core establishment stimulated altered responses and a fresh critique as an alternative discourse to nationalist and xenophobic reactions. This was one of the main explanations offered by participants in the study of why they refuse to enter such groups and have alternatively considered forming their own without an official character to it. Even with such local associations that had a gender perspective (e.g., women only), the critique was even fiercer, as my 20-40 year-old female returnees made clear when emphasising (to quote one of them): 'They are only interested in exchanging recipes over coffee and cake, talking about how wonderful their kids are and gossiping about others; besides, they are all my mother's and my grandmother's age'. The mobility of these women is a shifting in locations and identities. The reality of women's lives goes beyond simple dichotomies; it is a reality embedded in active engagement with subjecthood, identity and social transformations (Radcliffe 1993: 103). Theoretical spaces need to be explored, mapped, and contested while individuals are constantly on the move. Critical scrutiny is necessary for spatial conceptions that illustrate positionality, displacement, territory, locality and grounding. The autonomy of the gendered self, the women's self-agency, is contingent upon their individual capacity to produce meanings and to organise their activities as self-conscious expressions of daily and life practices, as clearly illustrated in the female returnees' extracts in the previous subsection.

The case of a cyber-networking group is a virtual diaspora community[8] of second-generation return migrants that accentuates the construction of the 'ethnic' component of identification as it transcends the simplistic communicative aspect of the new technologies and questions socio-political spaces. A prime example of this is the series of reactions in both 'home' and 'host' countries in response to the war in Iraq in 2003. From personal, phone and electronic conversations I had with informants, it became clear that despite intense anti-Americanism and anti-war sentiments in Greece, the majority of second-generation Greek-American return migrants had 'identified' with Greek mainstream political positioning. Some of them were appalled with some of the electronic communications they had with 'Greek-Greeks' in the United States who had adopted a pro-war perspective rationalised through argumentation of combating terrorism, thus identifying the war as a war against terrorism. Alternatively, other electronic communications with second-generation Greek-Americans permanently residing in the United States and with no intention to relocate, signified a mid-range apathy and indifference to world events but an intense concern with domestic security and personal safety on multiple levels (physical, professional, etc.).

The symbolic and pragmatic action plan of the 'official' organisations, ranging from national celebrations to fund-raising, presents itself as a transplantation of 'Greek-American' networking practices and practicalities whereas the existence of a hybridised, critical space created by returnee members of the second generation highlights the dynamic between the 'active-actor' (return migrant as agent) and the 'passive-structure' (constructions of national discourse in networks). Another point of departure that is illuminated is the generational gap that exists in the case of return networks. Surrounding all these dynamics is of course the social, political and historical context of the homeland structure in an era of developments as well as crises and conflicts. To sum up, the construction and ambivalence of the 'ethnic' component in networks, the generational gaps that seem to exist and the overall socio-political and historical circumstances of 'homeland' and 'hostland' contexts are all important features of return migrant networks.

The terminology of 'systems' has faded away since the 1950s and 1960s, but we are constantly told that we live in a 'network society' (Castells 1996). What we need to further explore is how these two components of Castells' vision interact and (re)produce themselves. Return migrant networks pose challenges in understanding contemporary transformations of social relations, cultural fields, etc. The argument is that society is a network of networks, consisting of processes involving individuals, the material world and symbolic elements, all networked with each other and the social environment. In this realm, we can examine how cohesive those components are and what the consequences of those dynamics of connections are for social outcomes and the study of return migration. Moreover, virtual ethnography (Hine 2000) leads us to rethink traditional ways of studying 'networks', 'culture', 'society' and 'migratory projects'.

At the core of the argument suggested in this section is that individual migrants as actors and collective subjectivities should be explored as dynamics in a context of interactive settings that include those selfsame dynamic relations. Social life is not static, but it is not completely fluid either. As Domingues suggests, 'The actual possibilities given in the concrete situations in which individuals and collectivities find themselves entangled must not be neglected either' (2000: 39). This kind of awareness may help us understand networks in a way that would avoid the pitfalls of essentialism while unveiling new transformations.

6.1.3   Immigration, ethnicity

The label 'The Balkans' inherently shares a kind of essentialism – it is a geographical identification, presupposing the existence of non-geographical characteristics. This is a self-evident, unquestionable presumption: the usage of the name points out that the Balkans exists as a region with certain common features, perhaps historical, cultural, and political, which establish a certain 'identity'. However, we need to enquire about the uncertain and dynamic relations between names, territorial landscapes, borders, social groups, individuals and identities.

There is a certain amount of ambivalence when we presuppose a specific Balkan existence. On the one hand, it claims that there are cultural and political characteristics localised on a territorial landscape, which could be described by a list of common features: religion, language, historical background and narratives, patterns of behaviour, everyday practices and rituals, political and economic traditions, works of art and literature, forms of imagination and other cultural expressions.

In the Balkans, there is an enormous reliance on and reference to the past as history glorified; recent events testify to how explosive and dangerous this is, but it is no less a means of legitimisation for the state. In 'Imagining the Nation' while 'Imagining the Balkans', we are confronted with many illusive (and elusive!) notions of self and other, insofar as the otherness is a reflection of the self. The Balkans cannot be illuminated enough; the construction of a Balkan identity and the 'balkanisation' of peoples of the region is the writing of history. To historicise the interactiveness of structures and agency is to locate the self in the context of socio-historical processes. This is even more comprehensible when we consider that 'history became each nation's search to locate the unique home from which the (national) "we" *comes* – the search to find *the first homeland* to which "we" will *return*' (Murphy 1998: 392; italics and quotes in the original).

Greece is the nucleus of much uniqueness and ambiguity for many reasons, not least its cultural and human personality and its historical and geographic setting. Both Balkan and Mediterranean, having access to the west by sea and sojourning, burdened by antiquity, an Orthodox Christianity and Ottoman rule, Greece was the first 'east' European country to have full independence in 1830 and in 1981 became the first to achieve membership of the European Community as its tenth member – although to this day, aside from the perceived economic and political benefits of accession, her 'Europeanness' and the country's identity as a European country are uncertain (Clogg 2002). This is precisely what one of the participants, Diomides, clearly described in Chapter four when he spoke about Greece's European, Eastern European and Middle Eastern side. It is also what Aristotle talks about below:

> Well, unlike other European countries, Greece...is in a very, very peculiar position. It's in the middle of three continents, you can say. (...) And I guess Greek people... traditionally, Greek people are very hospitable but very cultural. I wouldn't say closed but very traditional compared to other ethnic backgrounds. (...) I think even though we changed a lot since ancient times, we still carry the genes. We still have a lot of aspects of our ancestors. I think that Greece is not on a good track; I think there is a need for a lot of improvement. I think the 400 years of occupation from the Ottoman Turks have done more damage than people realize. I think Greece missing the Renaissance has really played a major role in its change of the culture. But I also think that the Greek spirit lives, and it lived throughout the Ottoman occupation, and it lived through a lot of hardships, and it will keep going, I think so. If we survived that, we can pretty much survive anything. A lot of people say that Greeks have to change now with the euro, and a friend of mine made a joke one day. He's like 'If you expect Greeks to change, forget it. It is most likely that the Europeans will change than the Greeks!' We are more traditional, I guess, and they are very passionate plus Greek people are very caring. I see that. They are very caring with each other, and they pretty much care about the rest of world too. I see it. (...) Of course, it's one of the first civilizations. Imagine what Europe would be without the Greek background, what Rome would be without the Greek background. The whole foundation started in Greece. Imagine if Europe hadn't followed the basic ideas of ancient Greece, and they had followed the basic ideas of, I don't know, the Assyrians, or the Indians or other cultures back in those days, what would Europe be? Of course I am proud. I am proud, but of course I am not happy that we haven't kept up with our ancestors with our responsibilities to our ancestors and a lot of Europeans see us as a country that is nice for a vacation and not much more. I expect Greece to be a little more active than that, but, yes, I am proud to be Greek. (...) So I think that's when it really comes out; given the chance, that's when I really think... again I can go back to the mingling with

other cultures besides the Greek. Again if it was just European culture, there would be no problem. Again I go back to that point if we were part of the Renaissance.... Again I go back to that point; we really wouldn't have any problems; the Greek culture would flourish, but for the Ottoman Turks, again I say it, I think the damage is far greater than people realize.

The issues presented above are all spaces of inbetweenness and hybridity as they relate to questions of identity and the constitution of subjectivity. In the previous narrative, the pride emanating from classical Greece is juxtaposed against a 'debilitating' Ottoman occupation. The 'greatness' of Greece is positioned against an epoch of 'decline' as the Greek subject is placed in opposition to the Ottoman 'other'. Reactive to this historical context is a passionate intent in showing that classical Greek civilization was the foundation of European culture and that contemporary Greek culture is directly descended from ancient Greece (Papanikolas 2002: 47). Although being descendents of the ancient Greeks fosters an ingrained sense of pride, this does not eliminate a critical stance for the neohellenic present circumstances of life in Greece. In the following extracts, we recognise the production of multiple identities where an interrelationship exists between history, tradition and multipart cultural forms:

> My identity as an outcome of my ethnicity is my own personal tool-kit, even a medicine cabinet, I can always reach out and fix things broken, mend those torn, glue those shattered, heal the wounds and eventually fill the glass that is constantly left half empty. It's my dictionary and literally my thesaurus. I feel a sense of wealth, the only wealth I experienced unbound, no losses, only gains. I feel such a great sense of pride in being Greek, for many reasons, the Greeks have made such huge contributions, our ancestors have offered so much to western civilization. Looking back is such a source of pride and inspiration for the future. (...) The Greek-Americans have the best of both worlds. The American life and the Greek heritage. This is both a blessing and a curse. When I moved to Greece I felt I had come home. I am infatuated with my Greek roots, the Greek spirit, the wealth of heart and spirit, the love of life and family and friends. But it is also a grand responsibility and a huge confusion to have to live in-between two worlds and to have to bridge the many gaps. (Hector, male, 36)

The sense of confusion that stems from having to bridge the manifold conspicuous or concealed disparities between two cultural worlds escalates when participants want to live a 'Greek-American' life in a Greece

that no longer corresponds to their imagined constructions of the ancestral homeland. Prior to their relocation, it is exactly that yearning
for 'Greekness' in their 'American' life that stimulates an inner need to
be immersed in the cultural context of a Hellenic lifeworld in the United States. Nevertheless, the returnees' plan for relocation to the ancestral homeland seems to be connected to their parents' longing for a
homeland return.

> *From the first couple of trips to Greece, when I was in elementary
> school and then on every summer, and sometimes during Easter, it
> made me want to identify more with my Greek side than the Ameri-
> can. I started reading more on Greece, Greek history, Greek literature
> and Greek Orthodoxy. I wanted to become fluent not only in modern
> Greek but also ancient Greek. I started listening to Greek music and
> learning Greek dances. I wanted to do just Greek things. My first
> couple of years at University were hard and lonely, I didn't meet any
> new friends there, I tried associating with Americans since there were
> no Greek-Americans in that part of the country and then as I was
> getting real miserable and depressed and ready to transfer to a school
> in my hometown, I then came across a bunch of graduate students, I
> was an undergrad at the time, all Greek-Greeks who were planning
> to form a 'Hellenic' social club. I was ecstatic, that was fantastic. Of
> course I changed my mind about transferring since I could now ex-
> perience Greekness with Greek-Greeks. I no longer felt out of place
> with that real connection with Greek culture. Sharing that unique
> bond and sharing stories, practicing my Greek, learning more about
> daily life in Greece, customs, traditions and lifestyle in the country of
> my heritage was the first intense stimulus to consider moving to
> Greece. I then started contemplating the dream of my parents, the
> one they hadn't achieved, to move back to their homeland. Just the
> idea only felt like home. My parents' understanding and support in
> this was the most precious gift they could offer. (Achilles, male, 33)

There appears to be an intense need to belong to a community and to
be bound by an ethnic container, a *topos* that will energise an otherwise
diluted identity split between two cultural worlds. Despite the overpow-
ering cultural confines, nostalgia for the homeland is a 'wound that
will not heal' (Papanikolas 2002: 249). Along with the values, customs
and traditions that exemplify 'Greekness', the children of immigrants
are incessantly directed to relentlessly endorse and preserve the Greek
culture, and in doing so, the parents' anguish of return is vibrantly present. Second generation relocation is the ultimate justification of this
struggle.

6.1.4 Memory, global events

Although individual memory is seen as a person's capacity to store and retrieve information and thus as a physiological and psychological function, memory is information processing, and the processes of remembering and forgetting are social (Christou 2003c). According to Evanthia Lyons, the social nature of memory is a threefold expression: firstly, the recollection of information is not a simple passive retrieval of an image stored in an individual's mind; rather, recollection is an active process of reconstruction. Secondly, remembering can take place collectively, either through conversation or in public commemorative ceremonies and rituals. Thirdly, the functions of these processes are social. Personal and social memories enable a person to construct their identity, to make sense of present events and to act in an intelligible manner. Most theories of the self and identity are indeed based on the assumption that people have the capacity to remember and to reconstruct information (1996: 32). Nevertheless, the production of ethnic memories does not entail a single process of identification and therefore should be analysed at specific intersections of racial, class, gender and ideological locations (Christou 2003c; Anagnostou 2004).

In examining the manner that ethnic forgetting and how the politics of memory is associated with the construction of an 'American Hellenic' identity, Anagnostou points to the ideological manipulation of ethnicity in order to serve dominant class interests, and these type of narratives are expressive of Greek-American assimilation that reproduces an ideology of America as a benevolent, egalitarian nation (2004: 27). Hence, immigrant forgetting is not simply an effect of nationalist discourse but a class-based strategic manoeuvring and an instrument of inclusive legitimisation. Specifically, ethnic amnesia becomes an autonomous choice and a strategic plan of belongingness. Anagnostou illustrates the narrative of cultural assimilation as follows: 'to forget means to habituate oneself into mainstream practices, to acquire the knowledge and cultural competence to embody and perform the newly fashioned self. Not uncommonly, this kind of cultural transformation is perceived as a deeply felt conversion experience, a liberating rebirth' (2004: 28). In this respect, the national and ethnic subject enters a subjective process that validates one's sense of belonging as a legitimating procedure that simultaneously entails conformity to the dominant socio-cultural and political establishment.

Remembrance in return migration is all about social dynamics and cultural imprints. It is about reprocessing cultural elements of the past, reshaping places and inevitably redefining selfhood in (return) migranthood. The processes of remembrance create spaces of connectedness and spaces of belonging: spaces of belonging are meaningful insofar as they are inhabited by '*living* memories' (Fortier 2000: 173; italics in the original), and the motions of re-membering are more about interconnectedness than simple reproduction or imitation (Braidotti 1994: 5). Furthermore, the rubric of 'migrant belongingness', which involves processes of (re)creating memories of place, culture and history, is deemed central to the definition and duration of identities because, as Fortier explains, 'memory becomes a primary ground of identity formation in the context of migration, where "territory" is decentred and exploded into multiple settings' (2000: 157).

The significance of memories in the construction of individual migrant and ethnic community identities has been attested by studies (Thomson 1999), highlighting the dialectical relationship between memory and identity. More specifically, 'our current identity (or "identities", a term which better expresses the multiple, fractured and dynamic nature of identity) affects how we structure, articulate and indeed remember the story of our life. The experience of migration...presents...an urgent need for...the construction of coherent identities and life stories' (Thomson 1999: 35). In the following excerpts, I focus on the most acute of processes of disjuncture and trauma, the events of September 11th 2001 as experienced by second-generation Greek-American returnees in the homeland. This is illuminated in the way returnees cope with homeland perceptions in their own diasporic terms and through what Basu calls 'networks of *sites of memory, sources of identity* and *shrines of self*' (2001: 338; italics in the original).

The post September 11th era as a 'new world order' is also characterised by much disorder in the global realm. Undoubtedly, Europe is in the forefront of several challenges and projects in achieving a transcultural and transnational civil society at *no risk* (Christou 2004a). Manolis Vasilakis' book, "*Καλά να πάθουνε!*" *Η ελληνική κοινή γνώμη μετά την 11η Σεπτεμβρίου* (2002), is quite relevant as an introductory remark to this section. It is difficult to provide a precise translation of the first part of the title; a free translation could have the following alternatives: 'Good that they suffered', 'Well-deserved', 'They had it coming to them', etc. The subtitle, which reads 'The Greek public opinion after September 11th', is easier to translate.

The book presents the reactions of Greek society after the events of September 11th, 2001. According to some of the introductory commentary provided by Stefanos Manos (former Minister of the National Economy and former Leader of the Liberal Party who is now an independent member of Parliament), the book's major usefulness is explained by its potential to show the bigger picture since it has gathered all the smaller pieces of the puzzle, mainly exemplifying that Greek society is deeply anti-Western but pro-Western politically when it can gain something from the West. But emotionally, it feels foreign towards the West; a society that is cynical and blames all others of being cynical. Moreover, Manos states the book's other major contribution is that it does not sweep under the rug what others have said or written in the media (journalists, politicians, academics, businesspersons, etc. in Greece and excerpts of reactions from Greek-Americans in the United States). The book mostly created turmoil rather than stimulate real discussion. Contrary to expectation, it was positively received by the majority of the participants in my study who considered it 'a courageous attempt' to discuss the issue.

The author begins his introduction to the book with a list of the names of 49 Greek-Americans confirmed to have perished during the events of 9/11. The final 'official' number had not, by the date of publication, been confirmed, he mentions, but in any case, numbers and ethnic origin could not make the event less tragic as any event (be it terrorism, war, genocide, accident) that takes away life and spreads disaster and devastation. The author ends his introduction with a quote from a poem by Lord Byron: 'For what is left [for] the poet hear;/For Greeks a blush, for Greece a tear', commenting that since these lines were written by Lord Byron, there is neither tear nor blush of shame or respect here any longer. It is not my intention here to debate, condemn or support either side of the issue. The attention given is to once again situate the point of discussion in the frame of 'home-host' constructions and media conversations in both countries on both sides. Vasilakis' book is above all a collection of media excerpts of Greeks (and Greek-Americans) on 9/11. If anything, it is a source, even if it is just excerpts from articles or newspaper cartoons. Additionally, *The National Herald* (Greek-American daily newspaper established in 1915 with offices in New York and Athens) held a special report on the events of 9/11 a year later (September 14-15, 2002 issue), participating in the general atmosphere of mourning and remembrance in the first commemoration of the 'black' anniversary.

In terms of the participants in the study, their narrativisation of the events is 'grounded' in the socio-cultural context of Greece as they experienced local reactions in everyday encounters with Greeks. Some of the most powerful narratives on the multifarious feelings in relation to 9/11 are as follows:

> I am animated and feisty. (...) Greek-Americans are abused here. In the post-September 11th environment, I felt radically disgusted by what these people are... totally given up on them... after September 11th, that's it; they are barbarians. I think there is a particular anti-American sentiment here. Yes. Absolutely. They don't like Americans; most of them don't even know why they don't like Americans. They are too stupid to figure it out,

but they just learned it from their parents. The first thing that I was told by my boss was, 'Too bad they couldn't catch the guilty parties', and then somebody told me Americans deserved it. (...) No dignity, no pride, no sense of purpose, nothing, nothing, but if you look at *Karagiozi* and what that is about, it's a national figure, very much the Greeks pride themselves in this cunning; they see this cunning as it has developed since Sparta, and the idea of organized theft is being part of the training of being adult. In reality, it's all about *Tourkokratia* as the Turkish influence is called. (...) They are corrupt to the bone; dignity is a key word, nothing, none of that, and because of that, they are fundamentally limited, and they don't realize the importance of dignity. They are fundamentally limited (...) handicap; it's as if they are limited in that way. It is very sad in a way. It's as if they underwent child beating, and they are handicapped. They are morally unable to deal with reality. They cannot imagine a world in which there is structure and organization and they are accountable for what they have to do, and because of that, they cannot survive in the real world, and because of that, (...) they can't get their act together. They basically can't. They are unable to do so. Can we stop this? (Sophocles, male, 28)

The participant became very emotional with the discussion, which he wanted to continue with the tape-recorder turned off. As his narrative developed, so did his rage and pain. Sophocles reiterated the tragedy of 9/11 with the traumatic after effects of Greek reactions to the events. Some of the female returnees had the same feelings about experiencing the post-September 11th atmosphere in Greece:

Like nothing is very secure anymore. I used to go to the subway and think nothing is going to happen in the States; nothing will happen in New York. (...) I used to work by the Twin Towers, and it was the most secure place for me. I think the bombing that happened in '92 was very bad. (...) How could that happen? I never expected something like this to happen, and I feel guilty that I left, and it happened. I have encountered anti-Americanism here in Greece. Yes. When that happened, first of all, I was very shocked, and I was very concerned about my relatives there because some of my cousins used to work by there, so I started calling New York, and of course all the lines were down, and I was going crazy, and I heard this co-worker say, 'Oh, wow', and stuff like that. They didn't believe it; they say stuff they didn't believe. I got into a huge fight, and in the end, I was all right. You are right, but I got this feeling that they were a little bit, most of the Greeks, anti-American. I don't think they were anti-American with the people. I think they were mostly with the government. They just said, because most of my co-workers knew that I used to work there, I would ask them, 'Would you be happy if I was there?', and they got scared. They said. 'Oh my God, we didn't mean anything like that'. So you could tell they didn't really think about it when they were saying stuff. (Phaedra, female, 27)

Both Sophocles and Phaedra describe encounters they had with their colleagues in Greece in their place of employment and perceived their attitudes on a level of anti-Americanism that mostly stems from hostility directed toward American governmental policy. Heated accusations against the United States for supporting the Colonels in imposing a junta and the ruthless authoritarianism of the seven-year dictatorship in Greece (1967-1974) and for CIA involvement in Greece has long ago activated an on-going sense of anti-Americanism (Papanikolas 2002: 256). For the participants, the intensity and duration of such an accusation seems incomprehensible and another thorny issue in their adjustment process that nonetheless strengthens their 'Americanness':

I was born in the States, and I think, you know, America is a wonderful country. It provides lots of opportunities, and I think anyone, where they are born, they have a strong tie to that place. Especially I realized that when 9/11 happened. I was very devastated. I was very upset. (...) I got very patriotic. Being here in Greece, it was very hard because there wasn't any understanding. I mean, because of anti-American sentiment, there wasn't a big understanding. People were not so upset about that. I mean, of course many people were devastated as well, but, you know, I had cab drivers tell me, *Kala na pathoune. Oi Amerikanoi pirane epitelous afto pou eprepe'* (Good that they suffered. The Americans finally got what they deserved), and I got very upset and very defensive, and it made me realize that I am mostly truly proud to be American. (Medusa, female, 21)

On the other hand, there were participants who adopted a less emotional stance and rationalised the events of September 11th, thus reflecting a more 'hybridised' perspective of both sides:

The thing is that I have the mentality of both worlds, which is very important. I can think like an American and a Greek. I know when Greeks are thinking and talking and behaving in a sarcastic way and things like that. I can relate with them; I can relate to the fears they've got. I think I can relate to feelings about anything that is an injustice because Greeks talk about things that are an injustice and things like that. But I can also relate to the American way of thinking. Greeks say, 'Why do the Israelis go into Palestine?', right, and 'Why are they killing Palestinians?' and this and that, but also you have to think, 'Why do the Israelis have to walk on the streets with the fear for their lives?' They go out, and the next minute they don't know if they are going to go back home. That is nasty stuff you know. So I can relate with both mentalities. (...) In regards to September 11th, again, I saw things from two perspectives. I saw first level, one, the American perspective, which was devastation, and I was extremely saddened, depressed and very worried about the people in New York because, like I said again, I love the US, especially I love New York, and it really touched me when this happened, but first, I was against anything anti-American in New York. In Greece you will find a lot of this sentiment. But I also saw another side, the Greek side: wait a minute; you guys are not seeing what the hell is going on outside New York. Not that you had this coming, but you only look after your own interests, and it is good for a country to look after its own interests but not at the expense of others. I think that is the sentiment here. The sentiment is not that you care only about yourself, and you don't care about anybody else, that you care about yourself at the expense of others. (...) I think it also plays a role on how countries think about super giants, super power. Everybody is against the big guy. Nobody likes the big guy. I think that mentality is also here a lot. They expect the US to be more fair. They expect the US as a superpower to be the mediator, to be the referee. Of course, the US is not going to do that; it is only going to do that selectively. It is going to do that only in areas that it has interest. It doesn't care what is right and what is wrong. It cares only if it is to its own interest. So I guess that is what people don't like. (Aristotle, male, 30)

There is something I want to say about September 11th. That bothered me because everybody in Greece kept interrogating the US, whatever, that they deserved it. I see now, I saw in the news. Maybe, they have a point, but in the US, it is a closed culture. I don't know how to describe it. You know about the rules, but I guess they were not as educated because I see here everybody is more educated. They know more about other countries, what is going on. Maybe they did not inform us the right way or something. (Hestia, female, 28)

September 11th, I must tell you that we felt here that it also hit here because it had to do with everybody and a lot of nationalities. I must tell you that there were a lot of people here who said, 'Well, they had it coming to them', but really deep down, I don't think they felt that. There were a lot of people from many countries involved. A lot of Greeks were involved. It really got them to start thinking. They started thinking that this could happen anywhere in the world. This could happen to us, and the Greek people, especially the older generation, started thinking differently, so I really think there is a purpose to everything. I know a lot of people left us, but it made the world think a little bit differently, so there is always something positive that comes out from something very, very, negative. I think it brought everybody together, especially in Europe. (Kalypso, female, 41)

Various layers and degrees of anti-Americanism by and large have dominated general public opinion in Greece, at least in everyday 'conversations', notwithstanding a radical shift in everyday practices that resonate with 'Americanised' behaviours of a lifestyle of consumption, as discussed in previous chapters and thoroughly depicted by some of the returnees' narratives. Deep-seated scepticism about American values and principles can be viewed as an ethnicised positioning firmly anchored in a context of power relations expressive of a particular dialectic of pervasive efforts to consolidate past Hellenic glory with present disgrace in an array of public scandals in the Greek government and the Greek Orthodox Church. The participants' statements epitomise an effort to rationalise this incommensurability of cultural ideals on a symbolic and moralistic level. The explosive ideological circumstances in the post September 11th, 2001 porous global environment call for a reconsideration of cultural spatialities. Primarily because 'in America in 11 September 2001, as the New York twin towers collapsed, new cultural borders were erected and borders closed around the United States' (Leontidou 2001; 2004). Returnees' narrations depict these open and closed cultural spaces, that is, the borders they stumble upon and those that they themselves construct.

6.2 'Transhybrid' identities: transformations and transitions within traditions

What is striking about social life is the extent to which an individual takes part in socio-cultural experiences and thus engages in actions whose subject-substance is not the individual but the group. In this way the collectivity is represented. A collective experience is not a representation of social relations in an 'idealistic-abstract' way but a reflection of 'temporalised' and 'spatialised' interactive events. The articulation of the group's identity through telling and retelling its 'story' explains the role of memory, history and narrative as a heuristic device that gives meaning to a community. We make sense of life by telling stories of our selves to ourselves and to others. So the collective is intertwined with the individual, and both are important in understanding social life. As Bourdieu instructs:

> Trying to understand a life as a unique and self-sufficient series of successive events (sufficient unto itself), and without ties other than the association to a "subject" whose constancy is probably just that of a proper name, is nearly as absurd as trying to make sense out of a subway route without taking into account the network structure, that is the matrix of objective relations between the different stations (2000: 302).

Hence, clearly, we need to take into consideration the collectivity as a matrix of socio-cultural relations and the return migrant as the 'active-agent' immersed within those interactions.

This chapter is slightly different from the other two previous empirical chapters where the material from the fieldwork study (the oral and written narratives) is presented, analysed and contextualised within the context of the theoretical debate. This section contains slightly longer and more extensive extracts from the participants' oral and written narratives. The reason for this is that this chapter exemplifies the core themes of my theoretical framework, namely the discussion on identities and identification, which is the essence of the study. In line with the methodological parameters set out in the study, there are no intervening comments of my own in this section on 'transhybrid identities'. This is in order to allow the voices of the returnees to directly communicate their views and feelings concerning identity. My methodological approach encourages the readers' comprehension of those experiences in connection with the storied lives of the participants to be an illumination of identifications in return migration through the use of the participants' own voices. In the concluding sections, I will provide an overview of a typology of identification that has emerged from the narratives. Therefore, here are some of the most powerful explanations of the formation of transhybrid identities in return migration:

> There are times, and I am sure you feel the same way, and other people might have told you the same thing: I feel like a split personality. (...) I understand both cultures very well. If I could have my way, I would live half the year, six months in the United

States and six months in Greece. Unfortunately, I can't do it because of my job, but it does give me opportunities to go back to the United States for business, conferences. I get my chance to go to the States, but most of the time I'm here. (...) Both places, no, both places are home for me. (...) It's what I said, split personality. I really don't feel Greek, and I really don't feel American anymore. When I'm back in the States, I feel American. I get it back. The longer I stay, the more I get back that feeling. Here, because I associate with a lot of Greek people, (...) usually because of my job, I try to get into their frame of mind. I try to understand them. I feel closer, I guess, in that respect, I feel more Greek because of that. My ethnicity... Quite few of my traits I acquired from my family, (...) so I owe a lot to my family, just as I suppose I owe a lot to both countries... (...) It's very difficult to pinpoint that feeling; it's very difficult. Sometimes I feel I have never clarified that with myself. Did you ever feel that way? That it's a decision that is still pending, that I will have to make that decision at some point. For a number of years, I kept feeling ok. This is not the end of the world, and maybe that's how I made my decision. (...) And maybe that's what helped me cope with the situation a little bit better. (...) And probably in the beginning, that's how I felt. Maybe I am contradicting myself here, but it is a contradiction in many ways. (...) You discover your strengths, your weaknesses. I think you become a better person, or at least I think I have become a better person with all the experiences that I have. (...) I don't detest this split, schizophrenic, two-country thing. No, no at all; it's a part of who I am. That's who I am, and I am proud of that. I am proud to be a split personality. I think I got the best of these two worlds. I had the best time in the United States, wonderful friends, wonderful education; I really enjoyed myself. I have so many fond memories. Maybe I did have bad experiences, but I don't remember. I chose to forget them, but I do not try to recall bad experiences, never, on the contrary. I had quite a few here. (...) It's quite obvious that I would have some bad experiences, and these bad experiences don't have to do with people. They have to do with life's difficulties, my mother's death, my father's illnesses because he has been in and out of the hospitals a number of times the last couple of years which would've happened in the States, too. No, I don't regret it at all, not any of it, not any of it. I think that it's what I told you before. It's all of that which has made me a better person, and it has made me grow faster. (...) Nothing is problematic. I am still living as a hyphenated person, and that's ok with me. It gives me a sense of balance. I've accepted that, I told you; I don't have any regret; that's who I am. (Iphigenia, female, 50)

It's very difficult for me, very difficult; sometimes in the beginning, I really didn't know where I was from. Someone would ask me in the beginning where I am from, born and raised in America, Greek parents, what does that mean? I feel that America and Greece, very special to me of course, but Greece somehow comes up. When I'm here, though, I feel American. When I am in America, I feel everything, Greek and American, because that's where it started. It's very difficult, a very difficult question, and it's a very mind-boggling one, and I don't know. That's all I can say on that. I can't go any further on that. That's where it stops right there. (...) It affected positive, not negative, no. You feel like you are from two different worlds. (...) But no, I can understand people easier. That's what it has done. I can understand people a lot easier. I'm not one-sided as I see a lot of people who were born and raised in one country. I can understand people here; I can understand the way people feel there, so it helps you but it helps others too. I guess in a way, maybe I don't realize it. You know my background, culture, it really played a part in bringing me back. Maybe it does play a part why I feel so good here... It was all of what I expected. I was never disappointed, never, at all. If I had problems, they would just solve themselves so that made it a lot more easier for me to stay here. But it was what I dreamed of, what I felt it was going to be. It's like I had a dream, and I knew this is what it was going to be. (...) Those feelings of sometimes being split between both worlds and that schizophrenic state of being, I like that, I like that. I like being bits and parts of everything because it wasn't monotonous; you had a little window here and a little window there, so you had a bigger view, right, instead of having one window and seeing the same thing over and over again, so it was a variety of things. I thought myself lucky, yes. (...) A view of the past, a view of the future, that's what I think I see when I look at it. I think I've come into the past because this country has a lot to offer from the past which I didn't know of. I've been to the future, which the United States has offered me, and I can balance things out. So that's what it has given me, a sense of balance, especially in my personal life and with relationships with other people, a balance which I don't think I would've had that if I didn't have this experience. (Kalypso, female, 41)

Unfortunately today I am trapped in a dual situation: as far as the Americans are concerned I am a Greek, while as far as the Greeks are concerned I am a person with strong American characteristics. The funny part, however, is that I am not aware of my American or Greek characteristics. I guess this is what makes me a Greek-American. Being a Greek for me means my heritage, the land where my grandfathers walked. It is always connected to my father's dream to come back. Being an American at the same time, means memories from my childhood, the land that gave my family an opportunity to achieve something, and the key that enabled us to have a better life. (Kallisto, female, 21)

After living there for a couple of years, I saw the differences between Greeks, Americans and Greek-Americans. The Greek-Americans living in the States are open-minded in a few factors, but in others, they are still in the mentality of the old village back in Greece in the 50s, and that's how they raise their kids. I loved living in the States, but I also love living in Greece. Personally, I am still in a confusing state. (...) I see from my own eyes many Greek-Americans complaining, for example my family here sometimes says why we moved back and so on. For me it is a privilege to have two identities because it opens my mind almost about everything. I have experienced things in two different views. In the States, I don' t think there is any discrimination to a point that it is a problem to the Greeks because it is a huge country, but in Greece people tend to see Greek-Americans in a different view. I believe in the States the Greeks are more ethnically fanatic because they miss their country. They tend to follow customs very strictly, even more some times than the Greeks living in Greece, especially the teenagers. At this moment of my life, I have decided where I would like to live. But I love both countries equally; when I am in the States, I wish I was in Greece and vice versa. I am proud to have two identities. (Thucydides, male, 23)

Ever since I can remember, I have always felt that home was in a different place. Home was a temporary term. As first-generation Greek-Americans, my Greek-born parents succeeded in raising my brother and me with actually three identities. At home, we were Greek. At school, we were American. In our social lives, we were Greek-American. What is my ethnic background you may ask? My response is: all of the above. We managed to maintain each successfully. I can say that now, after looking back and seeing that I was able to thrive in all of my identities. If there was one that would characterize me best now as an adult, I would say, I am Greek-American. I am never at home. When I am 'Greek' for a while, I feel like escaping into my 'American' identity and vice versa. I never fully relate to one or the other. There is always something missing from each, as there is always something missing when I am in Greece, and also when I am in America. For my family, it was not a question. They were Greek. They immigrated to America like many others because of need. The stayed in America because of opportunity. Like many others, they forever lived for the day that they would return to Greece, because that was 'home'. Our American address was temporary, and so was my mindframe. I was fortunate to have open-minded Greek parents who allowed us to travel, maintain friendships with people from other ethnic groups and choose where we wanted to be. (...) Once you assimilate to a new society, it is very difficult to completely strip yourself away from the place that you were living before. You are never at home. (...) Ironically, we made our decision to arrive in Greece as a 'final' destination, two weeks before the terrorist attacks in the United States. We came to Greece nine days later. America will always be a different place for me now. I am here, and I am adjusting. Am I home? I don't know. I don't think I will ever know. I am happy with my decision, and I believe I have completed a cycle that my family had begun about 100 years ago. For me, I'm settled on Greek ground now. I am still waiting for my family. I hope to one day become a mother and shelter my children from the confusion that has been such a great part of my psyche. I do however hope to allow them to feel as though they have a choice like I had. I hope to teach them and help them understand that an identity as a home is always in constant change and that feeling like Homer is just fine. (Iokaste, female, 30)

I am a Greek-American; I could live and interact and hold a conversation with the Greek societies and the Greek groups and basically go out and interact with people who were not Greek. So I basically... I guess my development there..., because I developed there by taking certain parts from both communities, if I can call them two communities, that is my..., if I can say my characteristics were not that sharp on either community. I wasn't that American-American, and I wasn't that Greek-Greek. (...) I think that is why I didn't have such a hard time adjusting in Greece, and I think that is the reason why I haven't been changed by Greece. I guess I was always somewhere in between, so developing I can say I was somewhere where I could have what I wanted from both communities or both cultures, both societies.

So, how do I say it? I was able to combine basically these two cultures and develop it and grow and mutate it in a way that it was Greek-American. (...) Well, starting off with the thing is basically being always in between. You are never 100 percent Greek, and you are never 100 percent American. You are always somewhere in between. So, I've always kind of liked that, in terms that I was never identical to the person next to me. I always felt kind of special in that way. Being able to adjust to a society, live in a society but not always work and live with the rules and mentality of the society. After making the conscious decision of coming back, I've always tried to maintain what I am. I never wanted to be 100 percent assimilated from the society I lived in. I always wanted to be somewhere off to the side, never wanted to be 100 percent. (...) I always wanted to be, again, different, not trying to be special but trying to keep the values I had taken in from marrying these two societies, or cultures or whatever. (...) Well, the process is still taking place. It's a process that I'm always afraid that if I stay too long, I'll fall into the trap, and I'll adjust 100 percent to the other people, to the other people in the society I live in. Basically, now that I reached an age where I know I am going to be living in Greece, I know that my career and my life is going to continue here most likely, it's kind of like me trying to put on extra work on maintaining and continuing that and evolving these characteristics, you can say, that I've always wanted to have. This basic marriage of two different things for me, in my life, Greece and the United States, are two different things. Being able to put these two things together, draw and take what I needed or what I thought, what I saw to be fit and adjusting it always to the environment that I lived in and the society that I lived in as well, is, what can I say, it's kind of hard to explain especially when I am talking about myself ...
(Plato, male, 30)

I see that we were able to compare our culture, which was good, so we could see the pros and cons of our own culture, and we could criticize it, and I think that is one of the reasons why the Greek Church in the United States tends to be different than the Greek Church here. I think it's more open. I think it's more... it opens up its arms, and it hugs you, and it tells you, and it consults you, and you learn more. It's not as strict. Here I believe you don't keep up much with your religion. But you were able to compare with other cultures; you were able to learn more, to adapt certain things. It was a way of knowing yourself more or learning how to find yourself. I think I wouldn't be the

person I am today if I didn't know both worlds. I hate the fact
that I did live in both worlds because I am torn apart between
them. I'd like the best of both worlds, but I think I am very privileged, and everybody that has lived the same thing I have is
very privileged, very privileged because they get to experience so
many things and open up their minds and their horizons. (...)
And all of a sudden, you put on a big smile, and you say, 'You
know what? I feel good'. Yes, this has been a self-discovery process. Everywhere you go, you tend to find yourself. You find all
these different threads. I think deep down I have realized things
very quickly. It was just a bit more quickly than I expected it to
be, and I feel excited that I know who I am. I feel excited that I
know what I want. I know the fact I am living here, and I want
that. (...) I am very proud. I am very happy to be able to have
these experiences to go back and forth, (...) being able to look at
yourself and smile and say, 'You know what? You have it all. You
really, really have it all'. You could have it all. It's up to you. It's
not up to anybody else. You create your own world wherever you
live. Like I said in the beginning, I love both countries. I feel at
home in both. (Andromache, female, 34)

6.3   Narrating the self upon finding the home: stories of 'who
we are' in the 'where we are'

Second-generation return migrants' stories that narrate the 'self upon
finding the home' are stories of the 'who we are' in the 'where we are';
these are performative and reactive acts of migrants' reinscribing, rein-
venting and reclaiming themselves within the writing of their new
world (the *geographia* of return migration). Their parents, first-generation migrants, had to construct spaces, bonds and bridges to cover the
cultural and social distances with the homeland. Interestingly, the recurring themes and patterns of the returnees' settlement and adjustment processes in their parents' country of origin reveal another kind
of struggle reminiscent of the previous one their parents had under-
gone in 'foreign lands'. The struggle itself is both the means and the
end of the returnees' journeyings to the homeland in search of a new
home and the (re)discovery of a new *self*. Identification processes in
journeys of return migration create a dynamic mode of interaction between the past and present in forming ways of constructing 'borderless
zones' of a future life in the ancestral homeland. To inhabit a 'borderless zone' in the homeland is to eradicate previous lives on the margin[9], previous struggles over 'hyphens' and 'loyalties'. Life in the United States, even for the second generation, entails negotiations of iden-

tities and integration processes, bounded spaces and 'ethnic boundaries' (Barth 1969). The homeland return envisioned as a return to
roots, heritage and culture poses, to say the least, an additional challenge when it includes requirements of a 'homeland acculturation' into
a 'modernising' and 'multiculturising' Greek society. Edward Said refers to the 'unhealable rift' to describe the pain resulting from the experience of exile (1990: 357). This 'rift' exists in the case of second-generation Greek-American returnees, and it is encountered as spaces of
'exile' and 'alienation' in the ancestral homeland. In the previous chapters I have presented several of those multi-layered 'exilic spaces' that
emerge in an antagonistic relationship with the imagined 'idyllic
spaces' of the homeland (Christou 2006c). These processes illuminate
the 'turbulence' (Papastergiadis 2000) of return migration and identification.

In referring to diaspora writing and the cultural transitions involved,
Peepre devises the following terminology: *ghetto narratives* and *heritage
narratives* when they focus on one culture, and *narratives of transition*
and *narratives of interaction* when they move between two or more cultures. A further division is the *intercultural narrative*, written by an
author who is the 'hybridised product of the fully realized multicultural
state and writes in a new space beyond the borders of any specific culture' (1999: 74). In my study, I have referred to the *geographia of return*
in describing that the return is the writing of the participants' new
world. Therefore, in this ethnography, we can point to three basic categorisations within which the return migrants, as both 'active' and 'reactive' agents, emerge as 'seekers of the *home*land and narrators of *self*',
thus justifying points of convergence between *place* and *identity*. These
are:

1. *Roots and heritage narratives* (ethnocultural identities)
2. *Narratives of transition* (transformative identities)
3. *Narratives of interaction* (transhybrid identities)

The above schema of narration is correlated to the return trajectory,
which exposes the 'diasporic experience' as one involving migrant subjectivity as a socially and politically understood figure in varying levels
of social interaction/construction in a newly formed state of migrancy
in the homeland. As a schema of identification, these varying levels of
action emerge as interactive processes of:

a. Transplanting seeds of the culture: transhybrid identities are trans-
    posed
b. Searching for the self in transition: othering identities are nego-
    tiated
c. Experiencing the future within a present of the past: longing identi-
    ties are remembered

d. Projecting links to an imaginative sequel: representational identities are depicted
e. Restoring fragmentation: symbolic identities are constructed

The schema of narration in concurrence with the schema of identification reflects the articulation of *ideologies of self* and *geographies of identity* process. The schema of narration corresponds to the possibilities of the 'who I am', thus disclosing abilities of the 'self' and the schema of identification corresponds to probabilities (that is, likely to happen) of the *'who* I am in the *where* I am', thus disclosing existing dimensions of the 'self' in the 'place'. More specifically, the *roots and heritage narratives* (ethnocultural identities) articulate belongingness emerging from adherence to cultural signifiers, such as language, religion, endogamy, participation in ethnic networks and organisations. *Narratives of transition* (transformative identities) articulate belongingness emerging from disruptive spaces of 'homeness' and 'alienation' where the 'self' meets the 'other'. Through the reconciliation of these transitions, transformative identities are formed and a sense of purpose, direction and well-being is achieved. Finally, *narratives of interaction* (transhybrid identities) refer to belongingness that is negotiated in the inbetweenness of the 'here and there', the spaces of interaction in 'home and host' constructs that 'translates' the 'self' through subjective and inner experience.

The above schema of identification illustrates the interactive processes of the returnees' states of being and becoming in the ancestral homeland. These processes narrate belonging. Excerpts of identification patterns show the five distinct categorisations mentioned above:

Transplanting seeds of the culture: transhybrid identities are transposed
This was clearly illustrated in returnee narratives that talked about working and studying in Greek-American academic and professional contexts and thus maintaining both worlds in the homeland environment. Additionally, their participation was noted in Greek-American 'official' and 'unofficial' networks and organisations as well as the celebration of American holidays in Greece (Thanksgiving Day, Memorial Day, Independence Day/4th of July). Olwig powerfully asserts the core point of this context: 'Viewing migrants as part of two or more worlds which are dynamically intertwined is vital for a fuller understanding of migration and migratory experiences, whether people are based in their country of origin, the United States, or Europe...Rather than presenting the "ends of the loom" as separate and oppositional (with migrants caught between two cultures), understanding origin and destinations as the same basic world provides us with greater insights' (1997: 148). The 'same basic world' has been termed *the transnational social*

field (Glick Schiller, Basch and Blanc-Szanton 1992; Basch, Glick Schiller and Szanton Blanc 1994), which is constituted by individual migrants and their social-migrant-business organisations.

Searching for the self in transition: othering identities are negotiated
Under this heading come all the changes the returnees had to make in their behaviour and life-style as well as all the 'pragmatic' negotiations they had to make (salary and job description/environment, housing, transportation/traffic, quality of life, healthcare, climatic changes) and emotional negotiations, too (language and communication with native Greeks, personal relationships and friendships, encountering discrimination or anti-American sentiments).

Experiencing the future within a present of the past: longing identities are remembered
Imagined and narrated stories of the past, memory and nostalgia can be classified under this rubric. Constructions of the national past are forged in the social and cultural landscape: the returnees' deep desire to teach and raise their children the ancestral way safeguards 'Greekness' (family, language, religion, tradition).

Projecting links to an imaginative sequel: representational identities are depicted
This process centres on the strong belief that second-generation Greek-American return migrants are the 'key to the future' and construct 'pragmatic' and 'imaginative' roles of contributing to the *patrida*, by giving back and thus securing the development of Greece.

Restoring fragmentation: symbolic identities are constructed
This is an expression of symbolic ethnicity and symbolic religiosity in ethno-cultural practices that occurs after the returned migrants understand the changes that have occurred in Greece and then have comprehended how Greece has changed them.

As Elizabeth Tonkin in her innovative and timely book *Narrating our Past: The Social Construction of Oral History* explains, 'It is open to any teller to construct a self, ...because the telling is "in person"' (1992: 48; quotations in the original). In this book, Tonkin uses an interdisciplinary approach to investigate the construction and interpretation of oral histories while arguing for a deeper understanding of their oral and social characteristics. At the same time, it is imperative to maintain an awareness of the story-telling process as an act of self-reflection and social-reflection:

The story-telling function, whether metaphorical or literal, is a social activity, and though we spoke of the self as audience to its own narration, the story of one's life and activity is told so much to others as to oneself. In our view the self is itself an interplay of roles, but clearly the individual is constituted in interpersonal transaction as well as intrapersonal reflection. It is one thing to speak of the social construction of the self, however, and another to inquire into the make-up of social entities as such (Carr 2002: 151).

6.4 Summing up

Any systematic attempt to define 'Greekness' in the case of second-generation return migrants must revolve around subjective perceptions that reveal cultural meanings, national underpinnings and ethnic manifestations of social relations as expressed by the diasporic subjects. In the case of diasporas (I have explained in previous chapters how and why my participants 'perform' and 'act' as a diasporic group in both 'home' and 'host' spaces), these processes that form an integral part of the identification process are primarily understood as attachment to home and feelings of cultural bonds that transcend geographical boundaries (Safran 1991; Cohen 1997). Home constructions materialise as objects of spiritual and nostalgic longing and are expressed through symbolic ethnicity and symbolic religiosity. This is a shared diasporic consciousness that is mediated through identification. Identification itself – whether fuelled by fervent nationalist sentiments, gender categorisations, anti-Americanism, ethnic pride, rootedness, connectedness, or simply life choices – stems from the lived experience of migrants' strategic actions (personal plan of action/unitive homing resolution): it is situated in larger historical processes; it is facilitated by social institutions, and it is marked by political, social and cultural relationships that define the parameters of the group in geographic and social space.

In this respect, Sinn has used the term 'mini-diasporas' (1999: 85) to refer to smaller diasporic networks. If I could subcategorise second-generation Greek-American 'mini-diasporas' in the ancestral homeland, I would most likely characterise them not only as *counter-diasporic* but also as 'adhesive-diasporas' in the sense that they 'adhere' to ethnic ties, cultural and religious practices, but also their own links are 'adhesive'. On the other hand, identification processes include both '(dis)ruptive' and (dis)jointed interactions. As adhesive as these networks appear to be, ethno-cultural dynamics also provoke 'fragmentising' tendencies in 'homogenising' contexts. There were several occasions in my observations of regular meetings of Greek-American organisations and return migrant associations during which intense arguments would burst out in relation to 'home-host' clashes over issues not unanimously welcomed by the members. I must, however, clarify that most of these heated discussions emerged during and soon after the large repetitive demonstrations of people throughout Athens protesting against the war that the United States and coalition forces had just initiated against Iraq. As the war escalated, so did the tear-gas lingering on the streets, launched by police against angry crowds of all ages. Attendance at association meetings was noticeably low during the months of March and April 2003 but not passive by any means. During my meetings with participants at this time, not only was the seriousness of the war situation discussed, together with the global state of affairs and the 'new order of things', but also above all, 'Americanness' and 'Greekness' were challenged and redefined by the country-wide anti-war and anti-American sentiment.

In the last stage of my fieldwork, in mid-late May 2003 during Mother's Day and Memorial Day celebrations and also in early July during Independence Day (4th of July) celebrations (American holidays) and June 16th (Holy Spirit/Greek Orthodox religious holiday, also a national holiday) but also earlier in the fall of 2002 during fundraisers for the 9/11 victims' families and other gatherings, I had an opportunity to meet up with separate groups of participants and to touch upon the subject of the wars in Bosnia, Afghanistan and in Iraq. Very often, the participants referred to the issue as 'traumatic' and 'painful' for them because by keeping silent, almost hiding from the public in self-imposed house arrest, they felt stripped of their identities, persecuted and hated. Yet, they did not consider departing for the United States, not even spending the Greek Orthodox Easter or Christmas holidays there. It was in those discussions that I realised even more how the fragility and fragmentation of 'disruptive' spaces was simultaneously a stimulant of agency and action negotiated in identity politics and the politics of identity. The latter formed an 'adhesive' identity that had filtered transnational, binational and plurinational constructions of 'Greco-Americanness' or 'American-Greekness'. This verifies once again that network analyses and identification processes cannot be comprehended in isolation; they are intertwined and interactive and historically, politically and socially situated in several contexts. They are deciphered through action, in time and within social spaces. They are grounded in the particularities of everyday life, and they venture beyond the localised activities of subjects (McKeown 2001).

The returnees' 'personal plan of action' incorporates ascriptive and self-selective aspects of ethnicity and culture, which are reformulated into a personal cultural system. This is the returnees' activity, consciously formulated, selective, and organised to fulfil specific personal purposes and plans. The triadic relationship between *place, culture* and *identity* reflects the interactive relationship between individual behaviour, group roles and social context, which should be viewed under the lens of a human geography that critically studies agency and structure in migration phenomena.

I have used stories of return to narrate the self as the self is constructed also through the return migration experience. It is an entire journey that spans generations and geography, past and present history. Both the journeys and the stories reveal multiple diasporic moments, diasporic spaces and diasporic events that shape diasporic identities because above all the returning migrants' identifications are mostly constructed through and negotiated in diasporic terms. There are inescapable implications of journeyings that illustrate this diasporic component:

> The story of the dispersed is always the story of a journey...Such journey stories have made the portal the natural 'home of the homeless'. What all diasporic groups have had in common is a sense of being 'at ease' in the space of perpetual journeying... The limited term 'return home', the eternal return of visitation, ...the only way left (in the epoch of the narration) to approach the grand narrative of the journey, the only way of answering a question that all diasporic people must address: *'where are we when we are at home?'*; above all, the only way of answering this question in diasporic terms, that is, that *'we are at home when we are abroad'* (Murphy 1998: 408-409; italics and quotations in the original).

Perhaps the most striking feature of such journeys is that the sense of place persists throughout migrant encounters. As Buttimer accurately explains, 'people's sense of both personal and cultural identity is intimately bound up with place identity' (1980: 167) as 'mobility and identity, like adventure and security, home and reach, are an intrinsic part of life itself – journey rather than a destination' (1985: 315). The journey of migrant life is one of mobility and identity, of grieving for a lost home and anticipation of an imagined home to be discovered. Several participants narrate their life as a search for balance and coherence in their aspiration for settlement and closure that a unitary self brings rather than the complex, multiple and contradictory regression of a diasporic existence. Perhaps participants will remain forever in diasporic delusion in their search for composure and coherence in their search for a 'home'. These processes are inextricably linked as the reconstruction of memories through cultural experiences composes feelings and identities that make migrants comfortable with their lives and identities (Thomson 1994; Einhorn 2000). In this direction, Goodson's reflective remarks underscore the very potential of migrant narratives: 'Life history work is interested in the way people actually do narrate their lives, not in the way they should. Here it seeks to avoid the fate of some postmodern fundamentalists. Life stories then are the starting point for our work. Such stories are, in their nature, already removed from life experiences – they are lives interpreted and made textual. They represent a partial, selective commentary on lived experience' (2001: 138).

I have used the life path as an 'existential' and 'socio-cultural' project, which corresponds to a migratory project. Return migration is one of many milestones in the returnees' lives and a marker of identity. We have seen it as a point of arrival but quite often too as a point of departure, a space of 'homeness' and a place of 'estrangement'. Nevertheless, the homeland return project is clearly demonstrative of identification: 'One's life/identity is a story in constant making and remaking, and in the systematic revision the person and the other people get equally involved. But ultimately, the self emerges from the encounter between the person in question and the multitude of her life narratives. What happens in this encounter?' (Ritivoi 2002: 64). To answer this last question, I shall respond: Perhaps it is because 'All things are in flux[10]' (Heraclitus, son of Vloson, born about 535 BC in Ephesos, spoken several thousand years ago), and identity is just one of those 'things'.

7 Conclusions

7.1 A three dimensional ideology: the return as a construction of place-culture-identity

This book has focused on the conceptual parameters of homeland and belonging in return migration through the voices of second-generation Greek-Americans. In so doing, I have sought to explore the return migration project as situated in an arena of discussion of *place, culture* and *identity*, extending across and beyond static territorial boundaries. The subjective terrain of the returnees' negotiating processes of place, culture and identity incorporates their *ideologies* and constructs their *geographies*. Both these key terms – 'ideology' and 'geography' – are used according to their original Greek linguistic meaning. For the former term, the meaning is 'study of ideas' or 'discourse', that is to say, the 'speech of ideas'. So, the participants' expressions of their ideas of *home, return* and *self*, the voices of the returnees, are their ideologies. The same holds for the usage of the term 'geographies', again from the Greek, which means 'to write one's world'. The geographies of place, culture and identity are the articulation of their new world. Hence their ideologies become the method of articulating their geographies. And here, too, I use the term 'method' from the Greek: 'a route that leads to the goal'. The participants' oral and written narratives were those ideologies – that is to say, 'speech of ideas' – that clearly reflected the geographies of their return migration.

Return migrants are simultaneously situated historical subjects and active actors. Their stories are about personal experiences, which are also national experiences. The stories unfold in the national time–space and are correlated with specific movements associated with and producing transitional phases during migrant life stages; they thus reveal the relation between social mobility and socio-cultural transitions. Many highly complex, abstract and volatile notions form a major part of the returnees' narrations. These are their personal, subjective constructions of ethnicity, place, culture, home, identity and belonging. Insight into those constructions helps us understand that socio-cultural constructions are at the same time multiple national and ethnic stories that are mediated by the intersection of national configurations with (trans)local experiences.

My analysis demonstrates that the stories narrated are perspectives of mediating agency; they are objectifications of self-understandings, discourses and images of the social world that return migrants inhabit and are inhabited by. Identity is a concept that figures prominently in return migration, combining the intimate or personal world with the collective space of cultural forms and social relations in the homeland (s). Identity is a product of self-consciousness and self-reflection, of both emotional and rational processes, the articulation and comprehension of a vision of both personal and social history that motivates the homeland return. Therefore, we are confronted with *identities*, the imaginings of self in 'home-host' worlds of action. Return migrant identities are lived in, negotiated, challenged and finally expressed through activity and have to be conceptualised as they develop in social practice in the (trans)national space. 'Belongingness' and 'homeness' are correlated with identification processes; they are part and parcel of the return migratory project, and they are the appropriate modes of narrativising the everyday life in a world of movement and uncertainty, which paradoxically intensifies boundary formation.

While I shaped the thematic analysis and the overall structure of this concluding chapter, the 'ideologies to geographies' construction maintained a powerful presence throughout the process (as it did throughout the book), challenging, questioning and helping me clarify the results of the answers given to the research questions presented in Chapter one. Although the answers to the research questions outlined in Chapter one have been dealt with in great detail in the empirical chapters four, five and six, here I would like to underline the core deconstructions of those answers:

1. As regards what has motivated second-generation Greek-Americans to relocate to their parents' country of origin, I have to stress that the motivation stems from a larger existential project to locate one's sense of self and place in the ancestral homeland, as an 'authentic' homeland. This type of 'existential project' is combined with a daily life plan of either an educational or a professional pursuit of self-development. Narratives of rootedness in Chapter four and narratives of belongingness in Chapter five articulate this well and give substance to the notion of the 'homeplace' in the ancestral homeland.

2. In terms of the coping mechanisms and strategies that the return migrants implemented in order to adjust to their new environment, the reliance on family and friends clearly stands out as well as the practice of forming networks (both official and unofficial as explained in Chapter six) and support groups. In a sense, this had the meaning of constructing new types of clusters of an alternative dia-

sporic life in the homeland. To some degree, the returnees had to make concessions and change their needs, attitudes and behaviour.

3. Although identity figures prominently throughout the book, it is vibrantly portrayed through a series of seven long extracts in Chapter six: those of Iphigenia, Kalypso, Kallisto, Thucydides, Iokaste, Plato and Andromache. The section that follows these accounts serves to classify identification processes into a typology (schema of identification) and to explain how the narratives (schema of narration) express the 'who I am' in the 'where I am' and hence articulate the 'ideologies of self and geographies of identity'. Moreover, narratives of the 'there' (United States), the 'here' (Greece) and the 'here and there' (the in-betweeness of identification in response to the ancestral homeland return project) illustrate both the 'personal plan of action' and the third space of homeness where transhybrid identities are formed.

4. In terms of the social and economic activities of the return migrants, the participants narrated in Chapter six in great detail their parents' humble beginnings and the economic hardships that led to the first westward, transatlantic migration. They also emphasised their gratitude for having the opportunity to pursue a better future educationally and professionally. However, the hardships that this generation of return migrants is currently facing are not due to financial restraints but because of the obstacles they have encountered living in modern-day Greece, as emphatically described by some of the participants in Chapter five but also in narratives of estrangement and alienation in Chapter four.

5. The impact of Greece on the returning migrants is multidimensional and deeply correlated with their identity construction. In the case of the female participants, identification is also clearly interrelated with gender and thus highlights multiple roles and reconciliations but also conflicts, as illustrated by the accounts of Hera, Pandora and Hestia in Chapter six. Greece has impacted on returnees also because Greece itself has changed; they see it as having disintegrated and lost its traditional style. They also recognise and process the mosaic of European, Southern and Eastern European, Middle Eastern and Balkan elements that synthesise the current portrait of Greece, as depicted by Diomides in Chapter four and further explained by Aristotle in Chapter six. We should also mention here the 'anti-American' component, evidenced in the accounts of Sophocles, Phaedra, Medusa, Aristotle, Hestia and Kalypso in the same chapter.

6. Finally, in terms of their current experiences and expectations as well as what they would do the same and what differently, there seems to be an ardent argumentation by the majority of participants

that there is not the least amount of regret in terms of their decision to return and their stay, despite the agonising moments of despair and frustration. In other words, they claim that they would not
have done it differently or have it any other way. In one respect, I
recall most of them used an old Greek saying that I paraphrase here
– 'It is best to have a shoe from your homeland than anywhere else
even if it is stitched' (meaning ripped, torn and defective) – to justify their choice of marrying Greeks and deciding to live in Greece.
On the other hand, such excerpts as those in the first part of Chapter five that stand against absolutist and fundamentalist views highlight an understanding of multicultural societies and Greece in particular. These perspectives underline the hope that participants expressed in contributing to their ancestral homeland and
recognising this as an important consideration in their decision to
relocate to Greece.

7.2   So, who then is this Greek-American return migrant?

Just a few years ago, on June 9, 2003, the Greek TV channels broadcast
the three-minute *zembekiko* dance of second-generation Greek-American twin brothers George Tenet[1], CIA director at the time, and Vasilis
Tenet, renowned cardiologist, at a Greek-American and Greek-Cypriot
celebration. In addition to the dance, the highlight of the newscast spot
was an excerpt from George Tenet's speech: 'The answer lies in being
blessed by a great family, a great heritage and a great religion'. While
processing Tenet's 'answer', I was reminded of Papastergiadis' question: 'Is the essence of a common language and shared history the only
guarantee for a collective identity?' (2000: 197). And then I went
further back in time and reflected on what Isocrates had declared,
namely that the Greek is the one who participates in Greek education[2].
This phrase resurfaced recently in the turmoil created when a handful
of Albanian students who had the highest marks in their classes were
selected by their teachers to hold the Greek flag during parades at national celebrations of the October 28th and March 25th national holidays[3]. I was left wondering how one can begin to attempt to negotiate
the quintessential image of 'Greekness' in a Europe that is itself struggling to define its 'European identity' in a multicultural and multifaith
context, a Europe which has incorporated ten new member states with
a distinct past and a heavy political history, and a Europe (and Greece)
which is struggling to deal with the 'fortress' of xenophobia and racism. How are second-generation Greek-Americans to negotiate their
place and *identity* in Greece, as a homeland, as an EU member state, as
a newly formed immigration/multicultural country? One of my partici-

pants told me that if the past is a foreign country because they do things differently there, then the present is a homeland by choice because they should do things the same there. Taking this thought a step further while having in mind second-generation returning migrants, I have to speculate if the future has to be some form of *hybridland* because things seem to be performed and understood both ways, in terms of *foreignness* and *sameness*.

7.3 Reflecting on the future: considerations for further research on diasporas new and old

In this book I sought to cast light on the 'dark' subject of identity and to explore the homeland return in relation to identification processes. The homeland return appears to be very much a relocation in search of home in the homeplace. This is not a return to a terra incognita; it is a return to a *patrida* that, nevertheless, encapsulates both spaces of homeness and spaces of alienation.

How might the research I have carried out for this study be further extended and developed? First, future research in the area could include a larger sample, embracing a comparative perspective and more diversity within the group of participants. Diversity could include what I already have attempted to a certain degree in my study, that is, a range of ages, and a variety of socio-economic, educational and professional backgrounds. The comparative perspective could be extended through different geographic locations of residence and include those Greek-American return migrants who are residing outside Athens, on islands or in villages and especially those who have decided to return to the regional/local ancestral place of origin, be that in the provinces or the islands. On a more complex level, further studies could include first-generation migrants as well as second-generation Greek-Australian, Greek-Canadian, Greek-German, etc. return migrants. It would also be interesting to undertake a similar study with children of second-generation return migrants who would be classified as third generation, both those born in the United States as well as those born in Greece subsequent to their parents' return migration. It would be extremely interesting and a challenge to explore ethnicity and identity issues in the third generation. In this respect, children are viewed as both objects of cultural adaptation and as active subjects who change the culture they were born into while simultaneously adapting to it (Knörr 2005).

Any endeavour to pursue further research focusing on the state of return migrancy and the cultural picture of present-day Greece cannot forget the past or ignore the future. No matter the subjectivity of the subject matter, it is imperative to contextualise the issue under discussion within the frames of history and society. The *anthropogeographia* of return migration in Greece is above all anthropocentric but revolves around axes of culture that intersect with praxes of migrants as they interact with both the others and the other within themselves. All this, of course, is not so neatly classified for researchers to delve into. Return migration research requires theoretical frameworks that consider and give attention to gender, class, ethnicity and race.

7.4   Revisiting reflections: mapping return migration, tracing place, mirroring identity, refiguring home, reframing belonging

I introduced this book by speaking about journeys, those of my participants and mine. It is only inevitable that the book has to arrive at the end of its own journey. Of course my participants' return journeyings, fluid and continuous as they are, will continue in the realm of more spaces and times as their life stories have generously demonstrated and as their lives continue to unfold. The end of my writing journey calls for a series of reflections on my part about what I have learned and what perhaps I should have done differently. Similar to my participants, in order to proceed to this reflecting mode, I gathered all my own journals of over a decade where I kept a log of my research progress, notes on earlier writings and thoughts on the overall project. I read my journals along with the chapters I had drafted. This was a whole new journey in itself.

In this concluding section I aim to offer a concise yet concrete presentation of the major findings of my study of second-generation Greek-American return migration and provide some key methodological, theoretical and fieldwork reflections. The narrow theoretical and empirical considerations regarding return migration will focus on *place, culture* and *identity* while the broader reflective discussion will centre on return migration as a phenomenon of situated migrant subjectivity.

7.4.1   Methodology

Without being bound into the emerging shifts in constructionist theories – from the structural indeterminism of post-modern approaches to the positive insistence on causal explanations – I found that a hermeneutic-interpretative approach is most useful mainly because it develops a nuanced conceptualisation of agency which bridges both the intersubjective understanding of migrants as 'active actors' while contextualising their agency in a socio-cultural historical environment. The end result is that this approach helps clarify the relations between agents and structures, hence leading to a contextual analysis of return migration as a multi-layered phenomenon. This is a more holistic approach that contextualises events and actors and helps us understand their meaning. Whether constructionism is considered an approach, a theory, a paradigm, an epistemology, an ontology or a method is a philosophical question that need not be replayed here. What is relevant, though, is that in my study, constructionism served well as a comprehensive device to clarify the complexities of return migration and the incoherencies of identification. In parallel to this, the use of a multi-interdisciplinary approach played a central role in looking at actors and structures as both mutually (trans)forming each other as much as they shape, (re)construct and (de)construct multiple layers of meaning of choice in decision making. In retrospect, my extensive reading of literature in several disciplines of the Humanities and the Social Sciences was valuable in creatively employing several theories and debates and deciding on a combination of methods for my research. I can only be hopeful that my study has offered some insight into second-generation Greek-American return migration and identity construction and that this project will stimulate further research.

The book has endeavoured to extrapolate the intricacies and interconnections between return migration and identity construction and to shed light on the notions of place and belonging, home and homeland, self in relation to 'Greekness' and 'Americanness' as well as the role of ethnicity and culture in the second generation. All these relations sustain dynamics of the 'home-host' discrepancies and verify the fact that return migration is a continuous movement of identities, not just of bodies and material objects. Furthermore, return migration for the second generation is a continuous process of negotiation. At times this negotiation becomes a polemic that polarises perspectives, poisons relationships and creates spaces of estrangement and alienation in the homeland that does not, in fact, feel like home. It is a continuous process of action even if at times dialogues disintegrate into monologues. The point being that action and agency are apparent in every step of the process of relocation and settlement, mainly due to the very pragmatic fact that modern-day Greece is a changed and a changing society. Greece is no longer a mono-cultural society and no longer a construction of a home that most participants seemed to long for. In their attempt to 'integrate' into their homeland, they encounter spaces of hostility and alienation. Their sense of self, their 'Greekness', to their surprise, is not an exact match to the native sense of 'Greekness'. As a result, their 'homeness' is even more confined to their own privatised, marginalized spaces. The participants' personal myths and imaginings of a welcoming homeland return did not include but were confronted by heterogeneities, exclusions, transitions and transformations of their traditions and traditional ways of celebrating the *patrida*. All of them were born and raised in a multicultural United States and claim aversion toward racist and xenophobic attitudes, but some returnees appear to express in their narratives a form of 'conversion' to these attitudes when they speak of the 'floods of foreigners' in their neighbourhoods, in their schools and in their lives. Being 'at home' for returnees was a construction of Greece as a culturally homogeneous space that encapsulated communal feelings of safety and security, a harmonious coexistence in an all-embracing homeland. Mostly the opposite is their lived experience of return. This highlights the very notion of home as a social construction and a product of social space in the mundane of everyday life. So although the homeland return is not exactly an 'impossible homecoming', it is nevertheless a 'conflicting homecoming' with few points of confluence between the two worlds, the world of the migrant and the world of the homeland(s). The returned 'exile' migrant translates a sense of belonging by invoking imaginary constructions of the *patrida*, flashes of memories and traces of heroic pasts. Hybrid identifications are states of spatial and temporal homelessness at home when return migrants confront the stranger in them by identifying the *other* within the *othering* state of modern Greece. Hence it becomes clear that different 'worlds' in motion permeate the entire process of return migration: at the individual level, the return migrant either in place or displaced is a traveller; at the collective level, Greek society is searching for its place in Europe and in the global scheme of things. For the migrant, the narrativity of return even does not bring closure; it has had a cathartic element in sorting out their 'story', and this has a partial sense of continuity when one pulls together all fragments of life and comes to terms with issues. Hence, return migration for second-generation Greek-Americans is a subjective journey during which the migrants develop strategies to cope with the major changes in their biography as constituted by the socio-cultural context of mobility. Retrospection is a component of their integration project and a mechanism that creates autobiographies of narrative transmission of their ethnocultural worlds.

In terms of the theoretical contribution of the book, a critical perspective on mobility and social processes advocates that 'processes of homing and migration take shape through the imbrication of affective and bodily experience in broader social processes and institutions where unequal differences of race, class, gender and sexuality, among many other relevant categories are generated (Ahmed, Castañeda, Fortier and Sheller 2003: 5). Mobility subjectivities are embedded in everyday life through the meanings conferred upon sociality and spatiality

as infused in daily practices. The emplacement of migrants and returnees in deeply structural contexts that also reflect their flexibility of
agency produces a dynamic process whereby global meanings and cultural spatialities socially construct identities. Such processes are also revealing of hierarchies, class differences and power relations saturating
both global and local fields of activity. Migrant life stories provide varying voices of such experiences and their narratives textualise differing
lenses for analysing instances of alienation and accommodation among
groups and communities. While maintaining critical awareness of such
categories and embodiments, in this book I aimed at illuminating the
complex and situational entanglements of migrant subjectivities and
cultural spatialities. I aimed at exploring identities in relation to the notions of home and belonging at the crossroads of an interdisciplinary
approach within an ethnographic context. More specifically, in reassessing questions of identity, ethnicity and gender in relation to broader
questions of diaspora, culture, nation and the multilocality of belongingness in space in time, I was interested in exploring identities as
neither essentialised, solid and frozen spatially and temporally nor utterly liquefied and fragmented in a vacuum. By perceiving the migrant-
actor within a context of social, economic and political coordinates, we
can decipher those forces that shape identification but also how migrants internalise them and act accordingly. Hence, returnee agency
produces a politics of self. This politicisation of return is an act of identification in response to the meanings of home and homeland.

7.4.2   Home and identification

The ancestral homeland is a site of home as a physical place (concrete
land/territory) and a site of homeness as a personal space of identification (place belonging). The construction of return migrants' identities
in their personal worlds of movement and fluidity is juxtaposed against
a modern-day homeland in flux, ever-changing in varying scales of national conceptualisations of its 'identity' (Hellenic, European, Balkan,
Mediterranean). Important symbolic markers of returning migrant
identification are the family, language and religion while for a changing Greece, immigration on a domestic level and the effects of such
global events as 9/11 have impacted on its identity struggle. The multiple understandings of belonging and home on the personal and national level demarcate Greek-Americans from Greeks because of feelings of inclusion and exclusion that reflect collective power structures
and individual agency (these are also identity searching processes).
These processes, conflictual as they may be, also highlight self-negotiations based on categorisations of gender, class and ethnicity in both
network interactions and memory constructions. It becomes rather

clear that the ancestral homeland for the returnees is a site of simultaneously 'shifting' and 'sifting' culture whereupon a process of culture
immersion is no longer vicariously constructed but pragmatically experienced, examined and even exempted from their sense of 'Greekness'. Hence, in addition to the multiplicity of a sense of self and the
diversity of a sense of home (as a result of interactive struggles and negotiations), there is an emergent politics of self and politics of home
that reveals:

1. Deep reflection and self-awareness does not necessarily include dialogue with the *other*. Return migrants observe, experience and process the 'othering' of the ancestral home but the *other* (Greeks) and
   the *others* (non Greek-American migrants) are not engaged in mutual collaborations with the self (Greek-Americans).

2. Second-generation Greek-Americans are not passive receptors of
   cultural and national confrontations of identity formation but co-
   constructors and co-creators of a hybridised reflexive identity in
   their marginalized space of belongingness as their compatriots do
   not embrace them as 'Greeks' but more so as Americans (*'Amerikanoi'*).

3. When the imagined homeland (Greece) becomes a home site of
   everyday life and belonging instead of a dissipating 'immigrant discourse', emergent 'diasporic discourses' intensify as individual and
   collective manifestations of alienation and marginalisation from the
   national community become a routine narrative of urban life because home is created through and unfolds during social relations
   of the ordinary everyday exchange in the city.

These are the most powerful dynamics that perpetuate the return migration project in relation to identification processes. Constructions of
identity and home in the narratives of second-generation Greek-American return migrants are expressive of *spaces of belonging* and ties to the
ethnic place. They cannot be emptied of their social and cultural contents and connotations, and they are not the least static; they are mobile in personal and global worlds of movement. But identification in
the homeland is not a smooth and harmonious process; it involves
sites of struggle, moments of discontent and spaces of alienation. All
of the participants in the study had dual citizenship and therefore did
not encounter any bureaucratic-administrative problems during their
initial relocation to Greece. The actual physical relocation to the ancestral homeland did not require second-generation Greek-Americans to
overcome bureaucratic and organisational hurdles, but their mental,
emotional and practical everyday life demanded a series of compromises in order to cope with, if not to completely overcome, obstacles.
Nevertheless, it almost seems that ethnicity, language and religion, the

'cultural stuff' of what returnees think makes up their 'Greekness', are not a valid passport but rather a temporary visa for their entrance onto Greek soil. Returning migrant identities are not always coherent and stable but *dynamic social constructions: reactions* and *actions* of context and not simply mirrors of inner selves. Identities are complex and situational and susceptible to contradictions and conflicts in a constellation of social relationships.

7.4.3   Between cultural fields and social spaces

In the social construction of identities, the emergence of the 'third space' or 'hybrid space' is intrinsically an inner space; in this sense it is a *psychic space* between the two 'homes', a space where an individual's identity is negotiated as the person relates dynamically to the two homelands. In terms of the narrative content in relation to the themes discussed, three observations emerge in how subjectivities produce fragmented and conflicting notions of identities:

First, we come across the idealisation of the Greek-American families and the use of the familiar 'rags to riches', 'America as land of opportunity', 'we were so close as family' kinds of rhetoric. Such tales are common, but it is still striking that participants' narratives very rarely recount conflict between parents and children or the intense disagreements and disaffections between them (or the complex psychodynamics between children, parents, grandparents), the wounds, dislocations, alienations, the very real pain, separation and deep family conflict that this first migration to the United States not uncommonly produced. That the latter kinds of stories don't get told in the research context is not completely surprising as it is an epiphenomenon of the research itself, which might be producing the 'party line', 'putting the best face forward for the group'.

Similarly, the largely positive (even 'ecstatic') accounts of participants on the their decisions to come and to stay in Greece required interrogation and framing. On the one hand, anti-Americanism, frustration with bureaucracy, etc. are noted, but again the need participants apparently felt to put all this in such a good light could be linked, more explicitly and powerfully, with certain needs of self-justification around a complex and contested decision to relocate and within the context of a potentially profound personal and social reconstruction of the self.

Finally, it is interesting to note the quite frequent internalisation of Greek national ideologies, as well as stereotypes of others, within the narratives, and this stimulates our awareness of the *limits* to critique. The migration experience has enabled some reflection on self and group, but it has not necessarily enabled a critical view of Greek or US societies in all respects. Maybe this is to be expected, and we have to remember that these are ordinary people, not social scientists – and the degree did vary between individuals. But one can recall another powerful text about 'home' written over two decades ago by a feminist scholar, Minnie Bruce Pratt, 'Identity: Skin, Blood, Heart', which showed just how powerful the questioning could be, and one is struck by the difference and the degree of self-reflexivity: 'Where does the need come from, the inner push to walk into change, if by skin color, ethnicity, birth culture, we are women who are in a position of material advantage, where we gain at the expense of others, of other women? A place where *we* can have a degree of safety, comfort, familiarity, just by staying put. Where is our *need* to change what we were born into? What do we have to gain?' (1984: 16; italics in the original).

Perhaps partly in response to the above, it is worth trying to think through these processes of self-transformation in relation to transnational movement, the two homes, the third space, the importance of national ideologies and discourses of national self/Other, specifically in relation to subjectivity. These processes of formation, change and re-evaluation, and the relation between self and society, agency and structure, subjects and discourses should be viewed through the return migratory project. The way 'agency' and 'structure' have been configured in the analysis, that is, translated into the terms of the migration experience, underscores the complex bond that exists between them particularly when gender is placed at the analytical centre and subtle expressions of power at an interpersonal and collective level surface. As such, the asymmetrical relations of gender generate particular conceptualisations about consciousness, experience, and the relations between social structure and human agency (Cowan 1990) as power is not simply exercised or resisted since compliance is complexly intertwined in hegemonic behaviours (see Williams 1977 and Foucault 1978; 1979) that occur not only in the midst of conflict but also in the centre of celebration. For the most part, the participants' life stories are revealing of how the family is narrated and presented as a site of belonging and a nexus of both an imaginary and performed unit through which transnational migrants seek to construct their identities (Chamberlain and Leydesdorff 2004). But the family is also a site of difference and continuing emotional adjustment in which migratory experiences are indicators of the ways in which culture shapes relations of conflict. This is indeed expressive of what Iphigenia describes in her narrative about the endless fights during family holiday dinners and festive events.

Return migration is a turbulent journey of rooted nostalgia through multidimensional routes of belonging in the mixed socio-cultural fields of 'home' and 'host' countries. Return migration is rich in spatial structures, and it is that dynamic arena in which returning migrants' socio-cultural life unfolds. This dynamic is the spatial medium through

which social relations and social constructions that impact on identification are (re)produced. Return migration and migrant identification
are phenomena saturated by social, cultural, political and historical elements. This mutual embeddedness, apparent in the narratives of return and belonging, is situated in the interactiveness of geographic
space (the nation and the ancestral homeland) and social space (the national discourse and migrant subjectivities). Return migrants as social
actors, situated in geographic space through their positionality and as
an outcome of their human reflection, construct the human geography
of return migration. *The human geography of return migration is the story
of migrant identification in migrant storied lives.* The lives of return migrants must be understood within, beyond and across national boundaries. At the same time, their boundaries of identification are embedded in multi-sited social spaces and multi-layered cultural fields.
Return migration cannot be viewed as a one-way process but as a dynamic process of (be)longing with fluid boundaries ascribed and chosen by migrants in differing social contexts. Belonging is constructed
within these contexts through channels of lived experience, memory,
nostalgia and imagining. There are no neat, culturally compartmenta-
lised and socially classified divisions of (pluri)local and (trans)national
connections as networks exist within the nation-state as well as in imagined communities of cybernetworks in migrants' everyday activities,
relationships and communications. In this sense, returnees as social
actors with access to information technology 'construct an imaginary
world dominated by the visual signifiers of Hellenic personal/national
identity: the mediascapes and ideoscapes of Hellenism in postmodernity' (Hamilakis 2000: 254). Such digital ethnoscapes indicate that 'the
projection of personal/national identities in cyberspace is often
grounded on the same essentialist and exclusivist notions which are
central to the national dream and imagination' (Hamilakis 2000: 258).
This type of imaginative heterotopia (Leontis 1995) creates a utopian
space of a representation of an 'authentic' homeland through migrant
social and cultural constructions that extends beyond territorial boundaries but is nevertheless a cultural spatial configuration of an idealised
ancestral homeland.

7.5   Epilogue

The writing of this book took place in Athens, Greece. I had decided
that in order to have a physical and mental immediacy with my participants and the field, it would be appropriate to temporarily renounce
my state of migrancy and become once again a returnee. By immersing
myself in the 'Greekness' of everyday life, I could fluctuate between 'in-

siderness' and 'outsiderness', bringing the field closer to the manuscript and producing a final written text collaborative of the field, my participants, my analysis and synthesis of all the above. So, in the midst of heavy construction in preparation for the 2004 Olympics in Greece, the six-month EU Presidency and the EU summit and enlargement treaty of ten new entrants, the war in Iraq, domestic political turmoil, national and international tension, municipal elections, the capture and trial of the November 17th terrorist group and much more (including temperatures regularly exceeding 40°C), my writing was set in a context shaped by particularly complex and challenging events. When I revisited my work and engaged in additional writing and subsequent revisions of the manuscript for publication, again, I had decided that this engagement would take place within a changing human geography of Greece, under new spatial and temporal conditions. Thus, once again, a 'devoted return migrant', I relocated to Athens from abroad. My (re)writing took place in a general atmosphere of transformations but also fixities in a context of an apparent diffusion of politics in most spheres of everyday life. In the spring of 2004, Greece witnessed the change of a socialist to a conservative government more than two decades later[4] while the rest of the world in the autumn of the same year during the US Presidential Elections saw the incumbent President Republican George W. Bush defeat the Democratic Senator John F. Kerry of Massachusetts. While this election campaign was widely seen as a referendum on the conduct of the 'war on terror', a global astonishment followed the election results. Then, the dawn of 2006 brought about a series of violent conflict that cost the lives of people and created much polarisation, namely the protests by Muslims in several countries spurred by the publication of cartoons of the Prophet Mohammed published by a Danish newspaper. For most of the first quarter of 2006, intense scepticism had come to dominate public debates on a domestic as well as international level. The 'cartoon war' had exacerbated attitudes of xenophobia and racism on a worldwide crisis level triggering negative emotions and questioning identities. Anti-immigrant attitudes and islamophobic feelings, often concealed in a selectively applied 'free-speech' argument, worked against any progress that had been made in achieving cultural pluralism and tolerance in a democratic context. In Greece, the beginning of 2006 brought about a series of new scandals publicly surfacing in relation to telephone interceptions, what Le Figaro has termed 'Watergrec' as more than 100 mobile phone numbers belonging mostly to members of the Greek government and to top-ranking civil servants – including those of the Prime Minister Kostas Karamanlis – were found to have been illegally tapped for a period of at least one year. Frequent demonstrations in the capital of Athens followed for most of the spring to protest economic

and educational policies planned to be implemented by the government and hence the growing financial crisis, unemployment and plans
to introduce an academic evaluation system in Greek public universities along with the constitutional recognition and establishment of private higher institutions in Greece. Ultimately, nothing had 'essentially'
changed in Greece during my absence.

However, when I had initially written this concluding chapter, I had
drawn much inspiration during my stay in the island of Rhodes in the
summer of 2003 when I participated and presented my work at the
*First International Conference on the Future and New Directions in the
Humanities*. During a simple but revealing stroll outside the massive
medieval walls of the old city of Rhodes, which was listed by the world
heritage as the largest inhabited medieval town in Europe, one needs
only to glance at the layers of history evident at every turn, from Gothic
buildings to mosques, synagogues and orthodox churches, all these
cultural influences are still obvious today in the fabric of this city, a cosmopolitan meeting point between East and West for two and a half
millennia. When I spoke with the locals, they all testified to how 'natural' the coexistence has been among Greeks, Turks, and migrants/for-
eigners: Christians, Muslims and Jews: 'No problem. We all live together. History brought us together; this is our *patrida*', a homeland
that is a home to all and an island that is a homeland for all. The pro-
fane and mundane of our everyday lives suggests the need to eventually secure a meaningfully rooted life. Home is mostly thought to be
both where you *place* your hat but also where your heart places you.
And thus the need to be intimately grounded corresponds to the human desire of continuity in the *sense of place*, anchored to its history
and bounded to its people. But for the return migrant, home does not
necessarily correspond to shared walls, shared memories and shared
experiences. Home, for most of the return migrants in my study, is
within and beyond their 'migranthood'. Ironically enough, the Greek
language has the same word for both stranger and guest/hospitality
(*xenos, filoxenia*). 'Greekness' should no longer be understood as property or essence, the culmination of 'Greek' norms or values, but alternatively must be understood in terms of the multiplicity of ways in
which 'being Greek' is always under a process of 'becoming' in an in-
scribed and negotiated relation to the collectivity and the processes associated with a global-modern Greece. *Identification in return migration
must be examined through the prism of situated subjectivity*. Ethnic membership is not just a process of imagining and remembering the nation; it is above all 're-membering' articulated by the returnees' perceptions and their reactions to others' perceptions of what constitutes the
'Greek', the particularistic processing of a self in relation to the other
and the otherness of modernity and post-modernity in the homeland.

It is only inevitable that *a critical human geography of return migration* must focus on both identities and locations (constructively not dogmatically) because people and place require understanding of all historical, cultural, social, political and geographical contours and perspectives involved.

Notes

Notes Chapter 1

1 I would like to clarify my usage of the term 'ideology'. I recognise that the term has become fortified throughout the history of the social sciences by complex meanings primarily around issues of power and political substance and is heavily loaded either from a Marxist, Althusserian, Gramscian or Foucauldian perspective; however, my intention is not to place it within or deriving from any of these theoretical contexts. I am using it in its most simplistic form, that of its linguistic origin, from the Greek *ideologia* (*idea* and *logos*) meaning the 'study of ideas' or the 'discourse' meaning the 'speech of ideas'. Therefore, my participants' expression of their ideas of home, return and self, that is, the voices of the returnees, are their ideologies. The same holds for the usage of the term 'geographies'. Again, this originates from the Greek, 'to write one's world'. The geographies of place, culture and identity are the articulation of their new world. Hence, their ideologies become the method of articulating their geographies, simply by using the term 'method' from the Greek: 'a route that leads to the goal'.

2 The distinction between social and psychological forms of constructionism is not within the scope of this section, nor is the analysis of differences in terminology and its usage. Briefly, for example, Phillips (1995, 1997a, 1997b) divides social constructivists from psychological constructivists while Gergen (1994a, 1994b) terms the former group social constructionists and the latter constructivists. In maintaining consistency with the *social* content of the discussion I use the term *constructionism* throughout the study.

3 In addition to many thorough annual surveys of feminist geography and related work published by the journals *Progress in Human Geography* (Bondi 1990, 1992; McDowell 1993a, 1993b) and *Professional Geographer* (in particular Nast 1994, vol. 46, no.1) that includes several articles, refer to Gluck and Patai 1991 and Sangster 1998.

4 Some claim phenomenology as a founding epistemology for qualitative inquiry, but as Schwandt convincingly argues, 'it is virtually impossible to discuss the relevance for qualitative inquiry of this complex, multifaceted philosophy in general terms without reducing the notion of phenomenology to a caricature. Phenomenology means something far more complicated than a romanticized notion of seeing the world of actors "as it really is"' (2000: 206; quotations in the original).

5 Researchers in the social sciences have used a variety of terms to refer to the people involved in the study, such as *actor, interviewee, informant, individual, participant, respondent, subject*. Although I will try to maintain consistency by using the term *participant*, there are instances when I need to emphasise that the participants are also *actors* and *subjects* as they are *interviewees* and *individuals*.

6 'Auto/ethnography' is a term used widely in the 1970s (first reference by Karl Heider 1975 and introduced formally by David Hayano 1979) to capture the experience of anthropologists looking at worlds of their 'own people'. It has acquired additional

meanings and developed further recently to include the reflexive and recursive life story, the observation of the self in sociological introspections. Guiding texts on this include Reed-Danahay, D.E. (ed.) (1997) *Auto/Ethnography: Rewriting the Self and the Social* among many others. A detailed overview of the term and a scrutinised presentation of the literature are provided by Ellis and Bochner 2000.

7   For a very challenging and critical paper that highlights the lack of engagement by population geographers with social construction and other recent developments in social theory while offering insightful suggestions of areas in which there is much potential for integrating these theories, refer to White and Jackson 1995.

8   We are then confronted with the issue of the self: Whose self? What self? Which self? This is a complex discussion that extends from the deconstructed 'authentic self' to the polyvocality of the 'post'-post period. For a very solid presentation of these issues, refer to Gergen and Gergen 2000.

Notes Chapter 2

1   Excellent interpretations of Lefebvre's theories can be found in Harvey 1989; Gregory 1994; Soja 1996.

2   Others have depicted this space as the 'thirdspace of political choice' (Soja and Hooper 1993: 198-199), drawing heavily on Foucault's (1970) notion of 'heterotopia', a place that captures the new cultural politics of difference.

3   Topophilia and the related idea of 'sense of place' are associated with the humanistic geography of the 1970s and despite the cross-cultural variation of degree of attachment to home-places that stimulated much discussion (progressive and reactionary – researchers have revealed a problematic side of topophilia manifested in the celebration of the nation-state through landscape aesthetic appreciation (aestheticisation of place and landscape). Topophilia however also promotes ethical behaviour that integrates feeling and thought.

4   Refer to Bourdieu, P. (1986) *The forms of capital.*

5   Only to consider that half a century ago, 164 definitions of culture were collected by Kroeber and Kluckhohn in their *Culture: a critical review of concepts and definitions* (1952), to be followed by several more attempts of comprehensive reviews (Singer 1968; Schneider and Bonjean 1973; Keesing 1974).

6   From the many studies on culture and of cultural processes, see Geertz 1973; Clifford and Marcus 1986; Herzfeld 1987.

7   As Mitchell suggests, 'culture is politics by another name' ...and when it is linked with geography – with the spaces, places, and landscapes that make it possible – it is a source of power and domination that must always be reckoned with. 'Culture', then, is *both* flux and stability, *both* a set of constantly changing relationships and a (socially produced) thing. (Mitchell 2000: 294; italics and parenthesis in the original).

8   This has been wonderfully accomplished by Eriksen (2002) in providing a careful review of the literature and the distinction between essentialist/primordialist and instrumentalist/constructivist accounts.

9   Transnational theory, from the early 90s on, has generated vital new analytical and methodological approaches within migration research and has added many articles and texts to the international literature. Kivisto's (2001) article, 'Therorizing transnational immigration: a critical review of current efforts', offers a thorough review and critique of the term as a conceptual construct and theoretical frame, ' as does Bailey's (2002) critical overview. Also, a special issue of the *Journal of Ethnic and Migration Studies* looks at 'Transnationalism and Identity': vol. 27, no. 4, October 2001. Trans-

nationalism in the second generation is explored in Levitt and Waters (eds.) (2002) *The Changing Face of Home: The Transnational Lives of the Second Generation*, New York: Russell Sage Foundation.

10 An overwhelming amount of work has been done on the 'nation' and 'nationalism', the nation-state and on 'nations' without states. From the classics, see Hobsbawm and Ranger 1983; Smith 1986; Hobsbawm 1990; Balibar and Wallerstein 1991; Anderson 1991; Gellner 1983, 1994.

11 Very thorough texts on the notion of 'diaspora' have been written by Safran 1991; Tololyan 1996; Cohen 1997; Vertovec 1997; Van Hear 1998.

12 Almost two decades before Anderson, the less well-known work of Cornelius Castoriadis (1965 French text; 1987 English text) analysed the nation as *imaginary signification* while suggesting comparisons with other cultural formations.

Notes Chapter 3

1 Even more limiting is the characterisation of Fairchild's book being permeated by a 'definite anti-Greek bias' and Burgess's book, in striking contrast, written by an 'enthusiastic Philhellen' (Vlachos 1968: 31).

2 Perspectives on whether *insider* or *outsider* scholarship is more 'appropriate' have been debated (Gefou-Madianou 1993; Panourgia 1995). I have addressed these questions as politically and socially embedded concerns that highlight the researcher's ethical responsibilities.

3 Special reference to the Saloutos tradition is made in the 'Moskos-Georgakas Debate': Georgakas, Moskos, Kitroeff (1987) in the *Journal of Hellenic Diaspora*, vol. xiv, no, 1-2, pp. 5-77.

4 Refer to Laliotou (2004: 191-195) for a critical review of Saloutos' comprehensive representation of the history of Greeks in the United States. Laliotou argues – and absolutely rightly so – that Saloutos' presentation of the absence of women from the history of Greek migration and the racist discrimination against migrants as natural matters of historical fact are, among other issues, 'illustrative examples of the ways in which Saloutos constructed a unidirectional and homogenizing representation of Greek migrants in the United States, which naturalized historical subjectivity and omitted the historicization of the studied categories and concepts' (2004: 195).

5 'America' used in the original by Sowell. My personal awareness is that the use of 'America' to mean US-American is problematic because it implies a hegemonic reproduction and power demarcation of the United States over the other American countries, and therefore I have tried to use the appropriate term. The migrants and returnees themselves at times use 'America' for the United States. This was neither contested nor argued and hence the returnee-narrator was not directed towards such understandings.

6 In addition to success stories interjected in the books listed below, one can consult Barkan (2001) *Making It in America: A Sourcebook on Eminent Ethnic Americans*.

7 For a more detailed account of this refer, among others, to Saloutos 1964; Vlachos 1968; Tavuchis 1972; Scourby 1984; Monos 1986; Georgakas 1987; Psomiades 1987; Kourvetaris 1997; Moskos 1999; Constantinou 2002 and for a quite comprehensive bibliographic guide on materials relevant to Greek-American Studies, although not relatively recent, see the one compiled by then librarian and head of the Bibliographic Control Department of the Columbia University Law Library, Zenelis 1982.

8 The former refers to external participation in the larger social system and the latter to the subjective feelings of becoming 'American' based on internalisation of new va-

lues. Initiated by Gordon 1964, there is a newly activated interest – the 'rethinking' in assimilation theories (Alba and Nee 1997; Gans 1999).

9   www.cnn.com/WORLD/europe/9911/20/clinton.trip.02
     http://news.bbc.co.uk/2/hi/world/Europe/529932.stm
     www.hollandsentinel.com/stories/112199/new_clinton.html

10   More on this and the politics of relations as well as politics and relations between the US and Greece can be found in Couloumbis and Iatrides 1980; Couloumbis 1983; Psomiades and Thomadakis 1993; Coufoudakis, Psomiades and Gerolymatos 1999.

11   For an excellent exploration of 'hybridity', terminologically as well as analytically, re-fer to Hutnyk (2005). Hutnyk's article offers a topographical survey of how the term hybridity has been used and misused along with its synonyms; however, it does not offer any alternative terms or concepts but concludes that, 'If some kind of hybridity appears, paradoxically, to be a good thing, a more radical analysis is needed to equip organized groups and achieve it in an equitable way' (99). Here, I must emphasise that my use of the term aims at highlighting biculturality as the product of diasporic migrant agency, thus going beyond 'romanticised', 'exoticised' and 'naturalised' cate-gories of a hyphenated self (the Greek-American). It is plausible then to consider the 'mixed' cultural/ethnic/national self as a subject and an agent experiencing space in the ancestral homeland with its social and political processes.

12   A thought-provoking article that questions assimilation assumptions in correlation to American political structures and proposes a 'binational identity' is Karpathakis 1999.

13   There are many sources (anthropology and ethnography of Greece) on the concept of 'philotimo'; among them see Herzfeld 1986 and Papataxiarchis 1991. A detailed defi-nition is also provided by Kourvetaris and Dobratz (1987: 5-6).

14   A very thorough discussion of Greek-American associations that highlights many in-teresting aspects of organisational activity can be found in Constantinou 1996 and Moskos 1999.

15   Greek return migration data are neither clear nor consistently documented; hence only approximations in terms of numbers are available. Fakiolas and King (1996) of-fer an insightful interpretation on the matter and a thorough review of the official figures. To this date and to my knowledge no precise data has been recorded on Greek-American return migrants (of any generation).

16   Recent research includes the following: For a synopsis and comparative analysis of the key literature on return migration in Italy in the 1970s and 1980s, refer to King (1988) and for a recent introductory historical overview King (2000). In terms of em-pirical case-study research, refer to the following: Beenstock (1996) on return migra-tion to Israel; Yamanaka (1996) and Tsuda (2001; 2003) on Japanese-Brazilians; Ta-kenaka (1999) on the Japanese Peruvians; Lorenzo-Hernandez (1999) on Puerto Ri-cans; Lomsky-Feder and Rapoport (2000; 2001), Remennick (2003), Yelenevskaya and Fialkova (2004), Fialkova and Yelenevskaya (2005), as well as Yelenevskaya (2005) on Russian-Jews; Baldassar (2001) discusses first and second generation 're-turn visits' of Italian-Australians; Hammerton and Thomson (2005) present return migration life histories of the British relocating from Australia; the edited volume by Long and Oxfeld (2004) offers an anthropological analysis on return through in-depth ethnographic case studies in Barbados, Bosnia, China, Eritrea and Ethiopia, Germany, Nicaragua, the Philippines, Rwanda and Vietnam while the edited volume by Potter, Conway and Phillips (2005) examines return migration in the Caribbean case, and Markowitz and Stefansson (eds.) (2004) *Homecomings: Unsettling Paths of Return* contributes ethnographic case studies while challenging the variety of ways in which return migration is imagined, motivated, practiced and experienced as invol-ving obstacles, suffering and continual diasporic sentiments. Such accounts, of both

possible and impossible *homecomings*, are evident in my study as well and will become apparent in the participants' narrations in the chapters that follow. Finally, Panagakos (2003c) is the only recent study on second-generation return migration to the ancestral homeland, and it examines the Greek-Canadian case.

17 The terminology has its own inherent ambivalence in the usage of home-host constructions and realities. I will clearly specify throughout the book the geographical location as well as cultural (dis)location of what *home* and *host* mean as expressed by the interviewees.

18 The terminology and typologies that have been suggested are based on various categories such as migrants' intentions (King, Strachan and Mortimer 1983; King 2000), classification based on the level of development of the host country (King 2000) and various stages of acculturation of migrants in the host countries (Cerase 1974; King 2000). For further commentary on definitions of terminology, refer to Bovenkerk 1974; King, Strachan and Mortimer 1983.

19 This paragraph is based on a concise interpretation of King's detailed review of the literature; see King 2000; King, Strachan and Mortimer 1983.

20 Also addressed as the 'illusion', the 'myth' or 'dream' of return, in particular when it never materialises.

21 For the Italian case ('Return and the problems of the second generation'), refer to King (1988: 87-89).

22 Refer to Chapter one, footnote 1, for a clarification of how I use the terms 'ideology' and 'geography' in my theoretical approach and analysis.

23 I draw inspiration for this in connection to David McCrone's claim that 'identities should be seen as a concern with "routes" rather than "'roots'", as maps for the future rather than trails from the past' (1998: 34). This is a core theme in my study of return migration and identity construction.

Notes Chapter 4

1   In order to demarcate my analysis from the return migrants' words, I have indented the participants' narratives. Furthermore, in order to distinguish the interview excerpts (oral narratives) from the participants' personal journals (written narratives), I have used the italic formatting for the written narratives while the oral ones are in regular print. One reason for making this choice is that the oral extracts are more numerous than the written ones, hence the former are placed in the more legible format.

2   That basically translates into a homogenous population consisting of Greeks, born to Greeks, raised the Greek way, married to Greeks, having and raising Greek children, following the Greek Orthodox faith, speaking Greek, basically behaving and practising all that is Greek.

3   The word 'pragmatic' is used in the Greek etymology of πραγματικός, meaning 'real'. Although reality is always negotiable, there is however a generally agreeable perception of major socio-cultural, political and economic changes in a country.

4   The usage of 'motherland' is a dual reflection of the gendered self and the nurturing, comforting fulfilment of the return project. The homeland return is relocation in search of home and self, the gendered self. The female returnees consistently employ the term. Moreover, such views of place that reverberate with nostalgia for something lost are coded female (Rose 1993; Massey 1994).

5   Only recently, in the summer–autumn of 2006 was a discussion initiated on the separation of Church and State in Greece. A recent series of corruption and other scandals in the Greek Orthodox Church, however, has led an increasing number of

Greeks to recognise the issue. The position of the Church of Greece and its relations with the State are set forth in Article 3, par. 1 of the present Constitution (1975/ 1986/2001). According to this article, (a) The Greek-Orthodox dogma is the prevailing religion, (b) The Church of Greece is inseparably united in doctrine with the Ecumenical Patriarchate of Constantinople and with all other Orthodox Churches, and (c) The Church is self-administered and autocephalous. A separation of Church and State would require an amendment of the Constitution.

Notes Chapter 5

1   I am borrowing a term used by Al Thomson in his work on return migration, an oral history project about post-war migration between Britain and Australia (Thomson 1999).
2   Refer to Bhabha 1990, 1994; Chambers 1996, and Chapter 2 for more on third space.
3   This is the terminology introduced by Appadurai 1991; see also Soja 1996.
4   For a very intriguing discussion of how migration as a literary theme has been used as a metaphor of death, including the work of Stratis Haviaras, a Greek migrant novelist and curator of the poetry collection in the Harvard University Library, refer to White 1995: 6-7.
5   Several interesting studies have been conducted in relation to the coffee shop culture and gender. Refer to Cowan 1990, 1991 and Papataxiarchis 1991 for more on this.
6   Seremetakis explains that this view is different from Danforth's (1982). She explains that in his model, 'xenitia as journey and passage bridges the opposition between life and death'. Seremetakis in her study shows instead that xenitia organises the opposition between life and death as that of inside and outside (1991: 244).
7   Recent discussions of the concept of Diaspora emphasise a tendency toward extending the definition to encapsulate many different migratory situations. See, for example, the Special Issue on 'Geographies of Diaspora', International Journal of Population Geography, vol. 9, no. 4, 2003 and specifically Paul White's article on the Japanese in Latin America, where the author points that, 'constructions of the continuing Japanese-ness of the diaspora population have been contested, and differences rather than similarities have been stressed' (White 2003: 309).
8   More or less there are at least two problematic aspects to these diasporic internalisations. On the one hand, it is highly contentious whether the United States is a truly multicultural society and on the other, for the most part Greek-Americans maintain social contacts within an insulated ethnic enclave and have very little meaningful contact with other ethnic groups. The latter correlates with their intensified quest for a return to an 'authentic' homeland.
9   Costantakos' (1993) study revealed the predominance of the family as a source of support and a consistent theme of attitudes of filial obligation toward aged parents cutting across three generations of Greek-Americans.
10 Although the official practice of dowries in Greece has been legally abolished, it is still very much implemented unofficially, mostly for brides but also for grooms. Again, there is a gender specific component in this discussion. Dating back to ancient times, a Greek woman had no rights in marriage and her father would offer a dowry or payment to any available and willing man to 'take the daughter off his hands' (Flacelière 2002; Papanikolas 2002).
11 For a very thorough bibliography of the social scientific perspectives on house and home that includes a synopsis of material drawn from a wide range of social science disciplines (theoretical work, government and policy documents, empirical research

reported in journal articles, book chapters, conference papers and monographs), refer to Perkins, Thorns, Winstanley and Newton (2002) 'The Study of "Home" From a Social Scientific Perspective: An Annotated Bibliography', (http://www.ssrc.canterbury.ac.nz/research/RPHS/hh/homepub.pdf). The authors state that 'the annotations span a wide time period, and represent various schools of thought, including the post-modern shift from grand theorising to temporally and spatially contextualised theorising' (3). Additionally, for an excellent interdisciplinary approach that examines the dominant and recurring ideas about 'home' represented in the relevant theoretical and empirical literature, refer to Mallet, S. (2004) 'Understanding home: a critical review of the literature', *the Sociological Review*, vol. 52, no. 1, pp. 62-89.

12 Former Prime Ministers, now both deceased, they dominated the politics of Greece in the later twentieth century. Papandreou (1919-1996) left for the US in 1938 after being arrested for alleged Trotskyist activity while a student, became a US citizen and followed a distinguished academic career. He returned to Greece, at the request of Prime Minister Konstantinos Karamanlis, in 1961 to head the Centre of Economic Research and Planning. He entered parliament for the first time in 1964. Arrested in 1967 under the dictatorship, he was allowed to leave the country where in exile he founded the Panhellenic Liberation Movement (PAK). He returned to Greece after the downfall of the dictatorship in 1974 and founded the Panhellenic Socialist Movement. Konstantinos Karamanlis (1907-1998), also President of the Republic for two terms (1980-1985; 1990-1995), led a self-imposed eleven-year exile in France, following defeat in the 1963 elections, disputes with the palace and a general feeling of disillusionment with politics. He was summoned back to preside over the return to civilian rule. He was instrumental in securing Greece's accession to the EC. Source: Clogg 2002.

13 George Andreas Papandreou (born June 16, 1952 in St. Paul, Minnesota) is a Greek politician and was Foreign Minister of Greece from 1999 to 2004. The son and grandson of Greek prime ministers, Papandreou became the leader of the Panhellenic Socialist Movement (PASOK) party in February 2004.

Notes Chapter 6

1   The core theme of the plot is reduced to a tale of intermarriage between a 'large and noisy Greek-American family' and a 'plain and polite Wasp family', with a lot of 'ethnic distress', 'stereotyping' and 'struggle' in between, on the part of the families and the 'mixed' couple.

2   The usage of 'motherland' is a dual reflection of the gendered self and the nurturing, comforting fulfilment of the return project. The homeland return is relocation in search of home and self, the gendered self. The female returnees consistently employ the term 'motherland'. Moreover, such views of place that reverberate with nostalgia for something lost are coded female (Rose 1993; Massey 1994).

3   Hybridity is a term that initially included mixed race debates and involved cultural discourses of racial purity. The new use of the term rejects issues of purity and focuses rather on paradigms of identity linked to the idea of 'non-essentialist new ethnicities', which involves a search for roots and grounding but does not include the above limitations. Much of Stuart Hall's work over the years concentrates on this idea (Hall 1993; Hall and du Gay 1996, etc.).

4   Although the term arises from linguistic theory, it is also powerfully introduced into feminist theory through the work of Judith Butler. The concept helps to draw a bit further from the fluidity and forever changing state of identities to an arena where identities are questioned in relation to their production, embodiment and perfor-

mance within socio-political contexts. Through the performative acts of gender and
ethnicity, social categories are mutually constructed (Butler 1990, 1993).

5   In her splendid book *Gender, Identity and Place: Understanding Feminist Geographies*
(1999), Linda McDowell examines the ways in which gender and place are interrelated and construct multiple identities in a variety of contexts including the nation-
state. My exploration of gender-nation-place is situated within this framework.

6   For a wonderful review of discussions about cultural constructions of identities and
subjectivities in relation to discourses of gender, ethnicity, race, class and culture with
special reference to the Greek diasporic condition, refer to Bottomley 1991, 1992.

7   The time of the post-modern is the time of neo-tribalism according to French sociolo-
gist Maffesoli (*Le Temps des Tribus*, 1988-*The Time of the Tribes*, 1996).

8   I found Martin Sökefeld's article, 'Alevism Online: Re-Imagining a Community in
Virtual Space' (2002), very intriguing as it explores such social and cultural spaces,
interconnections and transformations within cyberspace and the internet. Moreover,
it discusses the concepts of virtual community and virtual diaspora, the notions of
community and identity, while drawing clear conceptual distinctions between *social
virtual communities* and *cultural virtual communities*. Equally intriguing is a recent special issue of *Global Networks: a Journal of Transnational Affairs*, edited by Anastasia N.
Panagakos and Heather Horst and entitled 'Return to Cyberia: Technology and the
Social Worlds of Transnational Migrants' (2006).

9   *Marginality*, in sociological terms, refers to the uncertain position of persons experiencing two cultures but identified with neither; it can also include the idea, at a psychological level, of a *discrepancy* between in-group members' real and ideal identifications (Driedger 1996: 132).

10 In Plato's *Cratylus*. Quoted from Kirk, Raven and Schofield 1995.

Notes Chapter 7

1   George John Tenet was sworn in as Director of Central Intelligence on 11 July 1997
following a unanimous vote by both the Senate Select Committee on Intelligence
and the full Senate. While in this position, he was head of the Intelligence Community (all foreign intelligence agencies of the United States) and director of the Central
Intelligence Agency. He resigned on 3 June 2004 citing personal reasons.

2   Isocrates (436-338 BC) declared that being a Greek was no longer dependent on
blood but rather on participation in Greek education (*Παιδεία/Paideia*). Paideia refers
to both culture and formal education. Specifically, 'So far has Athens left the rest of
mankind behind in thought and expression that her pupils have become the teachers
of the world, and she has made the name of Hellas distinctive no longer of race but
of intellect, and the title of Hellene a badge of education rather than of common des-
cent', from the original: Και το των Ελλήνων όνομα πεποίηκε μηκέτι του γένους, αλλά
της διανοίας δοκείν τεκμήριον είναι, και μάλλον Έλληνας καλείσθαι τους της παιδεύσεως
της ημετέρας ή τους της κοινής φύσεως μετασχόντες (Ισοκράτους Πανηγυρικός Β, 50).

3   Refer to Tzanelli (2006) for a critical examination of the episode that took place in
northern Greece, 2000/ 2003, when an Albanian student, having the highest marks
in his class, was elected flag-carrier in a commemorative parade during a national
holiday celebration. The article discusses three versions of Greek identity emerging
in this particular context, namely, the first as based on civic understandings of identity, promoting the current Europeanist project of citizenship as belonging. The second version drawing upon the notion of 'culture' as an all-encompassing concept to
promote ideas of Greek cultural 'purity' that have roots in Greek ethnogenesis. The
third version adopts an understanding of the 'nation' in terms of racial affiliation,

thus transforming it into a natural category. The argument put forward is that in the context of the 2000/2003 episode, Greek self-perceptions are affected by the problematic economic and cultural position of Greece within Europe, and Greek discourses of identity are a form of resistance to processes of 'Europeanisation' that threaten traditional 'imagined communities' embedded in history. Tzanelli's argument resonates with the discussion put forward in the previous chapter on *ideologies of self* and *geographies of identity* and the section which focuses on the transitions and transformations in a 'modernising' Greece that have penetrated 'traditions' and hence have 'threatened' identities and the 'authenticity' of 'Greekness'.

4   Verney (2004) explores the interrelationship between European and Greek political spaces in addressing what she terms 'the end of socialist hegemony' in Greece following the results of the Greek Parliamentary Elections in the spring of 2004. Verney's article investigates the apparent paradox of European success followed by domestic electoral failure and suggests that the 'key to the 2004 Greek parliamentary election was popular fatigue with a party that had dominated government for the previous two decades, while the unpopularity of the euro undoubtedly aggravated popular discontent, Europe was essentially a "missing issue" from the campaign, and as a result, she emphasises, this landmark election which inaugurates a new phase in Greek political life may also open new prospects for Greek Euroscepticism'.

Appendix

Second-generation Greek-American return migration: participant profile

Migrant	Sex	Age on Return	Age now	Place of birth	Year of parents' emigration	Education	Occupation	Marital Status	Living Arrangements
1. Medusa	F	20	21	Boston, Mass.	1950, have not returned	Bachelor's	Student	Single	Renting
2. Kassandra	F	46	49	New York, NY	1949, returned 1968	Bachelor's	Secretary	Single	With Parents-Homeowners
3. Sappho	F	16	23	San Diego, CA	1975, returned 1995	Bachelor's	Student	Single	With Parents-Homeowners
4. Hestia	F	27	28	Astoria, NY	1974, have not returned	Bachelor's	Homemaker	Married	Homeowner
5. Artemis	F	31	32	Brooklyn, NY	1955, have not returned	Bachelor's	Homemaker	Married	Renting
6. Plato	M	23	30	Brooklyn, NY	1970, returned 1999	Bachelor's	Advertising	Single	Renting
7. Pericles	M	46	50	Chicago, Illinois	1950, returned 1969	Associate Degree	Real Estate	Divorced	With Parent-Homeowner
8. Iphigenia	F	24	50	Boston, Mass.	1948, returned 1985	Master's	Educational Administration	Single	Homeowner
9. Aristotle	M	29	30	Houston, Texas	1970, returned 2001	Bachelor's	Logistics	Married	Homeowner
10. Diomides	M	33	34	Columbus, Ohio	1950, have not returned	Bachelor's	Computer Specialist	Married	Renting
11. Aspasia	F	21	32	Astoria, NY	1965, returned 1994	Associate Degree	Stylist	Married	Homeowner
12. Kalliope	F	20	23	Washington, DC	1973, have not returned	Bachelor's	Student	Single	Homeowner
13. Lyssandros	M	24	28	Portland, Oregon	1966, have not returned	Bachelor's	Student	Single	Renting

Name	Sex			Place		Year	Education	Occupation	Marital Status	Housing
14. Nestoras	M	28	39	South Gate, Michigan	1962, returned 1984	1991	Master's	Business Owner	Married	Homeowner
15. Electra	F	18	22	Astoria, NY	1972, have not returned	1998	Bachelor's	Waitress	Single	Renting
16. Ariadne	F	20	24	Astoria, NY	1972, have not returned	1998	Bachelor's	Student	Single	Renting
17. Antigone	F	21	22	San Jose, California	1975, have not returned	2001	Bachelor's	Student	Single	Renting
18. Medea	F	21	22	Vallejo, California	1971, have not returned	2001	Bachelor's	Student	Single	Renting
19. Hercules	M	16	27	Bethpage, NY	1967, returned 1991	1991	Technical School	Bank employee	Single	With Parents-Homeowners
20. Hermione	F	30	31	Brooklyn, NY	1957, have not returned	2001	Master's	Dietician	Single	With Relatives-Homeowners
21. Nephele	F	25	32	Brooklyn, NY	1967, have not returned	1995	Master's	Lecturer	Married	Homeowner
22. Phaedra	F	25	27	Brooklyn, NY	1969, returned 2001	2000	Master's	Network Administrator	Single	Renting
23. Sophocles	M	24	28	Astoria, NY	1967	1998	Master's	Lecturer	Married	With Parents-Homeowners
24. Andromache	F	32	34	Brooklyn, NY	1967, returned 1995	2000	Master's	Production Manager	Single	Renting
25. Hera	F	47	70	Boston, Mass.	1916, deceased, did not return	1979	Associate Degree	Retired, Airline employee	Married	Homeowner
26. Pandora	F	18	43	Kingston, NY	1957, deceased, did not return	1977	Bachelor's	Lecturer	Married	Homeowner
27. Persephone	F	14	24	Oregon, Portland	1970, returned 1993	1993	Master's	Postgraduate student	Single	Renting
28. Thalia	F	33	68	New York, NY	1928, deceased, did not return	1968	Master's	Retired, School Teacher	Married	Homeowner

29. Kalypso	F	22	41	Flint, Michigan	1958, returned 1990	1984	Associate Degree	Administration	Single	With parents-Homeowners
30. Kallisto	F	12	21	Astoria, NY	1965	1992	Bachelor's	Student	Married	Homeowner
31. Iokaste	F	23; 30	30	Chicago	1970, have not returned	1994-97; 2001	Master's	Lecturer	Married	Homeowner
32. Hypatia	F	14; 23	30	Chicago	1957, have not returned	1985-88; 1994	Master's	Lecturer	Single	Homeowner
33. Polymnia	F	9	20	New York, NY	1960, returned 1990	1990	Bachelor's	Student	Single	With parents-Homeowners
34. Pythia	F	48	50	Ithaca, NY	1950, deceased, did not return	2000	Bachelor's	Secretary	Married	Homeowner
35. Thucydides	M	12	23	Chicago	1960, returned 1990	1990	Bachelor's	Student	Single	With parents-Homeowners
36. Xenofondas	M	8	22	New York, NY	1960, returned 1987	1987	Bachelor's	Student	Single	With parents-Homeowners
37. Aristophanes	M	18; 19	23	Poughkeepsie, NY	1975, returned 1996	1996; 1997	Bachelor's	Manages family business	Single	Homeowner
38. Achilles	M	25	33	Lowell, Massachusetts	1960, have not returned	1995	Master's	Lecturer / Translator	Single	Homeowner
39. Patroklos	M	30	37	Detroit, Michigan	1953, have not returned	1996	Bachelor's	Media / Advertising	Single	Renting
40. Hector	M	28	36	Seattle, Washington	1963, have not returned	1995	Bachelor's	Telecommunications	Single	Renting

Bibliography

Abu-Lughod, L. (1991), 'Writing against culture', in R.G. Fox (ed.), *Recapturing Anthropology: Working in the Present*, 137-162. Santa Fe, NM: School of American Research Press.

Adams, P.C., S. Hoelscher and K.E. Till (eds.) (2001), *Textures of Place: Exploring Humanist Geographies*. Minneapolis: University of Minnesota Press.

Ahmed, S. (1999), 'Home and away: Narratives of migration and estrangement', *International Journal of Cultural Studies* 2 (3): 329-347.

Ahmed, S., C. Castañeda, A-M. Fortier and M. Sheller (eds.) (2003), *Uprootings/Regroundings: Questions of Home and Migration*. Oxford: Berg.

Alba, R. and V. Nee (1997), 'Rethinking assimilation theory for a new era of immigration', *International Migration Review* 31(4): 826-874.

Alba, R. (1990), *Ethnic Identity: The Transformation of White America*. New Haven: Yale University Press.

Alcoff, L. and E. Potter (eds.) (1993), *Feminist Epistemologies*. New York: Routledge.

Alleyne, B. (2002), 'An idea of community and its discontents: towards a more reflexive sense of belonging in multicultural Britain', *Ethnic and Racial Studies* 25 (4): 607-627.

Allison, G.T. and K. Nicolaidis (eds.) (1997), *The Greek Paradox: Promise vs. Performance*. Cambridge, Massachusetts: The MIT Press.

Amitsis, G. and G. Lazaridis (eds.) (2001), *Legal and Sociopolitical Aspects of Immigration in Greece*. Athens: Papazisis (in Greek).

Anagnostou, Y. (2004), 'Forget the Past, Remember the Ancestors! Modernity, "Whiteness", American Hellenism, and the Politics of Memory in Early Greek America', *Journal of Modern Greek Studies* 22: 25-71.

Anderson, B. (1991), *Imagined Communities: Reflections on the Origins and Spread of Nationalism*. London: Verso.

Anemoyanis, V. (1982), 'Greek bilingual education in historical perspective', in H. Psomiades and A. Scourby (eds.) *The Greek American Community in Transition*, 171-179. New York: Pella.

Ankersmit, F.R. (2001), 'Six theses on narrativist philosophy of history', in G. Roberts (ed.) *The History and Narrative Reader*, 236-245. London: Routledge.

Anthias, F. (1998), 'Evaluating 'diaspora': beyond ethnicity?', *Sociology* 32 (3): 557-80.

Anthias, F. (2001), 'New hybridities, old concepts: the limits of 'culture'', *Ethnic and Racial Studies*, 24 (4): 619-641.

Appadurai, A. (1991), 'Global ethnoscapes: notes and queries for a transnational anthropology', in R.G. Fox (ed.) *Recapturing Athropology: Working in the Present*. 191-210. Santa Fe: School of American Research Press.

Baganha, M.I. (ed.) (1997), *Immigration in Southern Europe*. Oeiras: Celta.

Bailey, A.J. (2002), 'Turning transnational: notes on the theorisation of international migration', *International Journal of Population Geography* 7 (5): 413-428.

Baldassar, L. (2001), *Visits Home: Migration experiences between Italy and Australia*. Victoria: Melbourne University Press.

Balibar, E. (1996), 'The nation form: history and ideology', in G. Eley and R.G. Suny (eds.), *Becoming National: A Reader*, 132-149. Oxford: Oxford University Press.

Balibar, E. and Wallerstein, I. (1991), *Race, Nation and Class: Ambiguous Identities*. London: Verso.

Bammer, A. (1992), 'Editorial', *New Formations*, Issue 17: The Question of 'Home'.

Barkan, E.R. (ed.) (2001), *Making It in America: A Sourcebook on Eminent Ethnic Americans*. Santa Barbara, CA: ABC-CLIO, Inc.

Barth, F. (ed.) (1969), *Ethnic Groups and Boundaries. The Social Organisation of Culture Difference*. Bergen-Oslo: Universitetsforlaget (Scandinavian University Press).

Basch, L., N. Glick Schiller and C. Szanton Blanc (1994), *Nations Unbound: Transnational Projects, Postcolonial Predicaments, and Deterritorialized Nation-States*. New York: Gordon and Breach.

Basu, P. (2001), 'Hunting down home: reflections on homeland and the search for identity in the Scottish diaspora', in B. Bender and M. Winer (eds.), *Contested Landscapes: Movement, Exile and Place*, 333-348. Oxford: Berg.

Bauman, Z. (1993), *Postmodern Ethics*. Oxford: Blackwell.

Bauman, Z. (1999), *Culture as Praxis*. London: Sage.

Beenstock, M. (1996), 'Failure to absorb: remigration by immigrants into Israel', *International Migration Review* 30 (4): 950-979.

Benmayor, R. and A. Skotnes (1994), 'On migration and identity', in R. Benmayor and A. Skotnes (eds.), *International Yearbook of Oral History and Life Stories, Volume III: Migration and Identity*, 1-18. Oxford: Oxford University Press.

Berger, P. and T. Luckmann (1966), The Social Construction of Reality: A Treatise in the Sociology of Knowledge. London: Penguin Books, reprinted 1991.

Berger, P., B. Berger and H. Kellner (1973), *The Homeless Mind: Modernisation and Consciousness*. Harmondsworth: Penguin.

Berman, M. (1983), *All That is Solid Melts Into Air: The Experience of Modernity*. London: Verso.

Bernard, H.R. and S.Ashton-Vouyoucalos (1976), 'Return migration to Greece', *Journal of the Steward Anthropological Society* 8 (1): 31-51.

Bernard, H.R. and L. Comitas (1978), 'Greek return migration', *Current Anthropology* 19 (3): 658-659.

Bhabha, H. (ed.) (1990), *Nation and Narration*. London: Routledge.

Bhabha, H. (1994a), *The Location of Culture*. London: Routledge.

Bhabha, H. (1994b), 'Between identities: Homi Bhabha interviewed by Paul Thompson', in R. Benmayor and A. Skotnes. (eds.) International Yearbook of Oral History and Life Stories, Volume III: Migration and Identity, 183-199. Oxford: Oxford University Press.

Bilanakis, N., M.G. Madianos, and A. Liakos (1995), 'Demoralization and mental health: a community study among repatriated Greek immigrants', *European Journal of Psychiatry* 9 (1): 47-57.

Billig, M. (1995), *Banal Nationalism*. London: Sage.

Bodnar, J. (1985), *The Transplanted. A History of Immigrants in Urban America*. Bloomington: Indiana University Press.

Bondi, L. (1990), 'Progress in geography and gender: feminism and difference', *Progress in Human Geography* 14: 438-45.

Bondi, L. (1992), 'Gender and dichotomy', *Progress in Human Geography* 16: 98-104.

Bottomley, G. (1991), 'Culture, ethnicity, and the politics/poetics of representation', *Diaspora* 1 (3): 303-320.

Bottomley, G. (1992), *From Another Place: Migration and the Politics of Culture.* Cambridge: Cambridge University Press.

Bourdieu, P. (1977), *Outline of a Theory of Practice.* Cambridge: Cambridge University Press (trans. Richard Nice).

Bourdieu, P. (1986), 'The forms of capital, in J.G. Richardson (ed.), *Handbook of Theory and Research for the Sociology of Education*, 241-258. New York: Greenwood Press.

Bourdieu, P. (1989), *Distinction: a Social Critique of the Judgment of Taste.* London: Routledge.

Bourdieu, P. (2000), 'The biographical illusion', in P. du Gay, P, J. Evans and P. Redman (eds.), *Identity: a Reader*, 297-303. London: Sage.

Bovenkerk, F. (1974), *The Sociology of Return Migration: A Bibliographic Essay.* Publications of the Research Group on European Migration Problems, 20, The Hague: Nijhoff.

Brah, A. (1996), Cartographies of Diaspora: Contesting Identities. London: Routledge.

Braidotti, R. (1994), *Nomadic Subjects: Embodiment and Sexual Difference in Contemporary Feminist Theory.* New York: Columbia University Press.

Breakwell, G.M. and E. Lyons (eds.) (1996), Changing European Identities: Social Psychological Analyses of Social Change. Oxford: Butterworth-Heinemann.

Brettell, C.B. and Hollifield, J.F. (eds.) (2000), *Migration Theory: Talking Across Disciplines.* New York: Routledge.

Bromley, R. (2000), *Narratives for a New Belonging: Diasporic Cultural Fictions.* Edinburgh: Edinburgh University Press.

Burgess, T. (1913), *Greeks in America.* Boston: Sherman French.

Burke, P. (1997), 'An identity model for network exchange', *American Sociological Review* 62: 134-150.

Butler, J. (1990), *Gender Trouble: Feminism and the Subversion of Identity.* New York: Routledge.

Butler, J. (1993), *Bodies that Matter: On the Discursive Limits of 'Sex'.* London: Routledge.

Cain, M. (1986), 'Realism, feminism, methodology and the law', *International Journal of the Sociology of Law* 14 (3-4): 255-267.

Callinicos, C. (1991), 'Arranged marriage in Greek America: the modern picture bride', in D. Georgakas and C. Moskos (eds.), *New Directions in Greek American Studies*, 161-179. New York: Pella.

Callon, M. (1986a), 'The sociology of an Actor Network: the case of the electric vehicle', in M. Callonet al. (eds.), *Mapping the Dynamics of Science and Technology: Sociology of Science in the Real World*, 19-34. London: Macmillan.

Callon, M. (1986b), 'Some elements of a sociology of translation: Domestication of the scallops and the fisherman of St Brieuc Bay', in J. Law (ed.), *Power, Action and Belief: A New Sociology of Knowledge?*, 196-233. London: Routledge and Kegan Paul.

Campbell, J.R. and A. Rew (eds.) (1999), *Identity and Affect: Experiences of Identity in a Globalising World.* London: Pluto Press.

Carr. D. (2001), 'Narrative and the Real World: An Argument for Continuity', in G. Roberts (ed.) *The History and Narrative Reader*, 143-156. London: Routledge.

Carroll, N. (2002), 'Interpretation, history and narrative', in G. Roberts (eds.), *The History and Narrative Reader*, 246-265. London: Routledge.

Casey, E.S. (2001), 'Body, self and landscape: a geophilosophical inquiry into the place-world', in Adams, P.C., S. Hoelscher and K.E. Till (eds.), *Textures of Place: Exploring Humanist Geographies*, 403-425. Minneapolis: University of Minnesota Press.

Cassarino, J-P. (2004), 'Theorising Return Migration: The Conceptual Approach toReturn Migrants Revisited', *International Journal on Multicultural Societies* 6 (2): 253-279.

Castells, M. (1996), *The Rise of the Network Society.* Oxford: Blackwell.

Castells, M. (1997), *The Power of Identity.* Oxford: Blackwell.

Castles, S. and M.J. Miller (2003), *The Age of Migration: International Population Movements in the Modern World*. Third Edition. Basingstoke: Palgrave MacMillan.

Castoriadis, C. (1987), *The Imaginary Institution of Society*. Cambridge: Polity Press.

Cerase, F.P. (1974), 'Migration and social change: expectations and reality. A case study of return migration from the United States to Italy', *International Migration Review* 8 (2): 245-262.

Chamberlain, M. and S. Leydesdorff (2004), 'Introduction. Transnational families: memories and narratives', *Global Networks: a Journal of Transnational Affairs* 4 (3): 227-241.

Chamberlain, M. (1997), *Narratives of Exile and Return*. London: Macmillan.

Chambers, I. (1994), *Migrancy, Culture, Identity*. London: Routledge.

Chambers, I. (1996), 'Signs of silence, lines of listening', in I. Chambers and L. Curti (eds.), *The Post-Colonial Question: Common Skies, Divided Horizons*, 47-62. London: Routledge.

Chanfrault-Duchet, M-F. (1991), 'Narrative structures, social models, and symbolic representation in the life story', in S.B. Gluck One face, many masks: the singularity and plurality of Chinese identity', *Diaspora* 10 (3): 361-389.

Christensen, P., A. James and C. Jenks (2000), 'Home and movement: Children constructing 'family time', in S.L. Holloway and G. Valentine (eds.), *Children's Geographies: Playing, Living, Learning*, 139-155. London: Routledge.

Christou, A. (2001), 'The struggle, success, and national consciousness of the Greek diaspora in America', in L. Koski and K. Pajala (eds.), *American Studies at the Millennium: Ethnicity, Culture and Literature*, 125-135. Finland: University of Turku.

Christou, A. (2002), 'Greek American return migration: constructions of identity and reconstructions of place', *Studi Emigrazione* , Special issue: *Migration into Southern Europe: new trends and new patterns*, 145: 201-229.

Christou A. (2003a), 'Persisting Identities: Locating the *Self* and Theorizing the *Nation*', *Berkeley Journal of Sociology: A Critical Review*, Special issue: *Nationalisms: Negotiating Communities, Boundaries, and Identities*, 47: 115-134.

Christou A. (2003b), 'Migrating Gender: Feminist Geographies in Women's Biographies of Return Migration', *Michigan Feminist Studies*, Special issue: *Gender and Globalism*, 17: 71-103.

Christou, A. (2003c), '(Re)collecting memories, (Re)constructing identities and (Re)creating national landscapes: spatial belongingness, cultural (dis)location and the search for home in narratives of diasporic journeys', *International Journal of the Humanities* 1: 1-16.

Christou, A. (2004a) 'Human Rights and Migration – Theoretical Reflections and Empirical Considerations on issues of Social Justice, Ethics and Development: Towards a Redefinition of Civil Society', in V. Kyriakopoulos (ed.), *Olympia IV: Human Rights in the 21st Century: Migrants and Refugees*, 217-225. Athens: Sakkoulas Publishers.

Christou, A. (2004b), 'Reconceptualizing Networks through Greek-American Return Migration: Constructing *Identities*, Negotiating the *Ethnos* and Mapping *Diasporas* – Theoretical Challenges Regarding Empirical Contributions', *Spaces of Identity* 4 (3): 53-70.

Christou, A. (2006a), 'Crossing boundaries – Ethnicizing employment – Gendering labor: gender, ethnicity and social capital in return migration', *Social and Cultural Geography* 7 (1): 87-102.

Christou, A. (2006b), 'Deciphering Diaspora – Translating Transnationalism: family dynamics, identity constructions and the legacy of 'home' in second-generation Greek-American return migration', *Ethnic and Racial Studies* 29, in press.

Christou, A. (2006c), 'American dreams and European nightmares: experiences and polemics of second-generation Greek-American returning migrants', *Journal of Ethnic and Migration Studies* 32 (5): 831-845.

Clifford, J. and G.E. Marcus (1986), *Writing Culture: The Poetics and Politics of Ethnography*. Berkeley and Los Angeles: California University Press.

Clifford, J. (1988), *The Predicament of Culture: Twentieth Century Ethnography, Literature and Art*. London: Harvard University Press.

Clifford, J. (1997), 'Diasporas', in M. Guibernau and J. Rex (eds.), *The Ethnicity Reader: Nationalism, Multiculturalism and Migration*, 283-290. Cambridge: Polity Press.

Clogg, R. (1986) *A Short History of Modern Greece*. Second Edition. Cambridge: Cambridge University Press.

Clogg, R. (2002), *A Concise History of Greece*. Cambridge: Cambridge University Press.

Clogg, R. (ed.) (1999), *The Greek Diaspora in the Twentieth Century*. Basingstoke: Macmillan Press.

Cloke, P., C. Philo and D. Sadler (1991), *Approaching Human Geography: An Introduction to Contemporary Theoretical Debates*. London: Paul Chapman Publishing.

Cohen, A.P. (1985), *The Symbolic Construction of Community*. Chichester, Sussex: Ellis Horwood Limited.

Cohen, A.P. (1994), *Self Consciousness: An Alternative Anthropology of Identity*. London: Routledge.

Cohen, R. (1997), *Global Diasporas: An Introduction*. London: University College London Press.

Collins, P.H. (2000), 'It's all in the family: intersections of gender, race, and nation', in U. Narayan and S. Harding (eds.), *Decentering the Center: Philosophy for a Multicultural, Postcolonial, and Feminist World*, 156-176. Bloomington and Indianapolis: Indiana University Press.

Constantakos, C.M. (1982), 'Ethnic language as a variable in subcultural continuity', in H. Psomiades and A. Scourby (eds.), *The Greek American Community in Transition*, 137-170. New York: Pella.

Constantakos, C.M. (1993), 'Attitudes of filial obligation toward aging parents: a Greek American perspective', *Journal of Modern Hellenism* 10: 1-36.

Constantinou, S.T. and M.E. Harvey (1985), 'Basic dimensional structure and intergenerational differences in Greek American ethnicity', *Sociology and Social Research* 69 (2): 241-246.

Constantinou, S.T. (1989), 'Dominant themes and intergenerational differences in ethnicity: the Greek Americans', *Sociological Focus* 22 (2): 99-117.

Constantinou, S.T. (1996), 'Greek American networks', in G. Prevelakis (ed.), *The Networks of Diasporas*, 305-321. Nicosia, Cyprus: Cyprus Research Center.

Constantinou, S.T. (2002), 'Profiles of Greek-Americans', in K.A. Berry and M.L. Henderson (eds.), *Geographical Identities of Ethnic America: Race, Space, and Place*, 92-115. Reno and Las Vegas: University of Nevada Press.

Constas, D.C. and A.G. Platias (eds.) (1993), *Diasporas in World Politics: The Greeks in Comparative Perspective*. London: Macmillan.

Cosgrove, D. and P. Jackson (1987), 'New directions in cultural geography', *Area* 19: 95-101.

Coufoudakis, V., H.J. Psomiades and A. Gerolymatos (eds.) (1999), *Greece and the New Balkans: Challenges and Opportunities*. New York: Pella.

Couloumbis, T.A. and J.O. Iatrides (eds.) (1980), *Greek-American Relations: A Critical Review*. New York: Pella.

Couloumbis, T.A. (1983), *The United States, Greece and Turkey. The Troubled Triangle*. New York: Praeger.

Cowan, J.K. (1990), *Dance and the Body Politic in Northern Greece*. Princeton: Princeton University Press.

Cowan, J.K. (1991), 'Going out for coffee? Contesting the grounds of gendered pleasures in everyday sociability', in P. Loizos and E. Papataxiarchis (eds.), *Contested Identities:*

Gender and Kinship in Modern Greece, 180-202. Princeton: Princeton University Press.

Craib, I. (1998), *Experiencing Identity*. London: Sage.

Danforth, L. (1982), *The Death Rituals of Rural Greece*. Princeton: Princeton University Press.

de Lauretis, T. (1987), *Technologies of Gender*. London: Macmillan.

Demos, V. (1988), 'Ethnic mother tongue maintenance among Greek Orthodox Americans', *International Journal of Sociology of Language* 69: 59-71.

Denzin, N.K. (1997), *Interpretive Ethnography: Ethnographic Practices for the 21st century*. Thousand Oaks, California: Sage.

Dhruvarajan, V. and J. Vickers, J. (2002), *Gender, Race, and Nation: A Global Perspective*. Toronto: University of Toronto Press.

Dodgshon, R.A. (1998), *Society in Time and Space: A Geographical Perspective on Change*. Cambridge: Cambridge University Press.

Domingues, J.M. (2000), *Social Creativity, Collective Subjectivity and Contemporary Modernity*. London: Macmillan.

Dray, W.H. (2001), 'Narrative and historical realism', in G. Roberts (ed.), *The History and Narrative Reader*, 157-180. London: Routledge.

Driedger, L. (1996), *Multi-Ethnic Canada: Identities and Inequalities*. Toronto: Oxford University Press.

du Gay, P., J. Evans and P. Redman (eds.) (2000), *Identity: A Reader*. London: Sage.

Dubisch, J. (1995), *In a Different Place: Pligrimage, Gender, and Politics at a Greek Island Shrine*. Princeton: Princeton University Press.

Duncan, J. (1990), *The City as Text: The Politics of Landscape Interpretation in the Kandyan Kingdom*. Cambridge: Cambridge University Press.

Edensor, T. (2002), *National Identity, Popular Culture and Everyday Life*. Oxford: Berg.

Edwards, R. (2004), 'Present and absent in troubling ways: families and social capital debates', *The Sociological Review* 52 (1): 1-21.

Einhorn, B. (2000), 'Gender, Nation, Landscape and Identity in Narratives of Exile and Return', *Women's Studies International Forum* 23 (6): 701-713.

Elias, N. (1978), *The History of Manners*. Oxford: Blackwell.

Elliot, B. (1997), 'Migration, mobility, and social process: Scottish migrants in Canada', in D. Bertaux and P. Thompson (eds.), *Pathways to Social Class: A Qualitative Approach to Social Mobility*, 198-229. Oxford: Clarendon Press.

Ellis, C. and A.P. Bochner (2000), 'Autoethnography, personal narrative, reflexivity: researcher as subject', in N.K. Denzin Y.S. Lincoln (eds.), *Handbook of Qualitative Research*, Second Edition. 733-768. Thousand Oaks, California: Sage Publications.

Ellis, C. and A.P. Bochner (eds.) (1996), *Composing Ethnography: Alternative Forms of Qualitative Writing*. London: Sage.

Entrikin, N.J. (1991), *The Betweenness of Place: Towards a Geography of Modernity*. London: Macmillan.

Entrikin, N.J. (2001), 'Geographer as humanist', in Adams, P.C., S. Hoelscher and K.E. Till (eds.), *Textures of Place: Exploring Humanist Geographies*, 426-440. Minneapolis: University of Minnesota Press.

Epstein, A.L. (1978), *Ethos and Identity: Three Studies in Ethnicity*. London: Tavistock Publications.

Eriksen, T. H. (2002), *Ethnicity and Nationalism. Anthropological Perspectives*. Second Edition. London: Pluto Press.

Erikson, E.H. (1968), *Identity: Youth and Crisis*. New York: Norton.

Essays on Greek Migration (1967), *Migration Series no.1*. Athens: Social Sciences Centre.

Evergeti, V. (2006), 'Living and Caring between two cultures: narratives of Greek women in Britain', *Community, Work and Family* 9 (3), in press.

Fairchild, H.P. (1911), *Greek Immigration to the United States*. New Haven: Yale University Press.

Faist, T. (1999), 'Developing transnational social spaces: The Turkish-German example', in L. Pries (ed.), *Migration and Transnational Social Spaces*, 36-69. Aldershot: Ashgate.

Fakiolas, R. and R. King (1996), 'Emigration, return migration, immigration: a review and evaluation of Greece's postwar experience of international migration', *International Journal of Population Geography* 2 (2): 171-190.

Fakiolas, R. (1980), 'Problems and Opportunities of the Greek Migrants Returning from Western Europe', Athens: Centre of Planning and Economic Research.

Faubion, J. (1993), *Modern Greek Lessons: A Primer in Historical Constructivism*. Princeton: Princeton University Press.

Featherstone, M. and S. Lash (eds.) (1999), *Spaces of Culture: City, Nation, World*. London: Sage.

Fialkova, L. and M.N. Yelenevskaya (2005), 'Incipient Soviet Diaspora: Encounters in Cyberspace', *Croatian Journal of Ethnology and Folklore Research* 42 (1): 83-99.

Findlay, A.M. and L.L.N. Li (1997), 'An auto-biographical approach to understanding migration: the case of Hong Kong emigrants', *Area* 29 (1): 33-44.

Flaceliere, R. (2002), *Daily Life in Greece at the Time of Pericles*. New York: Sterling Publications.

Foner, N. (2000), *From Ellis Island to JFK: New York's Two Great Waves of Immigration*. New York: Russell Sage Foundation.

Fortier, A.M. (2000), *Migrant Belongings: Memory, Space, Identity*. Oxford: Berg.

Foucault, M. (1980), *Power/knowledge: selected interviews and other writings 1972-1977*. Brighton: Harvester.

Foucault, M. (1986), 'Of other spaces', *Diacritics* 16: 22-27, (trans. Jay Miskowiec).

Gans, H.J. (1979), 'Symbolic ethnicity: the future of ethnic groups and cultures in America', *Ethnic and Racial Studies* 2 (1): 1-20.

Gans, H.J. (1994), 'Symbolic ethnicity and symbolic religiosity: towards a comparison of ethnic and religious acculturation', *Ethnic and Racial Studies* 17 (4): 577-592.

Gans, H.J. (1999), 'Toward a reconciliation of 'assimilation' and 'pluralism': the interplay of acculturation and ethnic retention', in C. Hirshman et al. (eds.), *Handbook of Immigration: The American Experience*, 161-171. New York: Russell Sage Foundation.

Geertz, C. (1973), *The Interpretation of Cultures*. New York: Basic Books.

Gefou-Madianou, D. (1993), 'Mirroring ourselves through Western texts: the limitations of an indigenous anthropology', in H. Driessen (ed.), *The Politics of Ethnographic Reading and Writing: Confrontation of Western and Indigenous Views*, 160-181. Saarbrucken and Fort Lauderdale: Breitenbach.

Gellner, E. (1983), *Nations and Nationalism*. Oxford: Blackwell.

Gellner, E. (1994), *Encounters with Nationalism*. Oxford: Blackwell.

Georgakas, D. and C. Moskos (1991), 'Introduction', in D. Georgakas and C. Moskos (eds.), *New Directions in Greek American Studies*, 9-15. New York: Pella.

Georgakas, D. (1987), 'The Greeks in America', *Journal of the Hellenic Diaspora* 14 (1-2): 5-53.

Gergen, K.J. and K.E. Davis (eds.) (1985), *The Social Construction of the Person*. New York: Springer-Verlag.

Gergen, K.J. (1994a), Realities and Relationships: Soundings in Social Construction. Cambridge, MA: Harvard University Press.

Gergen, K.J. (1994b), *Toward Transformation in Social Knowledge*. Second Edition. Thousand Oaks, CA: Sage.

Gergen, M.M. and K.J. Gergen (2000), 'Qualitative inquiry: tensions and transformations', in N.K. Denzin and Y.S. Lincoln (eds.), *Handbook of Qualitative Research*. Second Edition. 1025-1046. Thousand Oaks, California: Sage Publications.

Ghosh, B. (ed.) (2000), *Return Migration: Journey of Hope or Despair?* Geneva: IOM and UN.

Giddens, A. (1984), *The Constitution of Society*. Cambridge: Polity.

Giddens, A. (1990), *The Consequences of Modernity*. Cambridge: Polity.

Giddens, A. (1991), *Modernity and Self-Identity: Self and Society in the Late Modern Age*. Oxford: Polity Press.

Giddens, A. and J. Turner (eds.) (1993), *Social Theory Today*. Oxford: Polity Press.

Gilroy, P. (1993), *The Black Atlantic: Modernity and Double Consciousness*. London: Verso.

Gizelis, G. (1974), *Narrative Rhetorical Devices of Persuasion: Folklore Communication in a Greek-American Community*. Athens: National Centre of Social Research.

Glazer, N. and D.P. Moynihan (1963), *Beyond the Melting Pot: the Negroes, Puerto Ricans, Jews, Italians and Irish of New York City*. Cambridge, Mass.: Harvard University Press.

Glazer, N. and D.P. Moynihan (eds.) (1975), *Ethnicity, Theory and Experience*. Cambridge, Mass.: Harvard University Press.

Glick Schiller, N., L. Basch and C. Blanc-Szanton (1992), *Towards a Transnational Perspective on Migration*. New York: New York Academy of Sciences.

Gluck, S.B. and D. Patai (eds.) (1991), *Women's Words: The Feminist Practice of Oral History*. London: Routledge.

Glytsos, N.P. (1991), 'Theoretical and Empirical Analysis of Migration Flow between Greece and Germany', Athens: Centre of Planning and Economic Research, (in Greek).

Goffman, E. (1969), *Strategic Interaction*. Philadelphia: University of Pennsylvania Press.

Gone, J.P., P.J. Miller and J. Rappaport (1999), 'Conceptual self as normatively oriented: the suitability of past personal narrative for the study of cultural identity', *Culture and Psychology*, 5(4): 371-398.

Goodson, I. (1998), 'Preparing for Postmodernity: The Peril and Promise', *Educational Practice and Theory*, 20(1): 25-31.

Goodson, I. (2001), 'The Story of Life History: Origins of the Life History Method in Sociology', *Identity: An International Journal of Theory and Research* 1 (2): 129-142.

Gregory, D. (1994), *Geographical Imaginations*. Oxford: Blackwell.

Grele, R.J. (1975), *Envelopes of Sound: The Art of Oral History*. Chicago: Precedent Publishing.

Grossberg, L. (1996), 'Identity and cultural studies–is that all there is?', in S. Hall and P. du Gay (eds.), *Questions of Cultural Identity*, 87-107. London: Sage.

Guba, E.G. and Y.S. Lincoln (1981), *Effective Evaluation: Improving the Usefulness of Evaluation Results through Responsive and Naturalistic Approaches*. San Francisco: Jossey-Bass.

Gurvitch, G. (1971), *The Social Frameworks of Knowledge*. Oxford: Blackwell.

Halfacree, K.H. and P.J. Boyle (1993), 'The challenge facing migration research: the case for a biographical approach', *Progress in Human Geography* 17 (3): 333-348.

Hall, S. (1987), 'Mimimal selves', in L. Appignanesi (ed.), *Identity. The Real Me. Post-Modernism and the Question of Identity*, 44. ICA Documents 6, London: ICA.

Hall, S. (1993), 'Cultural identity and diaspora', in P. Williams and L. Chrisman (eds.), *Colonial Discourse and Post-Colonial Theory*, 392-403. Hemel Hempstead: Harvester Wheatsheaf.

Hall, S. (2000), 'Conclusion: the multicultural question', in B. Hesse (ed.), *Un/settled Multiculturalisms: Diasporas, Entanglements, Transruptions*, 209-241. London: Zed Books.

Hall, S. and P. du Gay (eds.) (1996), *Questions of Cultural Identity*. London: Sage.

Hall, S. and T. Jefferson (eds.) (1976), *Resistance through Rituals: Youth Subcultures in Postwar Britain*. London: Hutchinson, Centre for Contemporary Cultural Studies.

Hammar, T., G. Brochmann, K. Tamas and T. Faist (eds.) (1997), *International Migration, Immobility and Development: Multidisciplinary Perspectives*. London: Berg.

Hammersley, M. and P. Atkinson (1983), *Ethnography: Principles in Practice*. London: Tavistock.

Hammerton, J.A. and A. Thomson (2005), *Ten Pound Poms: Australia's Invisible Migrants*. Manchester: Manchester University Press.

Hamilakis, Y. (2000), 'Cyberspace/Cyberpast/Cybernation: Constructing Hellenism in Hyperreality', *European Journal of Archaeology*, 3 (2): 241-264.

Handlin, O. (1951), *The Uprooted: The Epic Story of the Great Migrations that Made the American People*. Boston: Little and Brown.

Hardt, M. and A. Negri (2000), *Empire*. Cambridge, Massachusetts: Harvard University Press.

Harré, R.(1983), *Personal Being: A Theory for Individual Psychology*. Oxford: Blackwell.

Harrison, L.E. and S.P. Huntington (eds.) (2000), *Culture Matters: How Values Shape Human Progress*. New York: Basic Books.

Harvey, D. (1989), *The Condition of Postmodernity*. Oxford: Blackwell.

Harvey, D. (1993), 'From space to place and back again: reflections on the condition of postmodernity', in J. Bird, B. Curtis, T. Putnam, G. Robertson and L. Tickner (eds.) *Mapping the Futures: Local Cultures, Global Change*, 3-29. London: Routledge.

Harvey, D. (2000), *Spaces of Hope*. Edinburgh: Edinburgh University Press.

Hassiotis, I.K. (1993), *A Review of the History of the Modern Greek Diaspora*. Thessaloniki: Vanias (in Greek).

Hatziemmanuel, E. (1982), 'Hellenic Orthodox education in America', in H. Psomiades and A. Scourby (eds.), *The Greek American Community in Transition*, 181-189. New York: Pella.

Havelock, E.A. (1986), *The Muse Learns to Write: Reflection on Orality and Literacy from Antiquity to the Present*. New Haven and London: Yale University Press.

Hayano, D.M. (1979), 'Auto-ethnography: Paradigms, problems, and prospects', *Human Organization* 8: 113-120.

Hedetoft, U. (1995), *Signs of Nations: Studies in Political Semiotics of Self and Other in Contemporary European Nationalism*. Aldershot: Dartmouth University Press.

Hedetoft, U. (2002), 'Discourses and Images of Belonging: Migrants between 'New Racism', Liberal Nationalism and Globalization', AMID Working Paper Series, 1-25. Denmark: Aalborg University. www.humsamf.auc.dk/amid.

Hedetoft, U. (2003), *The Global Turn: National Encounters with the World*. Aalborg: Aalborg University Press.

Hedetoft, U. (2004), 'Discourses and Images of Belonging: Migrants Between New Racism, Liberal Nationalism and Globalization', in F. Christiansen and U. Hedetoft (eds.) *The Politics of Multiple Belonging. Ethnicity and Nationalism in Europe and Asia*, 23-43. Aldershot: Ashgate.

Hedetoft, U. and M. Hjort (eds.) (2002), *The Postnational Self: Belonging and Identity*. Minneapolis: University of Minnesota Press.

Hertz, R. (ed.) (1997), *Reflexivity and Voice*. London: Sage.

Herzfeld, M. (1986), *Ours Once More: Folklore, Ideology and the Making of Modern Greece*. New York: Pella Publishers.

Herzfeld, M. (1987), *Anthropology through the Looking-Glass: Critical Ethnography in the Margins of Europe*. Cambridge: Cambridge University Press.

Hobsbawm, E. (1990), *Nations and Nationalism Since 1780: Programme, Myth, Reality.* Cambridge: Cambridge University Press.

Hobsbawm, E. (1991), 'Introduction', in A. Mack (ed.), *Home: A Place in the World, Social Research* (special edition), 58 (1): 63-68.

Hobsbawm, E. and T. Ranger (eds.) (1983), *The Invention of Tradition*. Cambridge: Cambridge University Press.

Holland, D, W. Lachicotte, Jr., D. Skinner and C. Cain (1998), *Identity and Agency in Cultural Worlds*. Cambridge: Harvard University Press.

Holland, J. and Ramazanoglu, C. (1995), 'Accounting for sexuality, living sexual politics. Can feminist research be valid?' in J. Holland et al. (eds.), *Debates and Issues in Feminist Research and Pedagogy*, 273-291.Clevedon: Multilingual Matters/Open University Press.

Hutnyk, J. (2005), 'Hybridity', *Ethnic and Racial Studies* 28 (1): 79-102.

Ingold, T. (1993), 'The art of translation in a continuous world', in G. Palsson (ed.), *Beyond Boundaries: Understanding, Translation and Anthropological Discourse*. Oxford: Berg.

International Journal of Population Geography, Special issue on 'Geographies of Diaspora', 9 (4), 2003.

Jackson, P. (1989), *Maps of Meaning: An Introduction to Cultural Geography*. London: Unwin Hyman.

Jacobson, D. (ed.) (1998), *The Immigration Reader: America in a Multidisciplinary Perspective*. Oxford: Blackwell.

Janesick, V.J. (2000), 'The choreography of qualitative research design: minuets, improvisations, and crystallization', in N.K. Denzin and Y.S. Lincoln (eds.), *Handbook of Qualitative Research*, Second Edition. 379-399. Thousand Oaks, California: Sage Publications.

Jenkins, R. (1996), *Social Identity*. London: Routledge.

Jones, P. III (2001), 'Introduction: segmented worlds and selves', in Adams, P.C., S. Hoelscher and K.E. Till (eds.), *Textures of Place: Exploring Humanist Geographies*, 121-128. Minneapolis: University of Minnesota Press.

Journal of Ethnic and Migration Studies, special issue on 'Transnationalism and Identity', 27 (4), 2001.

Journal of the Hellenic Diaspora, 'Moskos-Georgakas Debate', xiv (1-2): 5-77, 1987.

Kalogeras, Y. (1985), 'Greek American literature: an introduction and a bibliography of personal narratives, fiction and poetry', *Ethnic Forum* 5: 106-128.

Kalogeras, Y. (1987), 'Greek-American literature: an essay and a bibliographic supplement', *Ethnic Forum* 7: 102-115.

Karakasidou, A.N. (1997), *Fields of Wheat, Hills of Blood: Passages to Nationhood in Greek Macedonia 1870-1990*. Chicago: University of Chicago Press.

Karpathakis, A. (1994), 'Whose church is it anyway? Greek immigrants of Astoria, New York, and their church', *Journal of the Hellenic Diaspora*, Special Issue: *Rethinking Greek America*, 21 (1): 97-122.

Karpathakis, A. (1999), 'Home society politics and immigrant political incorporation: the case of Greek immigrants in New York City', *International Migration Review* 33 (1): 55-78.

Karydis, V. (1996), *The Criminality of Immigrants in Greece*. Athens: Papazisis (in Greek).

Katakis, C. (1999), *The Three Identities of Greek Society*. Athens: Kedros (in Greek).

Keesing, R.M. (1974), 'Theories of culture', *Annual Review of Anthropology* 3: 73-97.

Keith, M. and Pile, S. (eds.) (1993), *Place and the Politics of Identity*. London: Routledge.

King, R. (ed.) (1986), *Return Migration and Regional Economic Problems*. London: Croom Helm.

King, R. (1988), *Il Ritorno in Patria: Return Migration to Italy in Historical Perspective*, Occasional Publication 23, Department of Geography, University of Durham, Durham.

King, R. (ed.) (1993), *The New Geography of European Migrations*. London: Belhaven.

King, R. (1995), 'Migrations, globalization and place', in D. Massey and P. Jess (eds.), *A Place in the World? Places, Cultures and Globalization*, 6-44. Oxford: Oxford University Press.

King, R. (2000), 'Generalisations from the history of return migration', in B. Ghosh (ed.), *Return Migration: Journey of Hope or Despair?* 7-55. Geneva: IOM and UN.

King, R.L., A.J. Strachan and J. Mortimer (eds.) (1983), *Return Migration: a Review of the Literature*, Discussion Papers in Geography 19, Oxford: Oxford Polytechnic.

King, R., J. Connell and P. White (eds.) (1995), *Writing Across Worlds: Literature and Migration*. London and New York: Routledge

Kirk, G.S, Raven, J.E. and Schofield, M. (1995) *The Presocratic Philosophers: A Critical History with a Selection of Texts*, second edition, Cambridge: Cambridge University Press.

Kivisto, P. (2001), 'Theorizing transnational immigration: a critical review of current efforts', *Ethnic and Racial Studies* 24 (4): 549-577.

Klinthäll, M. (1998) "Patterns of Return Migration from Sweden 1970-1993", Paper prepared for the TSER workshop on Labour Demand, Education and the Dynamics of Social Exclusion, Lisbon, 29 October – 1 November 1998, www.ekh.lu.se/ekhmkl/lisbon98.pdf.

Klinthäll, M. (1999), 'Greek Return Migration from Sweden 1968-1993', Paper prepared for the ESF-conference "European Societies or European Society? Migrations and Inter-Ethnic Relations in Europe", Obernai, France, 23-28 September, 1999, www.ekh. lu.se/ekhmkl/obernai99.pdf.

Klinthäll, M. (2003), *Return Migration from Sweden 1968-1996. A Longitudinal Analysis*. Stockholm: Almqvist and Wiksell International.

Knörr, J. (2005), *Childhood and Migration: From Experience to Agency*. London: Transaction Publishers.

Kondis, A.I. (1997), 'The research in Greece concerning the Greek diaspora' *The Review of Social Research* 92-93: 63-91 (in Greek).

Kopijn, Y. (1998), 'The oral history interview in a cross-cultural setting: an analysis of its linguistic, social and ideological structure', in M. Chamberlain and P. Thompson (eds.), *Narrative and Genre*, 142-159. London: Routledge.

Kourvetaris, G. (1997), *Studies on Greek Americans*. New York: Columbia University Press.

Kourvetaris, Y.A. and B.A. Dobratz (1987), *A Profile of Modern Greece: In Search of Identity*. New York: Oxford University Press.

Kroeber, A.L. and C. Kluckhohn (1952), *Culture: a critical review of concepts and definitions*. Cambridge, Mass.: Peabody Museum of Anthropology.

Labrianidis, L. and A. Lymberaki (2001), *Albanian Migrants in Thessaloniki*. Thessaloniki: Paratiritis (in Greek).

Laliotou, I. (2004), *Transatlantic Subjects: Acts of Migration and Cultures of Transnationalism Between Greece and America*. Chicago: University of Chicago Press.

Latour, B. (1987), *Science in Action*. Cambridge, MA: Harvard University Press.

Latour, B. (1988), 'The Prince for machines as well as for machinations', in B. Elliot (ed.), *Technology and Social Process*, 20-43. Edinburgh: Edinburgh University Press.

Law, J. (1988), 'The anatomy of a socio-technical struggle: The design of the TSR2', in B. Elliot (ed.), *Technology and Social Process*, 44-69. Edinburgh: Edinburgh University Press.

Law, J. (1991), 'Introduction', in J. Law (ed.), *A Sociology of Monsters: Essays on Power, Technology and Domination*, 1-23. London: Routledge.

Lawrence-Lightfoot, S. and J. Hoffman-Davis (1997), *The Art of Science of Portraiture*. San Francisco: Jossey-Bass.

Lawson, V. (1999), 'Questions of migration and belonging: understandings of migration under neoliberalism in Ecuador', *International Journal of Population Geography* 5: 261-276.

Lefebvre, H. (1991), *The Production of Space*. Oxford: Blackwell (trans. David Nicholson-Smith).

Leontis, A. (1995), *Topographies of Hellenism: Mapping the Homeland*. Ithaca, NY and London: Cornell University Press.

Leontidou, L. (2001), 'Attack on the landscape of power: An anti-war elegy to New York inspired by Whitman's verses, *City* 5 (3): 406-410.

Leontidou, L. (2004), 'The Boundaries of Europe: Deconstructing Three Regional Narratives', *Identities: Global Studies in Culture and Power* 11: 593-617.

Leontidou, L. (2005), *Geographically Illiterate Land: Hellenic Idols in the Epistemological Pathways of European Geography*. Athens: Hellenica Grammata (in Greek).

Levitt, P. and M.C. Waters (eds.) (2002), *The Changing Face of Home: The Transnational Lives of the Second Generation*. New York: Russell Sage Foundation.

Lianos, T.P. (1975), 'Flows of Greek out-migration and return migration', *International Migration* 13 (3) 119-133.

Lichtenberg, J. (1999), 'How liberal can nationalism be?', in R. Beiner (ed.), *Theorizing Nationalism*. 167- 189. New York: State University of New York Press.

Light, I. and S. Gold (2000), *Ethnic Economies*. San Diego: Academic Press.

Linde, C. (1993), *Life Stories: The Creation of Coherence*. Oxford: Oxford University Press.

Loizos, P. and E. Papataxiarchis (eds.) (1991), *Contested Identities: Gender and Kinship in Modern Greece*. Princeton: Princeton University Press.

Lomsky-Feder, E. and T. Rapoport (2000), 'Visit, separation, and deconstructing nostalgia: Russian students travel to their old home', *Journal of Contemporary Ethnography* 29 (1): 32-57.

Lomsky-Feder, E. and T. Rapoport (2001), 'Homecoming, Immigration and the National Ethos: Russian-Jewish Homecomers Reading Zionism, *Anthropological Quarterly* 74: 1-14.

Long, L.D and E. Oxfeld (2004), *Coming Home? Refugees, Migrants, and Those Who Stayed Behind*. Pennsylvania, Philadelphia: University of Pennsylvania Press.

Lorenzo-Hernandez, J. (1999), 'The Nuyorican's dilemma: categorization of returning migrants in Puerto Rico', *International Migration Review* 33 (4): 988-1013.

Ltd. New Zealand, 1-87. www.soci.canterbury.ac.nz/research/rphs/homepub.pdf.

Lyons, E. (1996), 'Coping with social change: processes of social memory in the reconstruction of identities', in G.M. Breakwell and E. Lyons (eds.), *Changing European Identities: Social Psychological Analyses of Social Change*, 31-39. Oxford: Butterworth Heinemann.

Maffesoli, M. (1996), *The Time of the Tribes*. London: Sage (trans. Rob Shields, originally published in French, *Les Temps des Tribus*, 1988, Paris: Meridiens Klincksieck).

Malkki, L. (1992), 'National Geographic: the rooting of peoples and the territorialization of national identity among scholars and refugees', *Cultural Anthropology* 7 (1): 24-44.

Mallet, S. (2004), 'Understanding home: a critical review of the literature', *The Sociological Review* 52 (1): 62-89.

Mann, C. (1998), 'Family fables', in M. Chamberlain and P. Thompson (eds.), *Narrative and Genre*, 81-98. London: Routledge.

Mann. M. (1986), *The Sources of Social Power, Vol. 1: A History of Power from the Beginning to A.D. 1760*. Cambridge: Cambridge University Press.

Mann, M. (1995), 'Sources of variation in working-class movements in twentieth-century Europe', *New Left Review* 212: 14-54.

Maratou-Alipranti, L. (1999), *The Family in Athens: Family Models and Spouses Household Practices*. Athens, Greece: National Centre For Social Research (in Greek).

Marger, M.N. (2001), 'The use of social and human capital among Canadian business immigrants', *Journal of Ethnic and Migration Studies* 27 (3): 439-453.

Markham, A.N. (1998), *Life Online: Researching Real Experience in Virtual Space*. Walnut Creek, California: AltaMira.

Markowitz, F. and A.H. Stefansson (eds.) (2004), *Homecomings: Unsettling Paths of Return*. Lanham, Maryland: Lexington Books.

Marvakis, A., D. Parsanoglou and M. Pavlou (eds.) (2001), *Immigrants in Greece*. Athens : Ellinika Grammata (in Greek).

Massey, D. and Allen, J. (eds.) (1984), *Geography Matters: a reader*. Cambridge: Cambridge University Press.

Massey, D. (1994), *Space, Place and Gender*. Oxford: Polity Press.

Massey. D. (2005), *For Space*. London: Palgrave.

McAdams, D.P. (1990), 'Unity and purpose in human lives: The emergence of identity as a life story', in A.I. Rabin et al. (eds.), *Studying Persons and Lives*, 148-200. New York: Springer.

McCrone, D. (1998), *The Sociology of Nationalism: Tomorrow's Ancestors*. London: Routledge.

McDowell, L. (1993a), 'Space, place and gender relations: Part I. Feminist empiricism and the geography of social relations', *Progress in Human Geography* 17 (2): 157-179.

McDowell, L. (1993b), 'Space, place and gender relations: Part II. Identity, difference, feminist geometries and geographies', *Progress in Human Geography* 17 (3): 305-318.

McDowell, L. (1999), *Gender, Identity and Place: Understanding Feminist Geographies*. Cambridge: Polity Press.

McKeown, A. (2001), 'Ethnographies of Chinese transnationalism', *Diaspora* 10 (3): 341-360.

Miles, M. and J. Crush (1993), 'Personal narratives as interactive texts: collecting and interpreting migrant life-histories', *Professional Geographer* 45 (1): 95-129.

Milner, A. (1999), *Class*. London: Sage.

Mitchell, D. (2000), *Cultural Geography: A Critical Introduction*. Oxford: Blackwell.

Mitchell, K. (1997a), 'Transnational discourse: bringing geography back in', *Antipode* 29 (2): 101-114.

Mitchell, K. (1997b), 'Different diasporas and the hype of hybridity', *Environment and Planning D: Society and Space* 15: 533-553.

Monos, D. (1986), The Achievement of the Greeks in the United States. Philadelphia: Centrum.

Morley, D. and K. Robins (1993), 'No Place Like Heimat: Images of Home(land) in European Culture', in E. Carter et al. (eds.), *Space and Place: Theories of Identity and Location*, 3-31. London: Lawrence and Wishart.

Moskos, C.C. (1999), *Greek Americans: Struggle and Success*. New York: Transaction Publishers.

Mousourou, L. and J. Kollarou, (1980), 'Return Migration', Athens: Center of Human Studies and Research, (in Greek).

Murphy, P. (1998), 'The Seven Pillars of Nationalism', *Diaspora* 7 (3): 369-415.

Nast, H.J., C. Katz, A. Kobayashi, K.V.L. England, M.R. Gilbert, L.A, Staeheli and V.A. Lawson (1994), 'Women in the field: critical feminist methodologies and theoretical perspectives', *Professional Geographer* 46 (1): 54-101.

Nelson, L. (1999), 'Bodies (and Spaces) do matter: the limits of performativity', *Gender, Place and Culture* 6 (4): 331-353.

Nielsen, G.M. (2002), *The Norms of Answerability: Social Theory Between Bakhtin and Habermas*. New York: State University of New York Press.

Norman, A.P.(2002), 'Telling it like it was: historical narratives on their own terms', in G. Roberts (eds.), *The History and Narrative Reader*, 181-196. London: Routledge.

Okely, J. (1992), 'Anthropology and autobiography: participatory experience and embodied knowledge', in J. Okely and H. Callaway (eds.), *Anthropology and Autobiography*, 1-28. London: Routledge.

Olwig, K.F. (1997), 'Toward a reconceptualization of migration and transnationalism', in B.F. Frederiksen and F. Wilson (eds.), *Livelihood, Identity and Instability*, 113-127. Copenhagen: Centre for Development Research.

Olwig, K.F. (1998), 'Epilogue: contested homes: home-making and the making of anthropology', in N. Rapport and A. Dawson (eds.) *Migrants of Identity: Perceptions of Home In a World of Movement*, 225-235. Oxford: Berg.

Olwig, K.R. (2001), 'Landscape as a contested topos of place, community, and self', in Adams, P.C., S. Hoelscher and K.E. Till (eds.), *Textures of Place: Exploring Humanist Geographies*, 93-117. Minneapolis: University of Minnesota Press.

Panagakos, A.N. (1998), 'Citizens of the Trans-Nation: Political Mobilization, Multiculturalism and Nationalism in the Greek Diaspora', *Diaspora: Journal of Transnational Studies* 7 (1): 53-73.

Panagakos, A.N. (2003a), 'Downloading New Identities: Ethnicity, Technology, and Media in the Global Greek Village', *Identities: Global Studies in Culture and Power* 10 (2): 201-219.

Panagakos, A.N. (2003b), 'In Search of Adonis: Marriage Strategies and Gender Identity in Greek Transnational Migration', in E. Tastsoglou and L. Maratou-Alipranti (eds.), Gender and Migration: Focus on Greece, (special issue), 77-106. *National Centre for Social Research* 110 A.

Panagakos, A.N. (2003c), *Romancing the Homeland: Transnational Lifestyles and Gender in the Greek Diaspora*. Unpublished PhD dissertation, University of California, Santa Barbara.

Panagakos, A.N. (2006a), 'From Napster to MEGA: Technology, Power and Gender in a Greek Canadian Community', in E. Tastsoglou (ed.), *En/Gendering Greek Diaspora Communities: Work, Community and Identity*. Lewiston, New York: Edwin Mellen, in press.

Panagakos, A.N. (2006b), 'Mapping Greektown: Identity and the Making of 'Place' in suburban Calgary, in C. Teelucksingh (ed) *Claiming Space: Racialization and Spatiality in Canadian Cities*. Waterloo, ON: Wilfred Laurier Press, in press.

Panagakos, A.N. and H. Horst (2006), 'Return to Cyberia: Technology and the Social Worlds of Transnational Migrants', *Global Networks: a Journal of Transnational Affairs*, 6 (2): 109-124.

Panourgia, N. (1995), *Fragments of Death, Fables of Identity*. Madison: University of Wisconsin Press.

Papademetriou, D. (1985), 'Illusions and reality in international migration: migration and development in post World War II Greece', *International Migration* 23: 211-224.

Papastergiadis, N. (1998), *Dialogues in the Diasporas: Essays and Conversations on Cultural Identity*. London: Rivers Oram Press.

Papastergiadis, N. (2000), *The Turbulence of Migration: Globalization, Deterritorialization and Hybridity*. Cambridge: Polity Press.

Papataxiarchis, E. (1991), 'Friends of the heart: male commensal solidarity, gender, and kinship in Aegean Greece', in P. Loizos and E. Papataxiarchis (eds.), *Contested Identities: Gender and Kinship in Modern Greece*, 156-179. Princeton: Princeton University Press.

Patrinacos, N.D. (1982), 'The role of the Church in the evolving Greek American Community', in H. Psomiades and A. Scourby (eds.), *The Greek American Community in Transition*, 123-136. New York: Pella.

Patterson, J.G. (1991), 'Greek and Romanian immigrants as hyphenated Americans: toward a theory of white ethnicity', in D. Georgakas and C. Moskos (eds.), *New Directions in Greek American Studies*, 153-160. New York: Pella.

Pattie, S. (1994), 'At home in diaspora: Armenians in America', *Diaspora* 3 (2): 185-198.

Peacock, J.L. and D.C. Holland (1993), 'The narrated self: life stories in process', *Ethos* 21 (4): 367-383.

Pecora, V.P. (ed.) (2001), 'Introduction', in V.P. Pecora (ed.), *Nations and Identities: Classic Readings*, 1-42. Oxford: Blackwell.

Peepre, M. (1999), 'Revising history in the diasporas: Sky Lee's *Disappearing Moon Café* and Denise Chong's *The Concubine's Children*', in J. Kaplan, M. Shackleton and M. Toivonen (eds.), *Migration, Preservation, and Change*, 73-90. University of Helsinki: Renvall Institute Publications.

Perkins, H.C., D.C. Thorns, A. Winstanley and B.M. Newton (2002), 'The Study of 'Home' From a Social Scientific Perspective: An Annotated Bibliography', Second Edition, Lincoln University, University of Canterbury and Institute for Environmental Science and Research.

Personal Narratives Group (1989), *Interpreting Women's Lives: Feminist Theory and Personal Narratives*. Bloomington: Indiana University Press.

Phillips, D.C. (1995), 'The good, the bad, and the ugly: The many faces of constructivism', *Educational Researcher* 24 (7): 5-12.

Phillips, D.C. (1997a), 'Coming to grips with radical social constructivism', *Science and Education* 6: 85-104.

Phillips, D.C. (1997b), 'How, why, what, when and where: Perspectives on constructivism in psychology and education', *Issues in Education* 3 (2): 151-194.

Phinney, J.S. (1990), 'Ethnic identity in adolescents and adults: Review of research', *Psychological Bulletin* 108 (3): 499-514.

Pile, S. (2002), 'Memory and the city', in J. Campbell and J. Harbord (eds.), *Temporalities, Autobiography and Everyday Life*, 111-127. Manchester: Manchester University Press.

Plummer, K. (2001), *Documents of Life 2: An Invitation to a Critical Humanism*. London: Sage.

Portelli, A. (1991), *The Death of Luigi Trastulli and Other Stories: Form and Meaning in Oral History*. Albany: State University of New York Press.

Portes, A. (1995), 'Economic sociology and the sociology of immigration: a conceptual overview', in A. Portes (ed.), *The Economic Sociology of Immigration: Essays on Networks, Ethnicity and Entrepreneurship*, 1-41. New York: Russell Sage Foundation.

Potter, R.B., D. Conway and J. Phillips (eds.) (2005), *The Experience of Return Migration: Caribbean Perspectives*. Aldershot: Ashgate.

Pratt, M.B. (1984), 'Identity: Skin Blood Heart', in E. Bulkin, M.B. Pratt and B. Smith (eds.), Yours in Struggle: Three Feminist Perspectives on Anti-Semitism and Racism, 11-63. New York: Long Haul Press.

Pred, A. (1985), 'The social becomes the spatial, the spatial becomes the social: enclosures, social change and the becoming of place in the Swedish province of Skåne', in

D. Gregory and J. Urry (eds.), *Social Relations and Spatial Structures*, London: Macmillan.

Pries, L. (1999), 'New migration in transnational spaces' in L. Pries (ed.), *Migration and Transnational Social Spaces*, 1-35. Aldershot: Ashgate.

Primpas-Welts, E. (1982), 'Greek families', in M. McGoldrick et al. (eds.), *Ethnicity and Family Therapy*, 269-288. New York: The Guilford Press.

Psomiades, H.J. (1987), 'Greece and Greek America: the future of the Greek American community', in S.D. Orfanos, H.J. Psomiades and J. Spiridakis (eds.), *Education and Greek Americans: Process and Prospects*. 91-102. New York: Pella.

Psomiades, H.J. and S. Thomadakis (eds.) (1993), Greece, The New Europe and the Changing International Order. New York: Pella Publishing.

Radcliffe, S and S. Westwood (1996), *Remaking the Nation: Place, Identity and Politics in Latin America*. London: Routledge.

Radcliffe, S.A. (1993), 'Women's place/el lugar de mujeres: Latin America and the politics of gender identity', in M. Keith and S. Pile (eds.), *Place and the Politics of Identity*, 102-116. London: Routledge.

Rapport, N. and A. Dawson (eds.) (1998), *Migrants of Identity: Perceptions of Home In a World of Movement*. Oxford: Berg.

Reed-Danahay, D.E. (ed.) (1997), *Auto/Ethnography: Rewriting the Self and the Social*. Oxford: Berg.

Reinharz, S. (1992), *Feminist Method in Social Science*. Oxford: Oxford University Press.

Reis, M. and J.G. Nave (1986), 'Emigrating peasants and returning emigrants: emigration with return in a Portuguese village', *Sociologia Ruralis* 26 (1): 20-35.

Relph, E. (1976), *place and placelessness*. London: Pion.

Remennick, L. (2003), 'The 1.5 Generation of Russian Immigrants in Israel: Between Integration and Sociocultural Retention', *Diaspora* 12 (1): 39-66.

Richardson, L. (1994), 'Writing: a method of inquiry', in N.K. Denzin and Y.S. Lincoln (eds.), *Handbook of Qualitative Research*, 516-529. Thousand Oaks, CA: Sage.

Richardson, M. (1989), 'Place and culture: two disciplines, two concepts, two images of Christ and a single goal', in J.A. Agnew and J.S. Duncan (eds.), *The Power of Place: Bringing together Geographical and Sociological Imaginations*, 140-156. Boston: Unwin Hyman.

Ritivoi, A.D (2002), *Yesterday's Self: Nostalgia and the Immigrant Identity*. Oxford: Rowman and Littlefield Publishers.

Robins, K. (1995), 'Cyberspace and the world we live in', in Featherstone and Burrows (eds.), *Cyberspace/Cyberbodies/Cyberpunk*, London: Sage.

Robolis, S., J. Boules, P. Souri and S. Pasadis (1989), 'An Investigation of the Economic Activity of Return Migrants and their Contribution to the Economic Development of the Region of East Aegean', University of the Aegean, Chios, Greece.

Robolis, S. and E. Xideas (1990), 'The economic determinants of Greek return migration to the Islands of the East Aegean', *International Migration* 34 (2): 297-319.

Romanucci-Ross, L. and G. DeVos (eds.) (1995), *Ethnic Identity: Creation, Conflict, and Accommodation*. Walnut Creek, CA: AltaMira Press.

Rosaldo, R. (1984), 'Grief and a Headhunter's Rage: on the cultural force of emotions', in S. Plattner and E. Bruner (eds.), *Text, Play and Story: The Construction and Reconstruction of Self and Society*, 178-195. Washington, D.C.: American Ethnological Society.

Rose, G. (1993), *Feminism and Geography: The Limits of Geographical Knowledge*. Cambridge: Polity.

Rose, G. (1996), 'As if the mirrors had bled: masculine dwelling, masculinist theory and feminist masquerade', in D. Duncan (ed.), *Body Space: Destabilizing Geographies of Gender and Sexuality*, 56-74. New York: Routledge.

Rushdie, S. (with Gunter Grass) (1987), 'Writing for a future', in B. Bourne et al. (eds.), *Writers and Politics*, from the Channel 4 television series Voices, Nottingham: Spokesman Hobo Press.

Sack, R.D. (1980), *Conceptions of Space in Social Thought: A Geographic Perspective*. London: Macmillan.

Safilios-Rothschild, C. (1968), 'Deviance and mental illness in the Greek family', *Family Process* 7: 100-117.

Safran, W. (1991), 'Diasporas in modern societies: myths of homeland and return', *Diaspora* 1 (1): 83-89.

Said, E. (1990), 'Reflections on exile', in R. Ferguson et al. (eds.), *Out There: Marginalizations and Contemporary Cultures*, 357-374. Massachusetts: MIT Press.

Saloutos, T. (1956), *They Remember America: The Story of the Repatriated Greek-Americans*. Berkeley and Los Angeles: University of California Press.

Saloutos, T. (1964), *The Greeks in the United States*. Cambridge, Mass.: Harvard University Press.

Saloutos, T. (1973), 'The Greek Orthodox Church in the United States and Assimilation', *International Migration Review* 7 (4): 395-407.

Sangster, J. (1998), 'Telling our stories: feminist debates and the use of oral history', in R. Perks and A. Thomson (eds.), *The Oral History Reader*, 87-100. London: Routledge.

Sayyid, S. (2000), 'Beyond Westphalia: nations and diasporas – the case of the Muslim *Umma*', in B. Hesse (ed.), *Un/settled Multiculturalisms: Diasporas, Entanglements, Transruptions*, 33-50. London: Zed Books.

Schiffrin, D. (1996), 'Narrative as self-portrait: Sociolinguistic constructions of identity', *Language in Society* 25: 167-203.

Schneider, L. and C.M. Bonjean (eds.) (1973), *The Idea of Culture in the Social Sciences*. Cambridge: Cambridge University Press.

Schwandt, T.A. (2000), 'Three epistemological stances for qualitative inquiry: interpretivism, hermeneutics, and social constructionism', in N.K. Denzin and Y.S. Lincoln (eds.), *Handbook of Qualitative Research*. Second Edition, 189-213. Thousand Oaks, California: Sage Publications.

Scourby, A.S. (1980), 'Three generations of Greek Americans', *International Migration Review* 14 (1): 43-52.

Scourby, A.S. (1984), *The Greek Americans*. Boston: Twayne Publishers.

Sennett, R. (2002), *Flesh and Stone: The Body and the City in Western Civilization*. London: Penguin Books.

Seremetakis, N.C. (1991), *The Last Word: Women, Death, and Divination in Inner Mani*. Chicago: The University of Chicago Press.

Shain, Y. (1999), *Marketing the American Creed Abroad: Diasporas in the U.S. and their Homelands*. Cambridge: Cambridge University Press.

Shaw, T.A. (1994), 'The semiotic mediation of identity', *Ethos* 22 (1): 83-119.

Shields, R. (1997), 'Spatial stress and resistance: social meanings of spatialization', in G. Benko and U. Strohmayer (eds.), *Space and Social Theory: Interpreting Modernity and Postmodernity*, 186-202. Oxford: Blackwell.

Singer, M. (1968), 'The concept of culture', in D.L. Sills (ed.), *International Encyclopedia of the Social Sciences*, 527-543. vol. 3. New York: Macmillan.

Sinn, E. (1999), 'Cohesion and fragmentation: a country-level perspective on Chinese transnationalism in the 1940s', in L. Douw, L. (eds.), *Qiaoxiang Ties: Interdisciplinary Approaches to 'Cultural Capitalism' in South China*, London: Kegan, cited in McKeown 2001.

Slim, H., P. Thompson, O. Bennett and N. Cross (2000), 'Ways of listening', in R. Perks and A. Thomson (eds.), *The Oral History Reader*, 114-125. London: Routledge.

Smith, A.D. (1986), *The Ethnic Origins of Nations*. Oxford: Blackwell.

Smith, A.D. (1991), *National Identity*. London: Penguin Books.

Soja, E. (1989), *Postmodern Geographies: the Reassertion of Space in Critical Social Theory*. London: Verso.

Soja, E. (1996), *Thirdspace*. Oxford: Blackwell.

Sökefeld, M. (2002), 'Alevism online: re-imagining a community in virtual space', *Diaspora* 11(1): 85-123.

Somers, M.R. (1994), 'The narrative constitution of identity: A relational and network approach', *Theory and Society* 23 (5): 605-649.

Sowell, T. (1981), *Ethnic America: A History*. New York: Basic Books.

Sowell, T. (1996), *Migrations and Cultures: A World View*. New York: Basic Books.

Spivak, G.C. (1998), 'Identity and alterity: a conversation with Gayatri Chakravorty Spivak', in N. Papastergiadis, *Dialogues in the Diasporas: Essays and Conversations on Cultural Identity*. 53-65. London: Rivers Oram Press.

Stryker, S., T.J. Owens and R.W. White (eds.) (2000), *Identity, Self, and Social Movements*. Minneapolis: University of Minnesota Press.

Tajfel, H. (1982), *Social Identity and Intergroup Relations*. Cambridge: Cambridge University Press.

Takaki, R. (1993), *A Different Mirror: A History of Multicultural America*. Boston: Little, Brown and Company.

Takenaka, A. (1999), 'Transnational community and its ethnic consequences: the return migration and the transformation of ethnicity of Japanese Peruvians', *American Behavioral Scientist* 42 (9): 1459-1474.

Tavuchis, N. (1972), *Family and Mobility among Greek-Americans*. Athens: National Centre of Social Research.

Tedlock, D. (1991), 'The speaker of tales has more than one string to play on', in I. Brady (ed.) *Anthropological Poetics*, 309-340. Savage, MD: Rowman and Littlefield.

Thompson, E.P. (1963), *The Making of the English Working Class*. London: Victor Gollancz.

Thompson, P. (1994), 'Between identities: Homi Bhabha interviewed by Paul Thompson', in R. Benmayor and A. Skotnes (eds.) *International Yearbook of Oral History and Life Stories, Volume III: Migration and Identity*, 183-199. Oxford: Oxford University Press.

Thompson, P. (2000), *The Voice of the Past: Oral History*, Third Edition. Oxford: Oxford University Press.

Thomson, A. (1994), *Anzac Memories: Living with the legend*. Melbourne: Oxford University Press.

Thomson, A. (1999), 'Moving stories: oral history and migration studies', *Oral History* 27 (1): 24-37.

Thomson, A. (2000), 'Anzac memories: Putting popular memory theory into practice in Australia', in R. Perks and A. Thomson (eds.) *The Oral History Reader*, 300-310. London: Routledge.

Tololyan, K. (1996), 'Rethinking diaspora(s): stateless power in the transnational moment', *Diaspora* 5 (1): 3-36.

Tonkin, E. (1992), *Narrating our Pasts: The Social Construction of Oral History*. Cambridge: Cambridge University Press.

Touraine, A. (2000), *Can We Live Together? Equality and Difference*. Cambridge: Polity.

Trimble, J.E. (1995), 'Toward an understanding of ethnicity and ethnic identity, and their relationship with drug use research', in G.J. Botvin, et al. (eds.) *Drug Abuse Prevention with Multiethnic Youth*, Thousand Oaks, CA: Sage, pp. 3-27.

Tsemberis, S., H. Psomiades and Karpathakis, A. (eds.) (1999), *Greek American Families: Traditions and Transformations*. New York: Pella Publishers.

Tsuda, T. (2001), 'From ethnic affinity to alienation in the global ecumene: the encounter between the Japanese and Japanese-Brazilian Return Migrants', *Diaspora* 10 (1): 53-91.

Tsuda, T. (2003), *Strangers in the Ethnic Homeland: Japanese Brazilian Return Migration in Transnational Perspective*. New York: Columbia University Press.

Tuan, Y.F. (1974), 'Space and place: humanistic perspective', *Progress in Geography* 6: 213-252.

Tuan, Y.F. (1977), *Space and Place: The Perspective of Experience*. Minneapolis: University of Minnesota Press.

Turner, V. (1974), *Dramas, Fields and Metaphors: Symbolic Action in Human Society*. Ithaca: Cornell University Press.

Tzanelli, R. (2006), '"Not My Flag!" Citizenship and nationhood in the margins of Europe (Greece, October 2000/2003)', *Ethnic and Racial Studies* 29 (1): 27-49.

Unger, K. (1986), 'Return migration and regional characteristics: the case of Greece', in R. King (ed.) *Return Migration and Regional Economic Problems*, 152-170. London: Croom Helm.

Unwin, T. (1992), *The Place of Geography*. Harlow, Essex: Longman Scientific and Technical.

Van Hear, N. (1998), *New Diasporas: The Mass Exodus, Dispersal and Regrouping of Migrant Communities*. London: University College London Press.

Vasilakis, M. (2002), *'Good that they Suffered': The Greek Public Opinion after September 11th*. Athens: Gnoseis Publications (in Greek).

Ventura, L. (1994), *Immigration and Nation: Collectivities and Social Positions under Transformation*, Athens: Mnemon (in Greek).

Vermeulen, H. (2001), *Culture and Inequality: Immigrant Cultures and Social Mobility in Long-Term Perspective*. Amsterdam: IMES.

Verney, S. (2004), 'The End of Socialist Hegemony: Europe and the Greek Parliamentary Elections of 7th March 2004', SEI Working Paper No. 80, Sussex European Institute, University of Sussex, Brighton, pp. 1-38.

Vertovec, S. (1997), 'Three meanings of 'diaspora', exemplified among South Asian religions', *Diaspora* 6 (3): 277-299.

Vlachos, E. (1968), *The Assimilation of Greeks in the United States*. Athens: National Centre of Social Research.

Waters, M.C. (1990), *Ethnic Options: Choosing Identities in America*. Berkeley and Los Angeles, CA: University of California Press.

Weinreich, P. (1997), 'Enculturation of a semi-alien: Journeyings in the construction and reconstruction of identity', in M.H. Bond (ed.) *Working at the Interface of Cultures: Eighteen Lives in Social Science*, 155-165. London and New York: Routledge.

White, P. (1995), 'Geography, Literature and Migration', in R. King, R., J. Connell and P. White (eds.) *Writing Across Worlds: Literature and Migration*, 1-19. London and New York: Routledge.

White, P. (2003), 'The Japanese in Latin America: on the uses of diaspora, *International Journal of Population Geography*, 9 (4): 309-322.

White, P. and P. Jackson (1995), '(Re)theorising population geography', *International Journal of Population Geography* 1 (2): 111-123.

Williams, R. (1976), *Keywords: A Vocabulary of Culture and Society*. Glasgow: Fontana.

Yamanaka, K. (1996), 'Return migration of Japanese-Brazilians to Japan: the Nikkeijin as ethnic minority and political construct', *Diaspora* 5 (1): 65-97.

Yang, M.M.C. (1972), 'How A Chinese village was written', in S.T. Kimball and J.B. Watson (eds.), *Crossing cultural boundaries: The anthropological experience*, 63-73. San Francisco: Chandler.

Yans-McLaughlin, V. (ed.) (1990), *Immigration Reconsidered: History, Sociology, and Politics*. New York: Oxford University Press.

Yelenevskaya, M.N. and L. Fialkova (2004), 'My Poor Cousin, My Feared Enemy: The Image of Arabs in Personal Narratives of Former Soviets in Israel', *Folklore* 115: 77-98.

Yelenevskaya, M.N. (2005), 'A Cultural Diaspora in the Making: Former Soviets in Israel and in Germany', in Moskovich, W. and S. Nikolova (eds.), Judaeo-Bulgarica, Judaeo-Russica et Palaeoslavica, *Jews and Slavs*, vol. 15, 265-279. Jerusalem-Sofia: The Center for Slavic Languages and Literatures of the Hebrew University of Jerusalem and The Cyrillo-Methodian Research Center of the Bulgarian Academy of Sciences.

Yuval-Davis, N. (1997), *Gender and Nation*. London: Sage.

Yuval-Davis, N. and F. Anthias (eds.) (1989), *Woman, Nation, State*. Basingstoke: Macmillan.

Zavalloni, M. and C. Louis-Guerin, C. (1984), *Identité sociale et conscience: Introduction l'ego-ecologie*. Montreal: Presses de l'Université de Montreal.

Zenelis, J.G. (1982), 'A bibliographic guide on Greek Americans', in H.J. Psomiades and A. Scourby (ed.), *The Greek Community in Transition*, 231-270. New York: Pella.